MICHAEL ROMANOV:
Brother of the Last Tsar
Diaries and Letters, 1916-1918

Translated by
Helen Azar

Annotations by
Nicholas B.A. Nicholson

MICHAEL ROMANOV:
Brother of the Last Tsar
Diaries and Letters,
1916-1918

Translated by
Helen Azar

Annotations by
Nicholas B.A. Nicholson

Academica Press
Washington – London

Library of Congress Cataloging-in-Publication Data

Names: Mikhail Aleksandrovich, Grand Duke of Russia, 1878-1918, author. | Azar, Helen, translator. | Nicholson, Nicholas B. A., editor.
Title: Michael Romanov : brother of the last Tsar diaries and letters, 1916-1918 / translated by Helen Azar ; annotations by Nicholas B.A. Nicholson.
Other titles: Brother of the last Tsar diaries and letters, 1916-1918
Description: Washington, [District of Columbia] : Academica Press, [2020] |
Includes bibliographical references and index. | Summary: "In Michael Romanov: Brother of the Last Tsar, translator Helen Azar and Romanov historian Nicholas B.A. Nicholson present for the first time in English the annotated 1916-1918 diaries and letters of Grand Duke Michael from the period in which he learns of the murder of Rasputin, attempts to preserve the throne for his brother Nicholas during the February Revolution, and finds himself named Emperor when his brother abdicates not only for himself, but for his son Alexei. Michael's diaries provide rare insight into the fall of the Empire, the rise and fall of the Provisional Government and the brief Russian republic, and the terrifying days of the February and October Revolutions after which Michael finds himself a prisoner who would meet his end in the Siberian city of Perm."-- Provided by publisher.
Identifiers: LCCN 2020022016 | ISBN 9781680539455 (hardcover) | ISBN 9781680539462 (paperback)
Subjects: LCSH: Mikhail Aleksandrovich, Grand Duke of Russia, 1878-1918--Diaries. | Mikhail Aleksandrovich, Grand Duke of Russia, 1878-1918--Correspondence. | Russia--History--Nicholas II, 1894-1917. | Romanov, House of. | Princes--Russia--Diaries. | Princes--Russia--Correspondence.
Classification: LCC DK254.M513 A3 2020 | DDC 947.08/3092 [B]--dc23
LC record available at https://lccn.loc.gov/2020022016

Contents

Acknowledgements vii

List of Illustrations ix

Introduction 1
Grand Duke Michael Alexandrovich: Biographical Sketch To 1916 1
Michael's Diaries 4
Note on the Text 5
Note on the Translation and Annotations 5
Note on Names and Dates 6

The Diaries of Michael Romanov 7
December 1916 7
January 1917 20
Letter to Natasha: 33
February 1917 35
March 1917 47
The Manifesto of the Grand Dukes 49
Letter to Natasha: 50
1 March, 1917 50
Grand Dukes at the State Duma. *Russkoe slovo*, 2 March 1917 51
Letter to Natasha: 54
The Act of Grand Duke Michael Alexandrovich 55
April 1917 64
May 1917 74

June 1917 84
July 1917 96
August 1917 109
September 1917 122
October 1917 131
November 1917 142
December 1917 155
January 1918 166
February 1918 178
March 1918 182
May 1918 185
June 1918 193
From *Izvestia*, 15 June 1918 197

Bibliography **199**
Books: 199
Articles: 200

Index **201**

Acknowledgements

The authors would like to thank and acknowledge for their assistance with this book Vasily Astankov of The State Archives of the Russian Federation (GARF); Christopher Forbes and Bonnie Kirschstein of the Forbes Collection, New York; Mike Aitken and the Pauline Gray Estate, UK, and Boris S. Stechkin. We are also indebted to Professor Paul du Quenoy, our reviewers, and the staff of Academica Press in Washington D.C., London, and India.

List of Illustrations

1. In Grand Duke Michael's hand: "The church in Vienna, where we were married." Circa 1912. Private collection

2. Travelling in Europe. Seated, Irina Nikolaevna Shilova, a friend of Natasha's. Circa 1914. From the private collection of Shilova's great-grandson, Boris Stechkin.

3. Norway: Michael on horseback. Irina Nikolaevna Shilova, third from left. Circa 1914. From the private collection of Shilova's great-grandson, Boris Stechkin.

4. V. N. Shilova at left, Irina Nikolaevna Shilova at Michael's right. Circa 1914. From the private collection of Shilova's great-grandson, Boris Stechkin.

5. Knebworth House. Circa 1914. From the private collection of Boris Stechkin.

6. Michael with singer Feodor Chaliapin and the Shleifers. Circa 1914. From a private collection.

7. Michael with his son George ("Baby") and Mrs Shleifer. Norway. Circa 1914. From a private collection.

8. Michael with his brother, Tsar Nicholas II, nieces and nephew, on the balcony of the Alexander Palace in Tsarskoe Selo. L-R: Grand Duchesses Maria, Olga, Tatiana, and Anastasia, Michael, Nicholas and Tsesarevich Alexei. Circa 1915-16. GARF. f. 640, op. 3, d. 25. l. 66ob. № 979

9. Michael on horseback, prior to 1917. From a private collection.

10. Michael and friends, at Gatchina in winter, prior to 1917. From a private collection.

11. Grand Duke Michael with his brother, Tsar Nicholas II, prior to 1917. From a private collection.

12. Michael and Natasha's house in Gatchina on Baggovutskaya Street. This house no longer exists. Circa 1916. From a private collection.

13. Natalia and Nicholas Johnson. Circa 1914. From a private collection.

14. Michael horsing around for the camera, prior to 1917. From a private collection.

15. Michael with the Russian ballerina Tamara Karsavina (in the foreground). Michael is in his swim suit, holding on to the boat. Circa 1914. From the private collection of Boris Stechkin.

16. Michael posing in front of the Kodak building on Nevsky Prospect in St. Petersburg, prior to 1917. From a private collection.

17. Michael playing the guitar, most likely circa 1916-17. From a private collection.

18. Michael visiting the 2nd Siberian Regiment, circa 1916. From a private collection.

19. Michael's written refusal to accept the Russian throne, signed "Mikhail," issued in Petrograd on 3 March 1917.

20. Likely the last known photo of Michael, taken in Perm in April 1918. With him is Pyotr Ludvigovich Znamerovsky, who has often been misidentified here as Nicholas Johnson. At least two copies of this photo exist: one at the State Archives of Russian Federation (GARF, f. P9440, op. 1, d. 1, l. 1991), which presumably belonged to Znamerovsky, as his landlady found it in his apartment after his arrest. The other copy is in the private collection of the Pauline Gray Estate.

21. On the back of the photo from the Gray collection, Michael wrote: "9 April 1918 – Perm. We were photographed during our walk in town, at the hay market, where the flea market is. The photograph was developed in 10 minutes. M. I had not shaved since the day of departure from Gatchina – (22 February/7 March)." Courtesy of Pauline Gray Estate.

Introduction

Grand Duke Michael Alexandrovich: Biographical Sketch To 1916

Grand Duke Michael Alexandrovich of Russia was the youngest son and fifth child of Emperor Alexander III and his wife, the Empress Maria Fedorovna (born Princess Dagmar of Denmark). Born in 1878, during the reign of his grandfather Alexander II, known as the "Tsar-Liberator" for having freed Russia's serfs, Michael was fourth in line to the throne after his father and two older brothers Nicholas II, who reigned from 1894 to 1917, and George, who died young in 1899. Michael came into the world in his mother's apartments in St. Petersburg's Anichkov Palace and enjoyed a close and comfortable childhood, dividing his time between the Anichkov Palace, Gatchina Palace outside of St. Petersburg, and the Livadia Palace in the Crimea. Known as "Misha" within the family, "Floppy" to his sister Olga, and later as "Uncle Mimi" to his nieces, Michael was raised in the same spartan manner as most Romanov men, with an emphasis on physical and educational excellence. A fine equestrian, Michael was taught by private tutors in history and government and received extensive religious instruction.

At the age of sixteen, Michael faced two important life events. His father, Alexander III, died unexpectedly on 1 November 1894, placing him third in line to the throne. Later that year, he left his family to attend the Imperial Artillery School located in Tsarskoye Selo on the corner of Sapernaya and Veliovskaya streets. After graduating, he joined Her Majesty's Own Horse Guards Artillery, under the patronage of his mother the Dowager Empress. In November 1898 he attained legal majority, and after his consumptive brother George's death in a motorcycle accident a few months later, he became Heir-Tsesarevich to his brother, Nicholas II. In 1904, Nicholas's son Alexei was born, and Michael fell back one place in the succession. As a sign of honor, he was designated Regent to the young Heir-Tsesarevich in the event anything should happen to the Emperor.

Very little was expected of Michael other than obedience and honorable behavior. He was required to uphold his oath to the Emperor and to fulfil his obligations as a dynast of the Russian Imperial House. Laws set down by his ancestor Paul I in 1797 required him to marry a princess of royal birth. In 1902, Michael dutifully fell in love with Princess Beatrice of Saxe-Coburg-Gotha, a granddaughter of Queen Victoria. Beatrice's mother, Grand Duchess Maria Aleksandrovna, and Michael's father, Alexander III were siblings, and marriages between first and second cousins "to the seventh degree" were prohibited by the Orthodox church. Nicholas could have given his permission to this otherwise acceptable marriage, but he refused on religious grounds. Michael and Beatrice were broken-hearted by the decision, and Michael quickly turned his attention to his sister Olga's lady-in-waiting, Alexandra Kossikovskaya, familiarly known as "Dina." When Michael asked permission to marry her in 1906, the Emperor, who had only recently exiled his first cousin Grand Duke Kirill Vladimirovich for marrying without permission, threatened Michael with the same punishment. Dina was dismissed, and the Dowager Empress took Michael to Denmark so that he might forget her. Other names romantically linked to Michael included Princess Patricia of Connaught, one of Queen Victoria's granddaughters, though news of the connection surprised them both.

In 1907, Michael met the woman who would change his life. Natalia Sergeyevna Wulfert (née Sheremetievskaya) was the wife of his fellow officer, Vladimir Vladimirovich Wulfert. She had been married once before, to Sergei Mamontov, a nephew of the famous industrialist and art collector Savva Mamontov. The marriage produced a daughter, but ended in 1905, when Sergei agreed to represent himself in Russia's notoriously difficult divorce proceedings as if he were an adulterous partner. In fact, it was Natalia who was unfaithful, and she went on to marry her lover, Vladimir. After two years of marriage, Natalia was introduced to Grand Duke Michael, and they began a close relationship. Their involvement soon became common knowledge and dangerous to Michael's position. Wulfert challenged the Grand Duke to a duel, and

Nicholas II had his brother transferred to another regiment far from St. Petersburg. By 1909, however, Natalia had become Michael's mistress, and by December of that year she was pregnant with his child. Wulfert agreed to a divorce, presenting himself, like her first husband, as the adulterous party. Natalia gave birth to Michael's son on 24 July 1910, before the proceedings were finalized, and the divorce decree was backdated so that the boy, named George after Michael's late brother, would be recognized as her illegitimate child, rather than Wulfert's. Nicholas II gave Natalia the right to live at Michael's estate, Brasovo, near Moscow, and Natalia and her son were permitted to use the surname "Brasov."

In 1912, without informing the Emperor, Michael and Natalia married secretly in a Serbian Orthodox Church in Vienna. Michael wrote his brother, "I know that punishment awaits me for this act, and I am ready to bear it" (Maylunas, 361). Nicholas quickly heard from his mother, who had also received a letter from Michael: "it has completely killed me" (Maylunas, 362). She begged that the marriage remain a secret, but the consequences were swift. Michael's position as Regent-in-waiting to Alexei was revoked. His funds from the Imperial appanages were confiscated in a way that made it seem as though the Grand Duke were insane or had lost his mental faculties. Michael was instructed not to return to Russia.

But time wore on, and after three years abroad as political and social exiles, Michael begged his brother to be allowed to return to serve Russia in World War I. Nicholas relented, and Michael and the Brasovs returned. Michael was restored to the army, promoted to Major General, and made commander of the "Savage" regiment, formed of Chechens and Daghestanis. After months of service, in March 1915 Nicholas recognized Natalia's son George and granted him the title of Count. From this time on, Natalia was known as "Madame Brasova" or even "Countess Brasova," though she was never legally accorded this title. After their return to Russia, she was never received by Empress Alexandra or the Dowager Empress, both of whom ignored her existence and began to suspect her motives. Gradually, however, Michael was reabsorbed into the Imperial Family, and began to take part in family activities, though Natalia and her son remained outside of Moscow at Michael's estate, where she received a stream of sympathetic artistic and political visitors and sponsored several military hospitals with her own funds.

Michael's Diaries

It is at this point that our annotated translation of Michael's diaries begins -- in December 1916, with a stay in Crimea just before Michael learned of the death of Rasputin while en route to spend Christmas at Brasovo.

Historians have only intermittently cited Michael's diaries, and their efforts, notably those of Donald Crawford in his 2012 book *The Last Tsar: Emperor Michael II*, have been very limited or extrapolated. Until now, there has been no full translation of them in English.

The diaries provide rare insight into the period of the February Revolution, which deposed Nicholas II in February 1917, and of Michael's brief moment as Russia's *de facto* Emperor and subsequent "deferral" of the throne in March 1917. They continue through the chaotic period before the October Revolution, when Russia was led by a Provisional Government, and after it, when it was ruled by the Bolsheviks. Michael's complete diaries shed new light on several critical moments in this period, including the Romanov family's efforts both to undermine Nicholas and Alexandra and also preserve the throne for them, a compelling account of Michael's relatively privileged detentions in 1917-1918, and details of the domestic life he enjoyed with his wife, her daughter by her first marriage, and their son at their estate at Brasovo and, later, at the Imperial Palace at Gatchina, outside St. Petersburg.

Michael was the first Romanov to be executed by the new regime. In March 1918 he and his private secretary Nicholas Johnson were exiled to Perm. Natalia, left behind, was determined to save them, but on 13 June of that year, they were killed outside Perm by local Bolsheviks agents acting with the approval of the Soviet government, just over a month before Nicholas II and his immediate family were murdered by the Bolsheviks at Ekaterinburg. Over ninety years later, on 8 June 2009, the Russian government declared Michael and Johnson rehabilitated and victims of unlawful repression. Despite intense searches that continue today, his remains have never been found.

Note on the Text

Michael's process of keeping a diary was quite different from that of his siblings and other Romanov relatives. Instead of writing in a journal by hand in the evening, Michael jotted down notes continually during the day, which he then turned over to Johnson, who would type them up. Michael might then make slight further notes in his own hand, and the sheets of typescript were bound together.

Michael's diaries and papers were returned to Natalia after his death. She arranged to have them removed from Russia via the Danish embassy to England where she had settled. Brasova lived in London and in. Paris until her death in 1952, when the diaries were inherited by her daughter, Natalia Mamontova Gray Majolier. The diaries were discovered after her death in 1969 by her granddaughter, Alexandra Majolier, who found them wrapped up and used to prop up a bed. An intermediary sold the diaries to the Forbes Collection in New York City in the 1980s, and the typescript diaries remained in its holdings until 2010, when they were deaccessioned and repatriated to Russia. They are now stored in Moscow, in the State Archive of the Russian Federation (GARF), where Helen Azar first read them in 2018.

Note on the Translation and Annotations

Helen Azar's translation of the diaries remains consistent with Michael's original text, in the hope that preserving its unusual grammatical syntax and punctuation will make the experience of reading the material as close as possible to the feeling of reading the original.

Michael's diaries were fully published in Russian with exceptional scholarly annotation by Russian scholar Vladimir Khrustalëv in 2012. Nicholas B. A. Nicholson has relied extensively upon Khrustalëv's annotations for structure, but his original notes are not translations of them. In most cases, they are expansions of information presented by Khrustalëv, which would be of use to Western audiences. Nicholson has crosschecked and cited the original sources used by Khrustalëv to aid further research. He has also drawn on the diaries of other Romanovs, as well as their intimates, courtiers, and newspapers and journals of the period, most never before published in English.

Note on Names and Dates

Core source materials in Russian used in the translation and annotations are cited in the bibliography. The problem of multiple transliteration systems plagues all authors of Russian history, as there is no universal standard. Grand Duke Michael himself used a variety of spellings and transliterations in multiple languages and single names are spelled a multitude of ways within the text. The authors have tried to standardize these inconsistencies in spelling, and have used a modified U.S. Library of Congress system, rendering familiar names in their English appellations: Nicholas, Alexandra, Alexei, etc. In some cases, they have used spellings currently used by the families mentioned in the text, such as Galitzine and Cheremeteff, rather than Golitsyn and Sheremetev. All dates in this book are given as Michael indicated, in the "old style," that is, according to the Julian calendar, in use in Russia until 14 February 1918. In the twentieth century, this was thirteen days behind the Gregorian calendar in use in the West.

Helen Azar & Nicholas B.A. Nicholson

The Diaries of Michael Romanov
December 1916

1 December. Thursday. Ai-Todor.[1] At 10 1/2 Natasha,[2] J[ohnson][3] and I went to Livadia.[4] Came out by the upper gate and walked on the horizontal path but made a mistake and walked on the old one, which leads to the Oreanda church,[5] there we had to walk up the real horizontal one, where we met up with Maria V[asilievna][6] and walked down along the vineyard to the big road, and, just before reaching Kichkine,[7] we got into an automobile and returned home. In the afternoon I went to see Xenia,

---

[1] **"Ai-Todor"** was a Russian Imperial estate at Gaspra, in Crimea. Built originally in 1864 by Grand Duke Mikhail Aleksandrovich, it was inherited in 1890 by his son, Grand Duke Aleksander Mikhailovich, who, together with his wife Grand Duchess Xenia Aleksandrova built a new art nouveau-style mansion in its place. The Dowager Empress and her family were later under house arrest there in 1917-1919.
[2] **Natalia Brasova** (née Natalia Sergeyevna Sheremetevskaya, later Madame Mamontova, Madame Wulfert, Madame (Countess) Brasova, and, in exile, Princess Romanovskaya-Brasova (b. Moscow 1860 – d. Paris 1952), was Grand Duke Michael's mistress and later wife.
[3] **Nicholas Johnson** (b. St. Petersburg 1878 – d. Perm 1918), private secretary to Grand Duke Michael.
[4] **Livadia** was the Crimean residence of Nicholas II and his family. Originally built in the 1860s for Alexander II by architect Ippolito Monighetti, in the reign of Nicholas II a new palace of the same name was built by Nikolai Krasnov between 1909-1911. It was the Imperial Family's preferred residence.
[5] **Church of the Protection of the Mother of God** was built from the stones of the Oreanda Palace, which had been destroyed by fire in 1882. It was consecrated in 1885, and the small cruciform church was a favorite place of worship for both Alexander III and Nicholas II.
[6] **"Maria V."** Maria Vasilievna Shelaputina (dates unknown). Daughter of a Crimean landowner, she directed the Russian Red Cross Health and Nutritional Unit, and was a close friend of Grand Duke Michael Alexandrovich and his wife.
[7] **Kichkine** Palace was built in 1908-1911 for Grand Duke Dmitry Mikhailovich by the architect N. P. Tarasov.

dropped by Vasya's,[8] who is in bed with high fever, and then Xenia[9] and I drove in my Rolls Royce to Livadia beach, where we took a little walk, then went up to the suite's house, and I drove Xenia via upper road, and I returned home. After tea I slept on the sofa. The weather was ideal until 2 o'cl, then it got cloudy, there was no wind, 10° in the shade, really hot in the sun. Today I found out that I received the Order of St. Vladimir, 2nd class, with swords.[10]

2 December. Friday. Ai-Todor. At 11 o'cl Natasha and I took a walk on our property and sat on the usual bench. In the afternoon we took a ride to Oreanda together, then to Koreiz via the upper road, there went down to Miskhor[11] and returned home via the lower road. I took one more walk on the Shelaputin property.[12] Xenia arrived at 4 3/4 and we had tea, after which the three if us sat in the sitting room until 6 1/2. Before dinner I studied with J[ohnson], and I was studying music. At tea we laughed a lot. The weather was sunny from 2 o'cl, mild, around 9 deg.

3 December. Saturday. Ai-Todor. At 11 o'cl Natasha, Maria V, J[ohnson] and I drove to Livadia, from the Grand Palace we walked to the sea and walked on the beach - there we got into an automobile and returned home via the lower road. In the afternoon Natasha rested, and around 3 1/2 N, Maria V and I took a ride in the automobile to Simeiz[13] and back, drove on the lower road. Having returned home at 5 1/4, we had tea, then the

---

[8] **"Vasya"** H.H. Prince Vasily Aleksandrovich of Russia (b. Gatchina 1907 – d. Woodside, CA, USA, 1989), youngest son of H.I.H. Grand Duchess Xenia Aleksandrovna, and nephew of Grand Duke Michael.
[9] **"Xenia"** H.I.H. Grand Duchess Xenia Aleksandrovna of Russia (b. St. Petersburg 1875 – d. Molesey, UK, 1960). Daughter of Emperor Alexander III and sister of Grand Duke Michael.
[10] **The Order of St. Vladimir** was founded by Catherine II in 1782. In 1916, Grand Duke Michael received it for his actions during the Brusilov Offensive while in command of the 2nd Cavalry Corps.
[11] **"Miskhor"** was the Crimean residence of the Princes Yusupov.
[12] **"Shelaputin property"** refers to the cliffside house "Swallow's Nest" and its gardens, built between 1911 and 1912 by the Anglo-Russian architect Leonid Sherwood for the Baltic German millionaire Baron von Steingel. In 1914 it was purchased by P. G. Shelaputin to be used as a restaurant.
[13] **"Simeiz"** is a picturesque resort town near Yalta.

ladies played *kosti*,[14] while J[ohnson] read a newspaper aloud. After dinner N[atasha] and Maria V played kosti. The weather was sunny and warm until 2 o'cl, 9 deg., no less than 20° in the sun.

4 December. Sunday. Ai-Todor. At 10 3/4 Natasha, Maria V, J[ohnson] and I went to Oreanda for liturgy, Mitya and Tatiana[15] were there. In the afternoon Natasha, M V, J[ohnson] and I went to the Miskhor beach, but did not stay there very long. From there our companions returned home, while we went to tea at Xenia's where Sonia D[16] and Princess Orbeliani[17] were too. Returned home at 6 o'cl. In the evening we studied music. The weather was sunny most of the day, 9°.

5 December. Monday. Ai-Todor. In the morning I wrote a letter to Mama. Then walked to Xenia's. She was supposed to go to Kiev today, stayed because of Irina,[18] who has a cold and is in bed. I also visited Vasya. On the way back, I got wet from rain. In the afternoon Natasha and Maria V went to Yalta, and J[ohnson] and I put together a letter to Muravev[19] in England. Returned to tea. Before dinner I wrote. In the evening I wrote telegrams, then played music. It was pouring rain all day, 8°.

6 December. Tuesday. Ai-Todor. In the morning I took a short walk. Around 11 o'cl Natasha and J[ohnson] went to Yalta, while I read until

---

[14] **"Kosti,"** or **"Bones,"** is a dice game similar to the modern game of craps.
[15] **"Mitya and Tatiana"** H.I.H. Grand Duke Dmitry Konstantinovich and his niece, H.H. Princess Tatiana Konstantinova of Russia.
[16] **"Sonia D"** Sofia Vladimirovna von Dehn (b. 1883- d. 1955), born Countess Cheremeteff, the niece of the daughter of Nicholas I, Grand Duchess Maria Nikolaevna of Russia. She married Dmitry Vladimirovich von Dehn, son of an Imperial Senator. "Sonia" was very close to Grand Duke Michael and his sister, Grand Duchess Olga, Duchess of Oldenburg, after 1917 Mme. Kulikovskaya.
[17] **"Princess Orbeliani"** Princess Vera Vladimirovna Djambakurian-Orbeliani (née Countess Kleinmichel, b. 1875 – d. 1948) was the wife of Prince Dmitri Ivanovich Djambakurian-Orbeliani, adjutant to Grand Duke Alexander Mikhailovich from 1910-1917.
[18] **"Irina"** H.H. Princess Irina Aleksandrovna of Russia, Princess Yusupova, Countess Soumarokoff-Elston (b. Peterhof 1895 – d. Paris 1970).
[19] **"Muravev"** According to Khrustalëv, Muravev was an unknown confidant on Grand Duke Michael's British property. (Khrustalëv, V.M., *Dnevnik i perepiska Velikogo Knyazya Mikhaila Aleksandrovicha 1915-1918*. Moscow, 2012, p. 744)

breakfast. Gen[eral] Spiridovich[20] had breakfast with us. Around 3 o'cl Xenia came to see us for a short time, and after her departure N, Maria V, J[ohnson] and I took a ride across the Yusupov estate from below up, reached Oreanda via the upper road and returned home via the usual road. After tea I wrote postcards to the children and others. At 7 o'cl Johnson, the birthday boy, went to Sevastopol in Maria V's automobile. He is going to Gatchina in tonight's train. The weather was very pleasant in the morning, although without sun, and from 3 o'cl there was a terrible shower, 11°.

7 December. Wednesday. Ai-Todor. At 11 o'cl Alyosha[21] arrived from Sevastopol, all wet from a terrible rain. Before breakfast I drove over to Xenia's, who is leaving for Kiev in the afternoon and will return here for Christmas. In the afternoon Koton[22] and I took a walk on the horizontal path, - walked for 1 hour 50 min. After tea Alyosha read newspapers aloud. In the evening Natasha played *kosti* with Maria V, while Alyosha with Koton. The weather was rainy until 2 o'cl, there was strong pouring rain, and then, although it was overcast, but the rain stopped, 11°. Natasha wasn't feeling well, she stayed in bed all day.

---

[20] **"Gen[eral] Spiridovich"** Alexander Ivanovich Spiridovich (b. 1873 – d. 1955) was a major-general of the military police who had accompanied and attended Nicholas II at Stavka. After 15 August 1916, Spiridovich served as mayor of Yalta. During the February Revolution, he returned to Petrograd, and was arrested and later released. In 1920, he emigrated to France. After the Second World War, he moved to the United States, where he wrote several histories of the late imperial period and Russian revolutionary movement. (Khrustalëv, p. 770).

[21] **"Alyosha"** Aleksei Sergeevich Matveev (b. 1871 – d. 1952) was Natalia Brasova's brother-in-law, the godfather of her son by Grand Duke Michael, Count Brassov, and one of Michael lawyers. In 1918, he emigrated to France, where he became an important member of the White Russian community. In 1952, he published a memoir in exile about Grand Duke Michael and the February Revolution of 1917. (cf. A. S. Matveev, "Velikii Knyaz' Mikhail Aleksandrovich v dni perevorota." *Vozrozhdenie*, No. 24, 1952).

[22] **"Koton"** Konstantin Antonivich Koton (dates unknown), was a court counsellor and assistant-practitioner of the Imperial Court Ministry of Medicine. (Khrustalëv, p. 727)

8 December. Thursday. Ai-Todor. At 11 o'cl I took a walk, took a "Savage" rifle[23] and walked to the upper highway, then on horizontal, but did not get to shoot. After breakfast Natasha, Maria V, Alyosha and I went to the Upper Massandra,[24] looked around the house and returned via Lower Massandra. After tea I read, in the evening too, while the others played dominoes. The weather was not sunny, but bright, cold wind, it rained in the evening, 8°.

9 December. Friday. Ai-Todor. At 11 o'cl Natasha, Maria V, Alyosha and I went to Nikitsky garden, took a walk there, on the way back we stopped to see the Izumrudnoe estate, purchased by Krivoshein, - it is right near Nikitinsky garden and leads to the sea. Returned home at 1 1/2. In the afternoon Koton and I took a long walk on the horizontal [path], then reached Xenia's house and returned home at 5 o'cl. Then Alyosha read, while I rested in the bedroom. The weather was sunny, cold wind, 8°.

10 December. Saturday. Ai-Todor. At 10 o'cl I went to Kichkine[25] to Mitya's. He lovingly showed me all his dominions. At 11 o'cl I went home, and then Natasha, Maria V and I took a walk and sat under a lighthouse and warmed in the sun. Wrangel and his wife came to breakfast with us. In the afternoon we all took a walk, initially at the bay, and then on Shelaputin land, across Malysheva's garden to Kharax,[26] where we dropped by Koton's and the Wrangels.' Having stayed there for some time, we went home and soon had tea. Soon I got a haircut, and then read. The weather was sunny, windy, 6°.

11 December. Sunday. Ai-Todor. At 11 1/4 we went to Oreanda for liturgy, Mitya and Tatiana. were there as well. Before breakfast we warmed in the sun. In the afternoon we all, i.e. Natasha, Maria V, Alyosha,

---

[23] **"Savage" rifle.** Savage Arms was founded in 1894 by Arthur Savage in Utica, New York. Before World War I they produced rifles, handguns, and ammunition for sportsmen and were a chief competitor of Colt.
[24] **"Massandra"** An imperial estate and vineyard purchased by Emperor Alexander III from Prince Galitzine.
[25] **"Kichkine"** the estate of H.I.H. Grand Duke Dmitry Konstantinovich of Russia.
[26] **"Kharax"** The Crimean estate of Grand Duke George Mikhailovich of Russia, built in the English style in 1905 and given a Greek name by the Grand Duke's wife, born Princess Marie of Greece and known as "Greek Minnie."

Koton and I, drove in two automobiles to Ai-Petri, through Eriklik. The weather was ideal and completely windless. We stayed upstairs around 20 min. Came down the same way, only drove past the Livadia farm. Got home at 5 1/2. Before dinner I played the guitar, then rested. The weather was sunny, 7°, while on Ai-Petri 1°.

12 December. Monday. Ai-Todor. At 11 o'cl I took a walk on the horizontal path and reached Oreanda, where the winemaking is, and returned. Natasha, Maria V and Alyosha went to Yalta before breakfast. At 3 o'cl Natasha and I went to Sonia D's who lives at Countess Kleinmichel's house. We stayed there until 5 1/2, Vera Orbeliani was there as well. Having returned home, Wrangel came to me with a report, stayed here for two hours. The weather was overcast, mild, 9°.

13 December. Tuesday. Ai-Todor. In the morning I took a walk with Konstantin An. Near the Swallow's Nest I shot at a cormorant, which was swimming away, and despite the distance I killed it. Then we went to Kharax, where we walked down to the sea, and there I killed another cormorant, I shot with the "Savage" rifle. After breakfast we all drove to Simeiz in two automobiles, from there drive up to Sevastopol highway and returned home. Before reaching home, we, the three men, walked to the sea (in Ai-Todor) and up to Kharax. With Volchok's help I found a cormorant and brought it home. At 5 o'cl the Spiridoviches came to tea with us. Before dinner I studied with Alyosha. The weather was sunny from 12 o'cl, almost no wind, 10°.

14 December. Wednesday. Ai-Todor. In the morning I walked with Wrangel to Xenia's children and sat at Vasya's, who is still lying in bed, we made paper flowers with him. Natasha went to Yalta. After breakfast we all went to Countess Kleinmichel's dacha in two automobiles to get Sonya and V. Orbeliani and then headed past Simeiz via coastal road to the Filiber estate, where we walked and sat by the sea. Drove up to the owner's house, thinking that the estate is for sale, but this did not turn out to be so, and we drove home. We liked the area, a lot of green space right by the sea. Before dinner I wrote business letters, and in the evening as well. The weather was pleasant, although overcast, mild, 10°.

15 December. Thursday. Ai-Todor. At 20 1/2 Natasha and Maria V went to Yalta, while Alyosha, Koton and I took a long walk, went via Rostislavskaya road, crossed to the horizontal, in Ai-Todor walked down to the sea and walked up in Kharax. F. F. Meltzer[27] came to breakfast. In the afternoon we all went to the bay, then walked around the Shelaputin estate. After that we got into an automobile, drove to the lighthouse, made a circle around Ai-Todor and circled Irina's house that's being built, which we did not like. After tea F. F. Meltzer left, - and I rested, after which I wrote a letter to Countess Tolstoy, and after dinner to Prince N. S. Putyatin.[28] In the morning the weather was bright, 11 deg., in the afternoon the strongest NW wind was blowing, like a hurricane, the temp went down to 3°, it calmed towards nighttime.

16 December. Friday. Ai-Todor. In the morning I walked to Ai-Todor to visit Irina and Vasya, who both feel better, Dmitri was there as well. Natasha came to get me with Maria V and we went to the post, then returned home. To breakfast came: Sonya D and princess V. Orbeliani. In the afternoon we walked to the bay, then walked around all of Shelaputin estate, - the guests all advised us to buy this land. At 3 1/2 The guests left, and in an hour N, Alyosha and I went to the Spiridoviches in Yalta, where we had tea. After we returned home Wrangel came to see me with a report. In the evening I studied with Alyosha. The weather was damp in the morning, it was snowing lightly, in the afternoon it was sunny, then a strong wind started to blow from the mountains, until 12 o'cl 8 deg., then 4°.

17 December. Saturday.[29] Ai-Todor. At 8 1/4 I went with the "Hoop" [coupé] with Koton and the Tatar [blank space] ... on Ai-Petri across Eriklik, but due to a heavy snowstorm we only reached Pendikule,

---

[27] "**F. F. Meltzer**" Feodor Feodorovich Meltzer (b. 1861 – d. 1945), merchant of the first guild, owner of the Meltzer furniture design studio and manufactory in St. Petersburg, brother of the court interior architect Roman Meltzer.
[28] "**Prince N. S. Putyatin**" Prince Nikolai Sergeevich Putyatin (b. 1862-1927) Rear-Admiral, and from 1903-1906 commander of Grand Duke Michae's yacht, the *Tsaritsa*. Head of the Black Sea Fleet Training Exercises (1916). Fled Russia and died in Paris.
[29] "**17/30 December 1916**" was the date of Rasputin's murder in Petrograd.

travelled for an hour and a half, - made a circle and drove back, but I with .... [blank] walked to Ai-Todor, - the snow depth was three vershoks,[30] it was raining down below. Came home at 12 o'cl and lay down to rest before breakfast, which was at 1 1/2, the Wrangel were here. Went to Sonia D and V. Orbeliani's for tea, Maria V came over there a bit later. We had dinner at 7 1/2, then went to the theater in Yalta, where they had a charity play, amateur, to benefit a daycare; Spiridoviches sat next to us, - Wrangel, Meltzer and Mme... [blank] stopped by our loge. Returned at 12 o'cl. The weather was very bad, windy, snow, rain, 5° in the morning, later 7°.

18 December. Sunday. Ai-Todor and departure to Brasovo.[31] At 11 o'cl. Natasha went to Yalta with Maria V, and I and Alyosha to Oreanda church for liturgy. N[atalia] and M V also came later. Then Mitya and I went to his place in Kichkine, where I took photographs in the garden. At 1 o'cl I arrived at home, and we had breakfast. Around 3 o'cl our luggage arrived in a truck to Sevastopol, and M V's people in a motor, i.e. servants. I wrote a letter to Prince Begildeyev, after which Koton and I went to the bay for the last time. At 4 1/2 we had tea, and at 5 o'cl 25 min. departed for Sevastopol, - I drove the Rolls Royce, with me rode: Natasha and Maria V, and in the "Hoop" [coupé] - Alyosha, Koton and Roza M. The Wrangels and police master Gvozdevich came to see us off. It was pouring rain like from a bucket, non-stop, - traveled well, arrived in Sevastopol train station at 8 o'cl 30 min and soon got into out train compartment and had something to eat, the provisions were ours. At 10 o'cl I went to the Marine library building with Alyosha, where I visited the ill Gen[eral] Alexeyev (Army Chief-of-Staff). Our train departed at 11 o'cl 40 min. Went to bed late. The weather was mild, overcast, around 6°.

19 December. Monday. The train. Got up late. Had breakfast in the compartment, ate the provision which we brought with us. Natasha played *kosti* with Maria V all day, while Koton [played] with Alyosha. In the

---

[30] **"three vershoks"** A *vershok* is an Imperial unit of measurement equaling 4.4 cm., or about 5 ¼ inches.
[31] **"Brasovo"** Grand Duke Michael's estate, which he inherited from his brother Grand Duke George upon his death in 1899, Natasha's official residence from 1915.

afternoon I played the guitar. The weather was overcast, around 12°. From newspapers we learned of Grigorii Rasputin's murder in Petrograd.

20 December. Tuesday. The train to Brasovo. Got up late. Got to Kursk around 9 o'cl instead of 7 o'cl. At the Dmitrievsk station the local representative of the nobility Volzhin presented Natasha and me with bread and salt.[32] (Forgot to mention that Maria V transferred in Kharkov tonight and went to Moscow). At 2 1/2 we arrived in Brasovo and at the overpass we were met by: Olga Pav. P.,[33] Praskovia Iv.,[34] Maria Nik.,[35] Johnson, Rosenbach, Bantle,[36] and at home the children, Miss Neame, and also Maria N's two girls were waiting for us. Initially we walked around the entire house, then I took a short walk, after which we had tea. Then we went to the wings [of the house]. Before dinner we played with the children, and the evening Domenici was here, and I played the guitar with him, initially downstairs, then upstairs. The weather was overcast, the sun was setting when we arrived, it was 8 deg., 12° towards the evening. A lot of snow.

21 December. Wednesday. Brasovo. At 10 1/2 I took a walk and made a circle in the grove, - returned home, after which I took another walk. In the afternoon the ladies went riding around with J, while I took a walk with Alyosha. After tea I played the guitar with Domenici.[37] After the children's dinner, Olga P, J[ohnson], Natasha and I played hide and seek

---

[32] **"bread and salt"** In the original text хлеб-соль, or bread-salt. The tradition of presenting bread and salt to visitors is an ancient Russian custom that became standard etiquette in welcoming a member of the Imperial Family or an important guest.

[33] **"Olga Pav. P."** Princess Olga Pavlovna Putyatina (b. 1877 – d. 1967) née Zelenaya, wife of Prince P. P. Putyatin, and mother of Olga, Natalia, and Michael.

[34] **"Praskovia Iv."** Praskovia Ivanovna Aberino ("Aunt Paranya"), a friend and neighbor of Natalia Brasova in Gatchina during the war, when Aberino worked as a sister of mercy. Lived in Petrograd, where she was also a friend of the great bass Fedor Chaliapin and the Minister of Justice N. A. Dobrovolsky.

[35] **"Maria Nik."** Maria Nikolaevna Trostyanskoi was a friend of Natalia Brasova's since her Moscow days during her marriage to Mamontov. She served at the front as a Sanitary nurse during the First World War.

[36] **"Bantle"** Gustav Adolfovich Bantle, manager of the Brasovo estate, lived in Altukhov.

[37] **"Domenici"** Guitar instructor to Grand Duke Michael. The Italian name was transliterated several ways throughout the original text by Grand Duke Michael; we use a standardized version common contemporary Italian spelling.

with the children. In the evening we all sat upstairs, while I played the guitar with Domenici. The weather was overcast, mild, 15°. Maria N's daughter Irina got ill with angina, in light of which Maria N and Kisa were isolated from us and stayed in the guest house with the sick ones.

22 December. Thursday. Brasovo. At 10 o'cl Natasha, Olga P, Praskovia Iv., J[ohnson] and I went to [hunt] wolves outside of the Vladimirsky hamlet via Altukhovkaya road. The circle was very close to the edge of the forest. We chased after three (Bantle, Koton and I), with me stood Natasha and Olga P. I killed a mature one, while Bantle wounded another one. Returned home at one and had breakfast. In the afternoon Natasha with the ladies, Alyosha and me took a walk, it was difficult to walk because of snow. After tea we had to bustle and arrange everything for the departure of Maria N to Moscow. During dinner we were notified of the unexpected death of poor Irina Lebedeva, she died of heart failure. Just this afternoon they were able to diagnose her with diphtheria, but the illness progressed at such a pace, that there was nothing that could be done to save her, it was lightning fast. Around 11 1/2 I went to Guest house, i.e. to the entrance, and said goodbye to MN, who is going to Moscow with Kisa this night. (Irina already turned 12). This is all so terribly sad. The weather was dark, 4° in the morning, 11° towards evening.

23 December. Friday. Brasovo. In the morning I went to the experimental field with Alyosha where we chose a fir tree and cut it down for tomorrow. Then we took a short walk with Vyazemsky. Forgot to mention that the Vyazemskys arrived today at 9 o'cl. In the afternoon princess O. P., P. I. and J[ohnson] went to ride in the grove, while Vyazemsky and I walked on foot. There was a whole lot of snow, and windy. After tea I played the guitar, after dinner as well. After the children's dinner O. P., P. I., J[ohnson] and I played with them. Natasha spent the day in bed, felt weakness. In the evening we had tea in her room. The weather was windy, overcast, 2°. They were unable to transfer the body of poor little Irina to Moscow today, but carried it from the Guest house to Lokot, and tomorrow it will be sent to Moscow.

24 December. Saturday. Brasovo. After 10 o'cl I took a walk with Miss Neame and the children; we took shovels and cleaned off the path at the

first clearing, a bit later Praskovia I. came over and helped us work, and towards us Vyazemsky was approaching, who was also working. After breakfast we decorated the tree, which was set up in the nursery. At 6 o'cl father Alexander gave an all-night vigil service, after which we lit up the tree. For additional liveliness, I played the guitar with Domenici. Sergei N was here as well, who stayed for dinner and the evening. In the large sitting room, we hung from a chandelier mistletoe which was brought from Crimea. Praskovia I. accompanied J[ohnson], besides that, Domenici and I played guitars. After tea the entire company moved to Alyosha's and J[ohnson]'s], I went there only for a few minutes. The weather was overcast, mild, 1°.

25 December. Monday. Sunday. In the morning I took a walk with the children, Miss Neame,[38] Olga P and J[ohnson]. Having returned to the house, all the others joined us, and we slid down the hill to the greatest pleasure of Tata and Baby.[39] Before breakfast *batushka* arrived with the crucifix. In the afternoon N and I took snapshots in the rooms, and at 3 o'cl we went to ride in three sleighs (Natasha, Olga P, Praskovia I.) - (the Vyazemskys and I) - (J[ohnson] and Domenici). We rode around the entire grove. Before tea V and I took a bit of a walk, and then lit up the tree and all sat in the nursery. I rested for a bit. At 8 o'cl Natasha and I went to the train station with the children, the children are going to Gatchina, in light of possible contagion, - Miss Neame, Koton and Alyosha are going with them, but the latter will wait for us in Moscow. Returned home at 8 3/4 and had dinner, then I played the guitar with Domenici, while the others played *zhelëzka*.[40] The weather was wonderful, sunny, mild, 8 deg. In the morning, and 0° in the sun, 15° towards the evening, moonlit night.

26 December. Monday. Brasovo. Got up late. I took a walk with V, it was difficult to walk because of snow. After returning home, we with Natasha, Vyazemsky and Rosenbach walked around the wings and chose wallpaper and borders for the rooms. In the afternoon we all, except Praskovia I. and J[ohnson], headed to the poultry yard in sledges, looked at the poultry, the

---

[38] **"Miss Neame"** Margaret Neame, a British-born governess to Tata Mamontova and George Brasov
[39] **"Baby"** Count George Brasov, young son of Grand Duke Michael and Natalia.
[40] **"***zhelëzka***"** A game of chance involving cards and a roulette wheel.

poultrywoman seems like a knowledgeable girl. Vyazemsky and I walked back. After tea I practiced the guitar until dinner, while the others played *zhelëzka*. In the evening we all played cards. The weather was dark, heavy snowstorm, 4°.

27 December. Tuesday. Brasovo. Got up late, then took a walk with V and Domenici. After breakfast we rode in three sledges (Prin. O. P. with me, P. I. with J[ohnson], V with Domenici, - navigated ourselves) to the village Brasovo, where we walked around the greenhouses. After tea I practiced the guitar. Rosenbach and Bantle came to dinner. We then sat in the nursery and lot up the tree for the last time. After 10 o'cl we went upstairs and played *zhelëzka*. Domenici also took part. Later I played the guitar with him. Parted late. The weather was sunny in the morning, 5°.

28 December. Wednesday. Brasovo and departure. In the morning I took snapshots of the rooms, then took a walk with Praskovia I. and Domenici, met up with Olga P and J[ohnson] and we all walked together. Before breakfast I had the chance to play the guitar for a bit. In the afternoon around 3 o'cl we went to ride in the sleighs, I navigated, with me rode Olga P and Praskovia I., behind us rode Vyazemsky and Domenici. We rode along the birch alley, turned left toward Lokot and returned home. After this, V and I knocked snow off trees. The poor trees are suffering all this time from the large amount of snow. After tea I practiced the guitar. Natasha hung paintings in the dining room and sitting room. Rosenberg and Bantle came to dinner (to breakfast too). At 9 1/2 we all went to the train station and took an extra train to Navlya, where we were hooked up to the Kiev train around 12 o'cl. We played *zhelëzka* until late. The weather was overcast, it was drizzling all day, 3° in the morning, and 1° later.

29 December. Thursday. Arrival in Moscow and departure to Gatchina. At 12 o'cl we arrived in Moscow and were met by Alyosha at the train station. We all went to the apartment of Kraft and Oboleshev to have breakfast. In the afternoon I went to the Natural with Alyosha, then to Kuznetzky to the photographer Mendel. From there, along with Sergei Aleksandrovich to their place on Vozdvizhenka, where we had tea, Sergei A[leksandrovich]'s two sisters with daughter and Kirusha were there. After 6 o'cl Alyosha and I went to the Strastnoi and dropped by a shop on the way. At 8 o'cl we all

headed to Maria Vasilievna's for dinner. Besides our whole Brasovo group there were: Yuliy Petrovich, F. M. Ruperti, A. I. Abrikosov, Obolishev. In the evening Olga A and Yablochkina arrived, the latter read poetry, and some of the guests were playing *zhelëzka*. At 11 3/4 we went to Nikolaevsky Station and went to Petrograd in the 12 o'cl train. With us are traveling: Princess Putyatina (until Bologoe), Alyosha, Vyazemskys and J[ohnson]. Went to bed late. The weather was overcast, 0°.

30 December. Friday. Arrival at Gatchina. Our train was very late, and we arrived in Tosno only around one o'cl. From there Natasha with Princess Vyazemsky and Alyosha went to Petrograd, while I went to Gatchina with J[ohnson] and Vyazemsky. Valyev accompanied us. Having arrived at home after 2 o'cl, J[ohnson], Vyazemsky and I had breakfast, and then Vyazemsky and I took a walk to the Malogatchinskaya forest dacha. After tea I wrote postcards to Olga P, Praskovia I. and Maria N. At 7 o'cl J[ohnson] and I went to the train station to meet N and prin. V. In the evening we settled in, i.e. unpacked our things. The weather was overcast, mild, 8°.

31 December. Saturday. Gatchina. At 10 3/4 Vyazemsky and I went to get J[ohnson] and with him through the Matrossky gates to the palace park, where we took a walk and went around the lake. By the palace near the Turkish gazebo we met up with Natasha and Prince V's children and a few times slid down the hill, which was built there for Krestianov's children. In the afternoon Vyazemsky and I took a ride in a sled: The Zoo,[41] the Black Gates,[42] the Priory.[43] After tea I rested a little, and at 6 1/2 we lit up the tree in the dining room, which the children cut down at the Zoo. Alyosha arrived. Around 8 o'cl Inna A arrived, and we had a bite to eat, there were only cold zakuski, the children are with us. At 9 1/2 arrived: the Shleifers and Vorontsovs. At 10 1/4 we all went to the palace church for molebna. At 12 o'cl we sat down to supper, Tata brought in the New

---

[41] **"the Zoo"** The Zoo (or "Menagerie") at Gatchina was established earlier than 1792 in the reign of Pavel I and functioned until the revolution.

[42] **"the Black Gates"** One of the main gates to Gatchina Palace.

[43] **"the Priory"** A picturesque building on the Black Lake at Gatchina from the reign of Paul I, built by the architect N. A. Lvov and presented to the Order of Malta by an imperial decree dated 23 August 1799.

Year for the first time. The tree was lit, and it was very lively. The guests left at 2 o'cl via the railroad. We went to bed around 3 3/4. The weather was overcast, mild, 7°, 2° in the evening.

January 1917

1 January. Sunday.[44] Gatchina. Got up late. Vyazemsky[45] and I drove down Tsarskoselskaya highway in an automobile, in order to find out if one can pass through. The road turned out to be bad due to snow. Returned home at 1 o'cl. At 2 1/2 Johnson and I took an extra train to Tsarskoe [Selo]. From the Alexander Palace, went to the Grand Palace with Nicky,[46] where they were receiving - the ministers, suite, the diplomatic corps. At 4 o'cl. I went to see Boris; Kirill and Andrei were there.[47] Stayed there until 5 1/2 then went to Gatchina. After dinner Natasha, the Vyazemskys,

---

[44] **New Year's Day**. In St. Petersburg, Emperor Nicholas II performed his regular duties by greeting the diplomatic corps in the Great Palace at Tsarskoye Selo, and baskets of fresh flowers were delivered to Empress Alexandra Fedorovna. At the diplomatic reception, there was friction between the Emperor and the British Ambassador, Sir George Buchanan, who was chastised by the Emperor for speaking with opposition members. The chairman of the (in 1917 currently dissolved) Duma, Mikhail Rodzyanko, refused to greet the Minister of the Interior, Alexander Protopopov, a favorite of both Nicholas and Alexanda (Spiridovich, p. 449).

[45] **"Vyazamsky"** Prince Vladimir Alexeevich Vyazamsky (b. 1875 – d. 1945) was a graduate of the Orlov Cadet Corps and served in the Moscow Dragoons. A close friend of Grand Duke Michael, the prince, when he was called up for service in World War I, was appointed an ordinary officer to the Grand Duke at the insistence of Natalia Brasova, and the Vyazamskys lived at Gatchina until after the February Revolution. When reports came that Grand Duke had escaped his captors in Siberia, Prince Vyazamsky went to Perm to find him, while Princess Vyazamsky remained with Natalia. The reports proved false, the Vyazemskys found each other in Siberia in 1919 and retreated with the White Army, settling in France, where the Princess had a restaurant on the Côte d'Azur called the "Café des Fleurs," which émigrés called the *"Vyazemskaya Lavra."* (The Vyazamsky Monastery).

[46] **"Nicky"** Emperor Nicholas II (b. 1864- d. 1918)

[47] **"Boris, Kirill, Andrei"** Grand Dukes Kirill (b. 1876 – d. 1938), Boris (b. 1877 – d. 1943), and Andrei (b. 1879 – d. 1956) Vladimirovich of Russia, first cousins of Nicholas II and Grand Duke Michael, and fourth, fifth, and sixth in line to the throne, respectively. They were sons of Grand Duke and Vladimir Aleksandrovich and Grand Duchess Maria Pavlovna "the Elder," née Duchess Marie Alexandrine of Mecklenburg-Schwerin.

J[ohnson] and I went to a concert at the *Realnoe* School.[48] The concert was a success. We returned at 10 1/2. The weather was overcast, 2°.

2 January. Monday. Gatchina. In the morning drove to the Kurakin gates with the children, and from there walked to the Black Gates. Returned home in a motor. In the afternoon Natasha, Mrs. Bennett, Inna A and I had a sleigh ride along the Priory. Forgot to mention that after breakfast Ditz[49] and Kavtarze[50] paid us a visit. After tea we lit up the [Christmas] tree for the children and Mrs. Bennett[51] who left after that, and Alyosha arrived at this time. I rested before dinner. In the evening played the guitar a little. The weather was overcast, 7°. At 10 1/2 we went to have tea at J[ohnson's], who had a cold and did not go out.

3 January. Tuesday. Gatchina. At 10 o'cl. Natasha, Alyosha, J[ohnson] and I went to Petrograd on a train. I went to Alyosha's apartment, and at 12 o'cl. went to visit Aunt Miechen,[52] where Andrei[53] and Boris were. To

---

[48] **"the *Realnoe* School"** A secondary school based on the German model of the "Realschule," which offered practical education with an emphasis on mathematics, science, and history.
[49] **"Ditz"** Vladimir Romanovich Ditz, a stalker of His Majesty's Imperial Hunt and well-known statistician.
[50] **"Kavtarze"** Nikolai Alexeevich Kavtarze (b. 1861 – d. 1931), after 1916, Gatchina's security chief.
[51] **"Mrs. Bennett"** Edith Rata Bennett. Miss Rata began as governess to Natalia Brasova's daughter Natalia Sergeevna "Tata" Mamontova. She went into exile in Britain with Michael and Natalia and lived with them at Knebworth House. She eventually fell in love with Knebworth's groom, Mr. Bennett, whom she married at the Marieevsky Church. The couple returned to Russia with the Grand Duke and his wife.
[52] **"Aunt Miechen"** Grand Duchess Maria Pavlovna the Elder.
[53] From Grand Duke Andrei's diary at the time, on the subject of their cousin Grand Duke Dmitry Pavlovich's exile to the Persian Front for his role in murdering Rasputin: "We wrote to Nicky [on 3 January 1917] asking for a softening of Dmitry's plight, and this is now seen as some kind of a family revolt. How this has happened is simply inexplicable. We sit at home peacefully, and they all say we boycott Kugaisov! [Count Konstantin Pavlovich Kugaisov (b. 1876 d. 1918), who accompanied Grand Duke Dmitry Pavlovich in exile] Why is all this happening? Who does it help? They appear to have a reason to keep the family in conflict, and more importantly, quarrelling with the Emperor. It is all very serious and we now must take steps to make sure that the Emperor understands us and knows how devoted we are to him." (Grand Duke Andrei, *Voennyi Dnevnik, 1914-1917*, p. 224) The family's plea for clemency was not granted and Dmitry remained in Persia, which ironically saved his life. Dmitry went from there

have breakfast, I came over to Alyosha's, Natasha and J[ohnson] too. In the afternoon I went to Frederick's, then to Sergei M's, after to the Chairman of State Duma M. V. Rodzyanko's.[54] We went to Gatchina at 6 o'cl 10 min. In the evening Natasha and I had a talk with Miss Neame. The weather was overcast, 16 deg., and late in the evening 19°.

4 January. Wednesday. Gatchina. At 11 o'cl Vyazemsky and I drove to the Matrossky gate and from there walked to the park, got into an automobile by the palace. In the afternoon wrote telegrams, then Vyazemsky and I took a walk along Olginskaya and Alexandrovskaya [Streets]. At 5 o'cl went to the palace to Krestyanovs,' where we had tea. After dinner we went to the Modern cinema and saw the drama *The Revenge of Land*. In the evening J[ohnson] came from Petrograd with the news - he went to see the new Minister of Justice N. A. Dobrovolsky. the weather was peaceful, overcast, in the morning 20°, and later 8°.

5 January. Thursday. Gatchina. At 11 o'cl Vyazemsky and I took a sleigh ride to Priory, then went to the Zoo from the Black Gates to the Kurakin, then returned home. Before dinner and in the evening, I reviewed least year's diary. Alyosha arrived at 5 1/4. The weather semi-bright, in the

---

to European exile, where he married an American heiress before dying in 1942. Their son Paul, granted the title Prince Romanovsky-Ilyinsky, served as mayor of Palm Beach, Florida in the 1990s.

[54] **"Rodzyanko's"** Mikhail Vladimirovich Rodzyanko (b. 1859 – d. 1924), former State Councilor and Chamberlain of the Imperial family, Chairman of the State Duma, and a leading figure during the February Revolution. Grand Duke Michael deliberately went behind the Emperor's back to assess the severity of the situation and approached Rodzyanko. Glinka reports that in this meeting, the Grand Duke asked point blank if revolution was coming, and who would be in charge: "On January 3, Grand Duke Mikhail Aleksandrovich visited Rodzyanko, and asked Rodzyanko whether he thought there would be a revolution, to which he [Rodzyanko] replied that there would not be, but that the situation was serious and that measures should be taken to replace the government with persons of public confidence who would assume these responsibilities once and only when irresponsible influences were eliminated. When asked who would be in charge, Rodzyanko answered that they should name him, Rodzyanko, and that he would not consider it possible to refuse if the aforementioned conditions were met. He [Rodzyanko] then asked [Michael] about everything that revolts society, in order to report it to the Tsar and ask him [Michael] to finally have an audience arranged for him. The Grand Duke promised to do so. (Y. V. Glinka, *Eleven years in the State Duma, 1906-1917*: *Diary and Memoirs*, p. 174)."

morning 4°, in the evening 12°. Today Baby received a gift from the [crew of the] yacht *Tsaritsa*, a model worked up by: Boatswain Kuzmenko and 4 sailors, ideally made, the model length 7 feet, can pick up 14 *puds*. Gen[eral] Shuvaev is out, Gen[eral] Belyaev was appointed Minister of War.

6 January. Friday. Gatchina. At 4 o'cl in the morning Miss Neame woke us up, as Baby had high temperature, 39.3°. We called [Dr.] Koton, who arrived in 3/4 of an hour. We then went back to bed. I got up at 9 1/2. Alyosha, Vyazemsky, Miss Neame, Tata and I went to the palace to church, then came out for the blessing of the waters at the Silver Lake. Then stopped by Krestyanovs.' Returned home by 12 1/4. Doctor Vyazhlinsky arrived, who with Koton gave Baby a checkup and diagnosed influenza in a heavy form. In the afternoon Vyazemsky, Tata and I took a walk, - strolled down Gernetovskaya St., and then down Mikhailovskaya, then down [to the] Priory along the lake, came out to Georgievskaya and returned home via Alexandrovskaya. - Stopped by the church for a minute. After tea in the divining room I studied with Alyosha. Natasha and I went to see Baby many times, who thank God felt better towards the evening, and temp. decreased. In the afternoon N[atasha] and the princess [A. G. Vyazemskaya] rode in sleigh. The weather was occasionally sunny, peaceful, in the morning 7°, towards the evening 10°.

7 January. Saturday. Gatchina. At 10 o'cl Alyosha, J[ohnson] and I took a train to Petrograd. Having arrived at Alyosha's I had to bandage two fingers on the right hand, which on the way I tore up on a pin Alyosha wears. At 12 o'cl went to the Moscow-Vindavo-Rizhsky train station to meet the Romanian Crown Prince Carol. The train could not be on time for 1/2. I accompanied him to the Winter Palace and then went to have breakfast at Alyosha's. Then received Klopov, and at 3 o'cl went to Bertenson's, and from there to the Naval Minister Grigorovich. At 5 o'cl arrived at Princess Putyatina's, where had tea, - Alyosha, J[ohnson] and A. Arapov were there too. Just and took the 6 o'cl train to Gatchina. Baby, thank God, feels much better today, temp. 37.7°. The weather was sunny, 7°.

8 January. Sunday. Gatchina. At 11 o'cl Natasha, Vyazemskys and I went to the palace for liturgy. Princess Putyatina arrived for breakfast with us. In the afternoon went riding to the Priory and the Zoo. Putyatina came for tea from Bologov. At 6 o'cl we all went to Petrograd. Had dinner at Alyosha's, that is Natasha, Vyazemskys, Olga P[avlovna], J[ohnson] and I, and then went to [see] a ballet. *Don Quixote* was playing. I sat with Ioannchik, Kostya and Igor.[55] During breaks went over to Natasha's loge.[56] Natasha, J[ohnson] and I took the 11 o'cl train to Gatchina. The weather was sunny until 3 o'cl. 2°.

9 January. Monday. Gatchina. At 12 o'cl the Chairman of the State Duma M. V. Rodzyanko arrived. At 3 o'cl took a sleigh ride with him. The Vyazemskys also took a ride with us. We dropped him off at the train station at 4 o'cl. At 5 o'cl I went to Tsarskoe [Selo] with J[ohnson]. Drove in an auto that was redone for winter work (skis under the front tires, and instead of rear tires - 4 rollers covered with rubber like a belt Kegress system). Kegress himself drove, another car followed him. Driving on tires was unimaginable due to snow. I went directly to Pavlovsk to Aunt Olga's,[57] where I spent an hour, then went to the Alexander Palace, where they had a dinner for the Romanian [Crown] Prince Carol, -- Alix, the children, all the Romanians and part of the suite were there too. Everyone left at 10 o'cl. I went to Boris's for J[ohnson] and home with him in the same automobile. The weather was overcast, 2°.

10 January. Tuesday. Gatchina. At 10 o'cl we all went to Petrograd. I went directly to Alyosha's, then visited Lavrinovsky, who had a cold. After breakfast Natasha again went to run errands, but I forgot to mention that before that we, that is she, Alyosha and I, went to the Academy to the posthumous exhibit of Krachkovsky's paintings, after which I received Colonel Heim and General Baranov at Alyosha's. At 5 o'cl Alyosha and I went to Princess Putyatina's, there were: the Putyatins from Bogolov,

---

[55] **"Ioannchik, Kostya, and Igor"** The brothers and Princes of the Blood Ioann, Konstantin, and Igor Konstantinovich.
[56] The Grand Duke did not sit with his own wife at the ballet, sitting instead with his cousins in the Imperial Box.
[57] **"Aunt Olga"** H.I.H. Grand Duchess Olga Konstantinovna of Russia, later Queen Olga of Greece (b. 1851 – d. 1926).

Shegubatov (Dmitri's adjutant), and also Natasha and J[ohnson]. At 6 we headed to the Warsaw Station and home. After dinner went to the Modern cinema, which was showing the drama *The First and Last Kiss*. The weather was sunny until 11 o'cl, 6 deg., towards the evening 12°.

11 January. Wednesday. Gatchina. Took a walk around the garden in the morning. After breakfast Natasha and I drove in the auto to the Priory and there walked from the Filkinsky Lake around the park, at the gates got into the auto and went home. After tea played with Baby, who is still lying down. In the evening Natasha went through photographs, and I reviewed the diary. The weather was overcast, peaceful, 5°.

12. January. Thursday. Gatchina. At 12 o'cl everyone went to Petrograd, and I got off at the Alexandrovskaya and went to Nicky and Alix's, where we had breakfast, and then had a talk with Nicky.[58] At 2 3/4 saw Yuzefovich there at the Alexander Palace, then drove in an auto (from the Imperial garage) to Petrograd to Alyosha's. It was difficult to drive, we were en route for an hour. After tea Natasha went to run errands, and I to visit Mavrikievna.[59] Aunt Olga was there, and then the children arrived, too. Had dinner at Alyosha's around 8 1/2. By 10 o'cl we all went to the Shleifers, who had lots of company on the occasion of Tatiana P[avlovna]'s name day – Gen[eral] Mikhailovsky, Colonel Kulikovsky, a few more officers of the 2nd Brigade, in total there were around 20 guests. Everyone was playing cards in different rooms, and our group was playing *zhelëzka*. At 1 o'cl we left on the extra train. The weather was dark, 5°.

13 January. Friday. Gatchina. Got up late. From 12 o'cl until 1 1/2 Vyazemsky and I took a walk, reached the cemetery, from there walked through Zagvoska to the Priory and home. At 3 1/2 we took the extra train

---

[58] Khrustalëv notes that on 12 January 1917, "From 2 o'clock, His Majesty made time to receive Grand Duke Mikhail Aleksandrovich and Princes Konstantin Konstantinovich and Igor Konstantinovich" (RGIA, F. 472, S. 42). Given Michael's surreptitious meeting with Vladimir's sons and later with Rodzyanko on 3 January, his meeting with the Konstantinovichi princes at the ballet five days later, and Rodzyanko's subsequent visit to Gatchina on 9 January, it seems likely that Michael, his cousins, and Rodzyanko were working together.

[59] **"Mavrikievna"** Grand Duchess Elizaveta Mavrikievna of Russia (née Princess Elisabeth of Saxe-Altenburg. (b. Meiningen 1865 – d. Leipzig 1927). Wife of Grand Duke Konstantin Konstantinovich.

to Petrograd. At 5 o'cl Natasha and I went to Aunt Miechen's (first meeting),[60] where we had tea. Andrei was there. At 6 o'cl Natasha went to run errands and I to Klopov's apartment. At 7 1/4 [I] arrived at the Putyatins' where we soon had dinner, and after that went to the Saburov Theater, where they showed *Romance*, translated from an English novel by Ed[ward] Sheldon. We were invited by the Bologov Putyatins, - Alyosha and J[ohnson] were with us. At 11 3/4 we went to Gatchina, Olga P saw us off to the train station. The weather was sunny until 3 o'cl, 13°.

14 January. Saturday. Gatchina. Got up late. At 1 o'cl Alexander L. arrived. At 3 1/4 he left. The Vyazemskys, Natasha and I drove to the Priory, where we got out and took a walk. After tea the children lit up the fir tree for the last time. At 6 1/2 N., Princess V and I went to the palace for an all-night vigil. After dinner the four of us went to the Modern cinema for *The Co-Ed*, a comedy with F. Bertini. The weather was overcast, 3°.

15 January. Sunday. Gatchina. At 11 o'cl Natasha and I went to liturgy. Princess Putyatina with Tata and the Tolstoys (cavalier guard and wife) came over for breakfast with us. In the afternoon we all took a ride in three sleighs at the Zoo and the Priory. Forgot to mention that Alyosha arrived at 2 o'cl. At 4 1/4 we arrived at Johnson's where we had tea, and then practiced music, - J[ohnson] played the piano, the princess sang, Domenici and I played guitars. At 6 o'cl the Tolstoys left, and we returned home, -

---

[60] **"first meeting"** Following the example of the Dowager Empress, no member of the Imperial Family would consent to meet Michael's new wife. Grand Duchess Vladimir was the first to do so. It would not be until after the Revolution that the Dowager Empress finally consented to meet her grandson, George Brasov. The news spread fast, and on 3 February 2017, Princess Elizaveta Naryshkina wrote in her diary: "A rush of blood to the head. Sad thoughts: the Empress [Alexandra] is abhorred. I believe danger will come from an unexpected source: Michael. His wife [Natalia] is very much a member of the intelligentsia, and, as such, lacks any constraints. She's already wormed her way through to Maria Pavlovna. Her box at the theatre is teeming with Grand Dukes; they will connive together with Maria Pavlovna. She will see to it that she's accepted by the Dowager Empress and the Emperor. I sense that they're plotting. Poor Misha will, in spite of himself, be implicated in this plot; first he will be regent, then he will be emperor. They will accomplish everything." (E. A. Naryshkina, "Iz dnevnika ober-gofmeisteriny kniagini E.A. Naryshkinoi," *Poslednie Novosti*, Paris, 10 May 1936.)

Alyosha, Vyazemsky and I walked. Dvorzhitsky[61] came for dinner and stayed until 11 o'cl., and Princess Putyatina with Tata [left] at 9 3/4. The weather was occasionally sunny, 5°.

16 January. Monday. Gatchina. We went to Petrograd on the 10 o'cl train. Before breakfast looked at two houses on Sergeyevskaya, Demodovsky and Alexandrov's house was nearby. But they weren't suitable for us. Had breakfast at Alyosha's, after which Wrangel[62] and Yuzefovich came to see me. At 5 o'cl they left, and Andrei came for tea, the day after tomorrow he is going to Kislovodsk for Easter.[63] Natasha, J[ohnson] and I took the 6 o'cl train to Gatchina. The weather was sunny, 15°. Vedikhov was hired as our chauffer. The garden thermometer in the evening showed 22°.

17 January. Tuesday. Gatchina. At 10 o'cl we went to Petrograd. I received a few individuals at the Control office, then went to Alyosha's with him, where we had breakfast, Wrangel was there too. At 1 o'cl Natasha, Alyosha and I went to church of the 1st Cadet Corps, where there was a

---

[61] **"Dvorzhitsky"** likely Georgi Konstantinovich Dvorzhitsky (b. 1887- d. 1962) Colonel of Her Majesty's Own Life-Guards Ulan Regiment. Member of the White movement, he emigrated to Serbia, and later to France. From 1956-1962, he was a member of the Chancellery-in-exile of the Head of the Russian Imperial House Grand Duke Vladimir Kirillovich (b. 1917 – d. 1992). He is buried in St. Briac, Normandy. France.

[62] **"Wrangel"** Baron Nikolai Aleksandrovich Wrangel (b. 1869 – d. 1927) Commander of His Majesty's Own Life Guards Cavalry Regiment. From 1901-1909 a member of Grand Duke Michael's suite, and from 1909-1912 personal secretary to the Grand Duke. From 1915-1917 served as personal adjutant to the Grand Duke. A cousin of Russian Civil War hero, Baron Peter N. Wrangel.

[63] Grand Duke Andrei took leave of the Emperor on 16 January and noted in his diary: "Today I was received at Tsarskoe Selo by Nicky on the occasion of my departure for Kislovodsk. My reception was quite ordinary and amiable, and with no mention of the past. It lasted five minutes, and I left." [Grand Duke Andrei, *Voennyi dnevnik*, p. 224.). He and his mother, Grand Duchess Maria Pavlovna "the Elder" departed for Kislovodsk, where they arrived on 22 January, intending to remain through the Lenten period until Easter. Ultimately, the two would remain there until their departure for exile on 13 February (new style) 1920. Some western sources indicate that the Grand Duke and his mother were sent by the Emperor into internal exile for a plot to overthrow him. This is first reported in Albert Stopford's *The Russian Diary of an Englishman: Petrograd 1915–1917*, published in 1919. While Stopford's stories repeat spurious articles from the Russian newspapers of the time, and the French ambassador Maurice Paléologue's diaries published in 1925 make similar accusations, there appear to be no period primary source documents which confirm this. (See also notes 104 and 118.)

prayer service for the occasion of the one-year anniversary of the St. George Committee. After the ceremonial prayer service, Natasha and Alyosha left, and I went with the members of the committee to the Grand Hall, where they brought me an icon, and then the meeting started, which lasted around forty minutes. At 2 1/4 I went to Wrangel's where saw V. V. Soldatenko, and then with Prince V. Volkonsky. At 5 o'cl went to Klopov's. On the way to the Tsarskoselsky train station I stopped by Alyosha's where I saw Natasha, who left for Gatchina at 7 1/2. I arrived at Tsarskoe Selo at 7 1/2 and dropped J[ohnson] off at Boris's, and myself went to dinner at Nicky and Alix's. At 10 1/4 J and I went to Gatchina. The weather was sunny, 15°.

18 January. Wednesday. Gatchina. At 10 3/4 drove to Dietz's in an auto, and from there [went] hunting with him in a troika. The troika slid off the road (caught) on the way to Salezi. Dietz held the right out-runner, I did the left one, but this didn't help, and we ran full steam ahead, luckily did not hit or encounter anyone. Having ridden this way for about a half of verst,[64] Epifan turned the root into a ditch, where we stopped successfully. On the way to Korpikovo 4 pheasant corrals were set up, Dietz killed 9, and I 15. By 1 1/4 I was already home. Krestyanov had breakfast with us and stayed until 2 1/2. In the afternoon I jogged around the park. After tea I played the guitar with Domenici, and Natasha, Princess Vyazemskaya and Tata played a game with Baby, which ended in a scene, - Baby got terribly angry at Tata and started to throw shoes at her. In the evening I wrote a letter to Nicky in Tsarskoe. The weather was sunny, 15°.

*19/I - 1917. Gatchina.

Dear Nicky,

Regrettably 3 days ago I completely forgot to tell you that Colonel Tolstoy, who was the cavalier guard under Dmitri's command, asked that you allow him to visit Dmitry in Persia. Tolstoy feels very burdened by the circumstances he is in and would like to visit him. Please notify me of your decision via a telegram.

---

[64] **"verst"** – A prerevolutionary Russian measurement of distance, about 1.1 kilometers or .66 miles.

I would also like to remind you about the old man Klopov, whom you agreed to receive. I am imploring you to do this within the next few days, i.e. prior to his departure to Stavka.

I gave Kira Naryshkin his address. I can add that I'm convinced and based on general consensus, the old man Klopov is loyal and deeply devoted to you.

I am leaving for Kiev this evening via Moscow, and farther to the front. Will see you at Stavka [Supreme Military Headquarters, at Mogilev][65] on the way back in. I embrace you firmly.

Your Misha*

19 January. Thursday. Gatchina. In the morning packed things for the trip. At 12 o'cl Mrs. Belyaeva came over to complete the deed on the house on Baggovutskaya Street near our garden; our assistant Kvyatkovsky acted as a notary, the witnesses: Vyazemskys and J[ohnson]. After breakfast I took a walk around the garden. At 4 o'cl we went to Petrograd; the train was late. We went directly to Moika to see the Pistolkors house #59. We liked the house, - the young Pistolkorses[66] showed it. From there went to Count Nirod's with whom I talked about Abas-Tuman. After that we all went to have dinner at Alyosha's. At 8 o'cl, having arrived at the Nikolaevich train station, they announced to us that there the train is late for more than an hour. We returned to Alyosha's and only got into our train car at 9 1/4. Traveling to Moscow with us are: Vyazemskys. Alyosha and J[ohnson]. The weather was sunny from 12 o'cl, 15°.

20 January. Friday. Arrival in Moscow. Arrived in Moscow one-and-a-half hours late and headed directly to the Vagankovsky cemetery, where in the new church the burial liturgy service took place in honor of the second anniversary of [the death of] dear Olga S. Only a short memorial

---

[65] **"Mogilev"** During World War I, the Belorussian city of Mogilev was the location of Stavka, the headquarters of the Russian Imperial Army. Nicholas II spent long periods there as Commander-in-Chief after he assumed that role in August 1915.
[66] **"the Young Pistolkorses"** The three children of the previous marriage of Princess Olga Paley: Alexander, Olga, and Marianna von Pistolkhors; stepsiblings of Grand Duke Dmitry and Grand Duchess Maria Pavlovna the younger, and half-siblings of Vladimir, Natalia, and Irina Paley.

service was held at the grave as it was too cold. Went to have breakfast on Strastnaya [Boulevard], only Gen[eral] Oboloshev was there, and Konstantin N [Kraft] did not come. Then Natasha went to run errands, and Alyosha and I walked to [the Hotel] National, on the way stopping by two shops. Before dinner studied with Alyosha. At 8 had dinner at Maria Vasilievna [Shelaputina], who had over: Kayutovs, Schuberts, Fanny Mavrikievna, Oboloshev, Yuliy P, Alyosha, J, Vyazemskys, M. F. Salomirskaya, a young lady pianist Mikhalchi and Maria V [asilievna]'s protégé - L. Veselova. Then we listened to the pianist for a little while, and when Sergei Aleksandrovich Shermetevsky and Olga A[lexandrovna] Rodkevich] arrived, we played *zhelëzka*, - and Natasha's bank went up to [blank] and she won 3860.[67] I went to [the Hotel] National before Natasha as it was late. The evening was very lively. The weather was sunny, 15°. Natasha arrived in 1/4 after me.

21 January. Saturday. Moscow and departure to Kiev. From 10 1/2 Alyosha and I took care of business. Then I received Prince Fazio, who is [there] for treatment and was wounded on 10 December; also there were directors from the Insurance community, Kayutov and Ensign [blank], who donated 12,500 r[ubles] to the St. George Committee. The last one there was the doctor... [blank]. After that Alyosha and I walked to Strastnaya Boulevard where we had breakfast, Gen[eral] Bogak was there. In the afternoon A[lyosha] and I headed by foot to the National, stopped by a shop, and I bought a blue down blanket and pillow. We studied until 5, then I went to the photographer [blank], where Natasha was being photographed and we were photographed together, after which we went to Olga Alek., where her mother and Maria N were, whom we had not seen since Brasovo. Having returned to the National I saw F[ather] Pospelov. At 7 o'cl Alyosha and I went to dinner at the Cheremeteffs.' There were: besides us four - Olga Aleksandrovna, Maria V, Guzhon, Fanny Mavrikievna and Kirusha. After they saw me off to the Bryansky train station, where the Vorontsovs, Oboloshev and Princess Vyazemskaya were. At 8 o'cl (Petrograd [time]) the train departed to Kiev. Going with

---

[67] 3,860 roubles in 1917 was a tidy sum. The 1915 Fabergé Imperial Red Cross Egg with Portraits cost 3,559 roubles and 40 kopeks. (cf. Faberge/Proler/Skurlov, p. 222)

me: Yuzefovich, Wrangel and Vyazemsky. The weather was sunny, 15°, and 23° in the morning. On 19 January I was appointed Inspector General of the Cavalry.

22 January. Sunday. The train. Did not leave the [train] wagon all day. Traveled with big delay. Arrived in Kiev instead of 6 o'cl all the way at 2 o'cl in the morning. Our wagon was detached and ended up sitting at the station. The weather was very cold, around 17°, overcast. Today Natasha is at the ballet.

23 January. Monday. Arrival in Kiev and departure to the Southwestern front. At 2 o'cl in the morning arrived in Kiev. At 10 1/4 I went to Mama's where I spent the entire day. Countess Mengden, Prince Shervashidze and Prince Dolgorukov came over for breakfast. In the afternoon Mama and I went to Olga's infirmary, - she had a slight cold and doesn't go outside. Returned for tea. At 5 3/4 I said farewells and went to see Shervashidze, and later stopped by Sandro's,[68] and [went] from there directly to the train station. The train departed for Tarnopol at 7 3/4. We had dinner in the railcar. The weather was sunny from 2 o'cl, 10°.

24 January. Tuesday. Around 2 o'cl afternoon arrived in Tarnopol. I received the commander, Governor Chartoriysky, and I. Orlov, who commands the [blank] Cossack Division. In the afternoon Yuzefovich, Wrangel, Vyazemsky and I took a walk to the city gardens. Vyazemsky and Wrangel then walked to the city, and Yuzefovich and I returned to the train, and after tea and before dinner I slept, had a slight headache. Yazykov had dinner with us. In the evening we all went to the cinema. The weather was sunny in the morning, around 7°.

25 January. Wednesday. Departure from Tarnopol and arrival at Nadvornaya. At 9 1/4 we drove off to Nadvornaya in automobiles. At 11 o'cl the commander of 7th Army, General-Adjutant Shcherbachev arrived and invited us to breakfast with Prince Massalsky, Gen[eral] Golovin and Gen[eral]-Adjutant Shch[erbachev]'s lieutenant [blank] were there. At 1 1/2 we travelled on, and by 4 o'cl 30 min we were in Nadvornaya. A convoy was lined up at the entrance in front of the house, in addition to all

---

[68] **"Sandro"** Grand Duke Aleksandr Mikhailovich

the staff officers. We sat down for tea right away, and I invited Prince Begildeyev, Panteleyev, Colonel Makarov, Doctor Angelov, Colonel Schavinsky and Rot. Afterward I played the guitar. Ivan enjoy came over for evening tea. The weather was overcast, light snow storm, 6°.

26 January. Thursday. Nadvornaya. At breakfast were: Lieutenant-Gen[eral] Khelmitsky, head of the 3rd Caucasus Cossack Division, with his chief of staff Colonel Lazare, Colonels Dragan, Kulyubyakin, and Mazalov. Before breakfast Prince Vadbolsky and Moshnin came to see me. In the afternoon Wrangel and I took a walk to the neighboring village. After tea I studied with Yuzefovich, then they showed us cinematograph in the garden, owned by the staff, which was set up on a cart and will be taken around the regiments of the corps. The show ended before dinner, to which were invited: Knyazev, Kadyan, Ber and Galperin (Corps quartermaster). In the evening I studied with Yuzefovich. The weather was sunny, 5° in the afternoon, and 10° in the morning and evening. Natasha and Tata went to the Popular Theater today where they performed *Eugene Onegin*.

27 January. Friday. Nadvornaya. At 11 o'cl we went to the farewell review of the 2nd brigade of the 9th Calvary Division and 2nd Brigade of Svodny Calvary Division (1st and 2nd Trans-Amur Regiments). Prince Vadbolsky, Prince Tumanov, Colonels Borodin, Yazykov, and Ensign Pernikov had breakfast with me. In the afternoon Prince Begildeyev and I went to Bitkuv, where oil is extracted. The work continues, but there are few workers, so the productivity is most pathetic. Gen[eral] Moshnin lives at the factory director's [quarters], which is the location of the 9th [Cavalry] Division's headquarters. After visiting Moshnin, we went to the machinist building and workshop. Yuzefovich, Wrangel, Vyazemsky, and Prince Vadbolsky went with us. The location there is very pretty, a ravine, with beech trees growing. Returned home at 6 o'cl. Prince Vadbolsky, Prince Tumanov, Colonel Gonchar, Colonel Navrotsky, Colonel Moraviasky, Major-Gen[eral] Karnisky, Colonel Skosarevsky, and artillerists: Colonel Butyagin, Captain Demyanovich, and Lieutenant-Colonels Munetrem and Ionov came to dinner. Prince Begildeyev has breakfast and dinner with me constantly. The weather was sunny, wonderful, [snow] melted in the sun, a rather strong frost in the morning and evening, around -10°. Staff Captain

Plyshevsky, who is transferring to the Nikolaevsky Calvary school, came to evening tea. I sent a letter to Natasha with him.

* 27 January, 1917. Nadvornaya.

Letter to Natasha:

I am awfully glad to have the chance to send you a letter with Staff Captain Plyshevsky, who has until now served at the headquarters of my corps, and is now starting at the Nikolaevsky Calvary School. - Well here I am again here at the army, that is at Darmy [sic], although this time only for a few days. It's not hard for a short time, but staying here for long is very hard. The contrast between life here and in Petrograd is huge; as if one is living in another country and all that worries the brain in Russia is cancelled out in general, and in both capitals, in particular. Thank God, my mood is cheerful and spirit firm [to be cont[inued.]

28 January. Saturday. Nadvornaya. At 10 3/4 we drove in automobiles to the village of Krasnoyarsk (12 versts), where I made a farewell review of the Arkhangelsk and Irkutsk Regiments. Then moved to Maidahn-Gorne where said goodbye to the equestrian batteries: 16th, 17th, 25th, 26th and 1st Turkestan Equest[rian]. After that we went to the meeting of the equestrian artillerists, where the master was Prince Cantacuzène, and they treated us to breakfast. The trumpeter of the Kazan Regiment played, then Ensign Starosvetsky sang. In general, it was all very charming and adorable. Around 3 1/2 we went to our place, and took a short walk before tea. Commanders of brigade regiments came to dinner, as well as Prince Cantacuzène with officers of 9th Calvary Division. Colonel Serebrennikov (Commander of the 7th Hussar regiment) also arrived. In the evening we went out to the garden, where a movie was shown to us. The public was somewhat cold. At 11 o'cl everyone left. Cherepanov came over for evening tea. The weather was ideal, March-like, and in the sun it was simply warm and everything melted.

29 January. Sunday. Nadvornaya. At 9 1/2 we drove in automobiles to Maksimetz Okhotnichy house, to the headquarters of 163rd Lenkoransky-Mashenburgsky Regiment. We drove through the villages Pnyuv, Pasechna and Zelena. From there climbed into sleigh and headed to

altitude 1036, where artillery position was, one platoon from our corps, - drove through the ravine to the altitude 883, where the district reserves were, a battalion of 163rd Regiment and riflemen of the 9th [Cavalry] Division. There I thanked the riflemen for their service, tasted the food, reviewed the wooden barracks of the lower ranks, and then we entered a dugout (for officers) and had a snack, - the provisions were our own. After breakfast, we drove ahead to the outpost of the infantry, 3 versts along the valley, or rather along the ravine of Bystritza-Solovinskaya. From there returned to 853 and drove through the ravine of Bystritza to house of the division commander. We left the sleigh there and went on foot to the top of Negrov Mountain, where our outpost is located. Prince Begildeyev, Wrangel and Kulyubyakin just started to ascend and did not go farther. Prince Vadbolsky, Pukovsky and I reached the tip in an hour and a half. Before us rose the bare tip of Sivul, where the Austrian outpost is, and behind us the mountain Bayarin, also bare, where our other outpost is stationed. Before of our eyes the Svodny Division was being relieved by the 9th [Cavalry] Division. In the officers' dugout they offered us tea. After 40 min. Yuzefovich arrived, and 10 minutes later we began descending, - it was around 5 1/2 o'cl. Pukovsky and I were running down. We flew at breakneck speed and in about 1/2 hour were at the bottom of the mountain, where the little house is. Prince Vadbolsky and Colonel [blank] came after 13 min., after which we rode back to the 163rd Regiment's headquarters in a sleigh, where we waited for Yuzefovich, who arrived after 1/2 hour. From there we returned to our place in an automobile. Prince Vadbolsky and Pukovsky had dinner. (We came home at 8 3/4). The weather was sunny from 12 1/2 o'cl. The snow is deep in the mountains. The mountains are overgrown with fir and pine trees. Paths are competently made by patrols. We ascended on foot to about 800 meters. Natasha had over: Boris, Gabriel, Princess Putyatina, Mme Donich, Dobrovolsky and Alyosha. Today it was drizzling all day, in the morning 3°, in evening 7°.

30 January. Monday. Nadvornaya. In the morning individuals from various medical organizations serving our corps presented themselves to me. After breakfast, to which Staff Captain Novitsky, Ensign Illyasov and Staff Captain Lubinsky were invited, I gave out my photographs and gifts to some in the staff ranks. At 3 1/2 we went to the realm of our intendant,

where we watched breadbaking, soapmaking and blacksmithing, and at the station reviewed warehouses and harnesses of four dogs who pull 10 *puds* in a sled. After tea Panteleyev came to see me. Tsurikov came to dinner. Then we listened to the terrace and watched a cinematic show. The weather was sunny part of the day, slight frost in the shade.

31 January. Tuesday. Nadvornaya and departure to Kamenets-Podolsk. At 11 o'cl I made a farewell review of the 1st Brigade of the 9th Calvary Division, which was lined up between Nadvornaya and Pnyuv. On a wide street at Nadvornaya were lined up: my convoy squadron, the 7th Samokratny Company and all the teams of our corps, along with all the staff officers and officials, - in the lineup there were 490 of the lower ranks, but only 42 officers and officials. After the farewell and awards of St. George's medals they all marched ceremonially. To breakfast came: Nikitin (he is now serving at headquarters of the 7th Army), Semenov, Colonel Davydov and Ivanenko. At 3 o'cl I took photos with the entire staff, after which Vyazemsky and I took a walk towards Bystritza. Then I took photos with my convoy and also dropped by to see the chancery rooms, and dropped by to see Yuzefovich and Prince Begildeyev. At 4 3/4 had tea. At 8 o'cl I had dinner for the entire staff, besides officers there were officials too, altogether there were around 50 of us. Dinner took place in a former little restaurant along with a cinematograph. Canvas and multicolored materials were stretched on the walls, and everything was very nicely decorated. I sat between Yakov D and Prince Begildeyev. I had to give a farewell speech. Prince B[egildeyev], Yuzefovich and Angelov also spoke. Trumpeters of the Kazan regiment played. After dinner we went to the cinematograph. At 10 3/4 we drove to the train station. Everyone saw me off, along with the convoy squadron with trumpeters, - it was touching and sad. Going with me are: Yuzefovich, Wrangel, Vyazemsky and Colonel Dragan of the Bugsky regiment. The weather was sunny, [snow] melted, 2° with frost in the shade.

February 1917

1 February. Wednesday. Arrival in Kamenets and departure to Kiev. At 11 o'cl we arrived in Kamenets, the commander of the Southwest Front, Gen[eral] Brusilov came into my railcar with his chief of staff [Sukhomlin]

and Governor Myakinin. At 12 o'cl we went to [Sukhomlin]'s, and at 1 o'cl we had breakfast with Brusilov in his room. Then Vyazemsky and I drove to visit Bishop Mitrofan, then to Myakinin's. He lost his wife in June, poor thing, and is very sad, - his two sisters are currently visiting him. Wrangel and Yuzefovich came over too - they treated us to tea and showed us engravings. Having returned to the train at 5 1/2, I received Prince Massalsky, then played the guitar. Prior to train departure Brusilov and Myakinin came to see me. At 6 o'cl 30 min the train moved [from the station]. The weather was sunny, 4°.

2 February. Thursday. Arrival in Kiev and departure to Gatchina. At 12 3/4 we arrived in Kiev. I went directly to Mama's.[69] They were just finishing breakfast and there were: Ducky,[70] [Crown Prince] Carol (Romanian), and Sandro. Soon they left and I had breakfast. At 4 o'cl I paid a visit to Carol, who was on the train, then returned to have tea at Mama's. Sandro was there. After that Wrangel and I went to the second-hand dealer Berkhovich. I bought a few things. Before dinner I went to Shervashidze's, who was lying in bed with a cold. At 8 o'cl had dinner at Mama's: Ducky and Olga.[71] Then put away the puzzle. At 11 o'cl 30 min Wrangel and I went to the train, which left at 12 1/4. Yuzefovich and

---

[69] **"Mama's"** Kiev's Mariinsky Palace, commissioned in 1744 by the Russian Empress Elizaveta Petrovna and designed by Bartolomeo Rastrelli, was the Imperial Family's official residence in Kiev. Dowager Empress Maria Fedorovna of Russia had left for Kiev in 1916 and would never return to the capital. She noted in her diary that day that she met with Grand Duchess Viktoria Fedorovna, Crown Prince Carol of Romania, and Grand Duke Alexander Mikhailovich, with Grand Duke Michael arriving later. "Sandro is troubling me and speaks constantly of my need to go to Petersburg. I do not wish to go, as I think I cannot do anything there. Baby, Ducky, and Misha came to dinner." (Empress Maria Fedorovna, *Dnevniki imperatritsy Marii Fedorovny, 1914–1920, 1923 gody*, Moscow, 2006, p. 684)

[70] **"Ducky"** H.I.H. Grand Duchess Viktoria Fedorovna of Russia (née H.R.H. Princess Victoria Melita of Edinburgh, Princess of Saxe-Couburg-Gotha, b. Valetta, Malta 1876 – d. Amorbach, Germany 1936). Wife of Grand Duke Kirill Vladimirovich of Russia, former wife of Empress Alexandra's brother, Grand Duke Ernst of Hesse and by Rhine.

[71] **"Olga"** Grand Duchess Olga Alexandrovna of Russia (b. Gatchina 1882 – d. Toronto, Canada 1960), later Mrs. Nicholas Kulikovsky. Younger sister of Emperor Nicholas II, and Grand Duke Michael's closest sibling.

Gen[eral] Mannerheim,[72] commander of the 12th Calvary Division [who] arrived from Romania, are going with me. Vyazemsky is going to Popelevo. The weather was sunny, windy, 8°.

3 February. Friday. The train. Travel delayed by three hours, most likely due to snow storm; I say most likely because it's impossible to get the real reason - everything is a mess. In Mogilev Gen[eral] Ivanov, who permanently lives at Stavka, dropped by. Got to Mogilev only at 7 1/2. The weather was sunny, around 0°.

4 February. Saturday. The train and arrival at Gatchina. In Semerino my companions transferred to another car and continued traveling to Petrograd, and I was taken to Gatchina with the extra caboose, where I arrived at 7 1/4 instead of 12 o'cl, i.e. the train was almost eight hours late. Natasha and Johnson met me. Maria V and Fanny Mavrikievna are staying with Natasha for almost a week. After dinner we played *zhelëzka* and I won 655 r[ubles]. The weather was sunny, 16°.

5 February. Sunday. Gatchina at 11 o'cl Natasha, Maria V, Fanny M and I went to church at the palace, then visited part of the palace, in the center part [of it] upstairs, in the theater, in my rooms and Olga's. Yuliy P came to breakfast. At 4 o'cl we all went to Petrograd directly to Alyosha's. Once there, all the ladies brushed their hair and got dressed. After dinner we all went to the ballet (except Yuliy P), [and saw] *Ruses d'Amour* and *Harlequinade*. I sat with Ioannchik, Gavriil, Igor and Boris.[73] During breaks went over to Natasha's loge, where the Shleifers and Alyosha were. At 11 1/2 Natasha, J[ohnson] and I rode down Baltiyskaya in an extra train. Got home at 12.40. The weather was sunny, 16°, during the night it was around 20°.

6 February. Monday. Gatchina. At 12 3/4 took the extra train via Baltiyskaya Road to Petrograd, took less than 3/4 of an hour. We went directly to Nerodovsky's apartment (in a museum). There we looked at the

---

[72] **"Mannerheim"** General Baron Carl Gustaf Emil Mannerheim (cf. entry for 8 January 1917, p. 54) served 30 years in the Imperial Russian Empire and later became president of his native Finland after its secession from the Russian Empire.
[73] Interesting to note once more the gathering of the Konstantinovichi and Vladimirovichi branches with Michael at the ballet (cf. January, 1917.)

tapestry – decorative, of the Elizabethan Era. From there went to Alyosha's, where I saw Wrangel, Oboloshev, who just arrived from Moscow, and then Klopov. At 4.25 I went to Tsarskoe [Selo] to Nicky, where had tea. At 6 1/2 I went to the Alexandrovskaya [train station] where I joined Natasha, who was going to Gatchina with Maria V and Fanny M. After dinner we played *zhelëzka*, Natasha's bank rose up to 10,000 r[ubles].[74] Dispersed late. The weather was sunny, 14°.

7 February. Tuesday. Gatchina. At 11 o'cl I took a ride on horseback, rode around the Priory, from the Black Gates rode to Kurakin and home through town - I rode Vityaz. After breakfast we went to a wolf hunt. Natasha rode with Maria V and Fanny M, and I in another sleigh with Dietz. Chirikin's house was left behind on the right, the circle was around 3-4 versts past the train tracks. Maria V also stood with a rifle. The wolf came toward Natasha and me, I killed him with one shot, - and the wolf was very large, dark gray, very beautiful. At the end of corral, we rode back and returned home at 6 1/2; it was light until 6 o'cl. Altogether we rode 34 versts. Before dinner played in nursery. To dinner came [the following]: Alyosha, Oboloshev, the Shleifers. In the evening played *zhelëzka*. At 11 1/4 Boris arrived from Petrograd, where he had attended a dinner with English officers. We kept playing until 1 3/4, then had supper, after which Boris left for Tsarskoe in automobile sleigh. Other guests took extra train at 3 o'cl. The weather was sunny, - when we returned from the hunt it was 18°.

8 February. Wednesday. Gatchina. At 22 3/4 went to Petrograd via Baltiyskaya [railroad], had breakfast in train. In the city I went to Alyosha's, - at first rested on the sofa, and after tea studied with Alyosha, later sat with Oboloshev, also played the piano. At 7 o'cl we had dinner. Natasha, Maria Vasilievna and Fanny Mavrikievna came over at dinner. Oboloshev went to Moscow on the 8 o'cl train. He is going to the front in next few days, where he will receive, or rather form, a new division. At

---

[74] **"10,000 r[ubles]."** In 1916, the approximate exchange rate was 6.7 rubles to one U.S. dollar. In 2020 terms (with one 1916 dollar = $24.95 2020 dollars) it appears that Natalia had thus won close to $37,238.62. (Source: www.dollartimes.com, viewed 30 December 2019.)

9.40 Natasha, J and I went to Gatchina, - arrived only at 11 1/2. The weather was windy, snowing, 10°.

9 February. Thursday. Gatchina. At 10 1/2 Natasha, Tata, Miss Neame, J[ohnson] and I went to Petrograd via Baltiyskaya. Had breakfast at Alyosha's, Maria V and Fanny M were there. At 1 o'cl Tata and Miss Neame went to the ballet, and I went to Evropeiskaya Hotel at 2 o'cl, where I saw the chief of staff, Gen[eral] Gurko, on some business. From there went to Klopov's, where stayed until 4 1/2. After that I went to Aunt Miechen's, where I had tea. Kirill was there. We returned to Gatchina on the 6 o'cl train. With us rode Inna A and Sofia N Khodakovskaya. They stayed at our place until 10 3/4. The weather was sunny until 1 o'cl, from 8° to 13°.

10 February. Friday. Gatchina. Walked in the garden before breakfast. Tata and Miss Neame went to Tsarskoe [Selo] at 10 1/2 to [see] the Tolstoys. After breakfast Natasha, Baby and I headed to Tsarskoe [Selo] in a sleigh- automobile. Rode for an hour. N went to the Tolstoys', and I received Yuzefovich on business at the Alexander Palace. Then had tea at Nicky's, after which had a talk with him.[75] At 6 1/2 picked up Natasha, stayed at the Tolstoys' 1/4 of an hour, then went to Gatchina. The weather was sunny, 3° in the sun, 12° in the shade, and 17° in the evening.

11 February. Saturday. Gatchina. At 10 1/2 Natasha, Tata, Miss Neame, J[ohnson] and I went to Petrograd via Baltiyskaya. Had breakfast at Alyosha's, except Tata and Miss Neame, who had breakfast at the Shleifers' and went to the ballet with them. In the afternoon I received at the entrance: Gen[eral] Ostrogradsky (former general inspector of the cavalry), Gen[eral]. Stakhovich, 2 Chernigov Hussars, Colonel Kalinin and Adjutant-Gen[eral] Yaroshev, Yuzefovich and Klopov. From 4 1/2

---

[75] **"had a talk with [Nicky]"** Other records for this day suggest a more complicated situation. The palace journals for February 10 (Khrustalëv, citing RGIF, f. 472, s. 42) show that Empress Alexandra dined alone, and then met with Grand Duke Aleksandr Mikhailovich. Later, "Sandro" described the meeting as fraught with resistance to his warnings about impending revolution. Empress Alexandra responded, "I refuse to continue this dispute ... You are exaggerating the danger. Someday, when you are less excited, you will admit that I knew better." (Grand Duke Alexander Mikhailovich, *Once A Grand Duke*, New York: 1931, p. 284) The journals also note that on the same day at 4 o'clock, Nicholas II met with Rodzyanko together with Grand Duke Michael.

until 5 1/4 I was at Sandro's, where M.V. Rodzyanko was. After that I dropped by Alyosha's, where I saw Wrangel, then J and I went to the train where we met with Natasha, Tata, Miss Neame and Domenici, with whom I studied after dinner until 10 1/2. The weather was overcast, snow storm, 7°

12 February. Sunday. Gatchina. At 11 o'cl we went to church to the palace with the children. After breakfast Tanya and Marina came over. From 2 1/4 until 3 1/2 I rode on horseback, rode through the Zoo and Priory. Prince P. P. Putyatin came to tea, then he left and Maria V, Fanny M and Alyosha came over. After dinner we sat down to play *zhelëzka*. The guests planned to leave at 11 o'cl., but Natasha did not let them, so they stayed overnight. I went to bed at 12, while the others continued playing until 1 1/2. The weather was overcast, the sun occasionally peeked out, it was snowing, the temp[erature] kept changing between 2-6° tomorrow is the start of Great Lent.

13 February. Monday. Gatchina. At 10 1/2 we went to Petrograd via Baltiyskaya- had breakfast in the train. Alyosha and I went to his place, and then to Lidval's for a fitting. Having reunited with Natasha, the ladies and J[ohnson], we went to the Imperial Porcelain Factory, where we bought a few things, Strukov was there. From there I went to George's,[76] where I also saw Sergei. We, Gatchintzy returned home on the 6 o'cl train. Koton came over to evening tea. The weather was overcast, from 2° to 6°. The first week of Great Lent.

14 February. Tuesday. Gatchina. At 11 o'cl I went to the church to the palace. Princess Vadbolskaya came to breakfast, and at around 2 o'cl Prince R. F. Bagration. At 4 o'cl we had tea, after which they left. Then Natasha and I took a little walk around the garden. At 5 o'cl R. F. Meltzer arrived, - we talked to him about our Petrograd house. At 6 1/2 he left, and Natasha and I went by sleigh to the palace for an all-night vigil. In the

---

[76] **"George"** H.I.H. Grand Duke Georgiy Mikhailovich (b. 1863 – d. 1919).

evening pasted into album newspaper cutouts in the nursery. The weather was overcast, 5° at 2 o'cl there was an opening of the State Duma.[77]

15 February. Wednesday. Gatchina. At 10 1/2 we went to Petrograd via Baltiyskaya. I presented myself to the War Minister Belyaev on the occasion of my new appointment, then went to Alyosha's, from there to visit Count S. D. Cheremeteff, then to Kulimzin's. Having returned to Alyosha's, we went to the Putyatins together at 4 3/4, where we had tea. The Bologov Putyatins were there and Mme Donich, Olga P was not well and did not come out. We returned to Gatchina on the 6 o'cl train. (Krestyanovs travelled with us in the morning and in the evening.) In the evening I played the guitar with Domenici. The weather was overcast, 5°. In Petrograd Maria V and Fanny M came to the train station in order to travel to Gatchina, but in light of them losing the bag with money and documents they were forced to stay and look for the cab where the bag was left. Having returned to Gatchina, we learned via telephone that everything was found and they successfully departed for the front via Baltiyskaya railroad. Natasha went to the train station to say goodbye.

16 February. Thursday. Gatchina. At 11 o'cl we went to church at the palace. Before breakfast ran around the garden with the children. From 2 1/4 until 3 1/4 I rode Vityaz, - rode on Krasnoselskaya highway, then turned at Pudost mill and returned home along the Zoo. After that Natasha and I rode to the Priory in a sleigh, where we took a walk. After tea Natasha rested, and I played with Baby. At 6 o'cl we went to church. At 7 1/4 George came over. He stayed with us until 10 3/4. After dinner we sat in

---

[77] The opening of the State Duma was a day of confusion, power plays, and betrayals within the establishment. Khrustalëv notes that even after Kerensky announced that it was "the historical task of the Russian people in this moment to overthrow the medieval regime immediately" and that after Miliukov had interrupted him to note that such talk was "an insult to the Duma," Kerensky went on to assert that what needed to happen was "what Brutus did in the time of ancient Rome." Miliukov, horrified at Kerensky's statements, urged that they be stricken from the record. A day later, Rodzyanko received a request from the Minister of Justice to strip Kerensky of his parliamentary immunity so that he could be prosecuted for a crime against the State. After receiving this note, Rodzyanko invited Kerensky to his office and said "Don't worry – the Duma will never betray you." (from Khrustalëv, pp. 605-606, citing Kerensky, *Zapiskie*, p. 131-132)

the bedroom and looked at photographs. The weather was semi-sunny, it was snowing, 7°

17 February. Friday. Gatchina. Got up like all the other days, late and at 11 o'cl went to church. Before breakfast Natasha and I took a walk around the garden. At 2 1/2 I took a ride Vityaz, rode around Priorat, and at 3 3/4 Natasha and I took a sleigh ride across Priorat to the Black gate, and then to Kurakin and home. At 5 o'cl Prince Cantacuzène, commander of the equestrian artillery of the 9th Cavalry Division, arrived. Around 5 1/2 Alyosha arrived, and at 6 o'cl we went to the palace for a service, after which we confessed to Father Strakhov. After dinner Alyosha studied for a bit. The weather was sunny, wonderful lighting, in the afternoon 11°, and in the evening 17°.

18 February. Saturday. Gatchina. At 10 o'cl Natasha, the children, Alyosha and I went to the palace, where we took communion, Johnson, the Krestyanovs, too, and the palace staff as well. Having returned home we had coffee. Before breakfast Alyosha and I walked around the garden. Father Strakhov came to breakfast. In the afternoon Father V. Seibuk, who is giving lessons to Tata, dropped by. From 3 until 4 1/4 Alyosha and I took a walk, walked along Olginskaya [Street], and then along Priorat. At 5 o'cl Dietz came over. At 6 1/2 we went to an all-night vigil. After dinner we played guitars with Domenici. The weather was sunny, in the afternoon 12 deg., in the evening 14°. Alyosha is spending the night here. Last night it was 23°.

19 February. Sunday. Gatchina. At 11 o'cl Alyosha and I went to the palace for liturgy. Natasha and J[ohnson] went to Petrograd at 12 o'cl. After breakfast I went with Dietz to [hunt] wolves (Tsarskoslavyanskaya dacha), the circle was in the 21 quarter, to the right of the road and two versts from the sentry box. I felled one old wolf, and two others tore through the left side. At 3.50 we went back and got home at 5 1/4. After tea Dietz left. I studied with Alyosha. At 7 1/4 Natasha returned from Petrograd and brought over Dvorzhitsky. Dvorzhitsky and Alyosha left at 9 3/4. The weather was sunny, in the afternoon 11°, in the evening 16°.

20 February. Monday. Gatchina. In the morning walked in the garden. In the afternoon Natasha and I went to the Priory in an automobile and took

a walk there with J[ohnson]. Got into the automobile at another gate and returned home at 4 1/4. At 7 o'cl the three of us went to Tsarskoe [Selo] to the Tolstoys,' where we had dinner, there were: Olga P, Mme Donich, Countess Mengden, Rita Khitrovo, Lazarev (cavalier guard), Ensign Bezobrazov and the young Prince Putyatin (sharpshooter). After dinner balalaika players performed and a choir of the 1st Railroad of His Majesty's regiment sang and played wonderfully well. I forgot to mention that Count Kutaisov also was at dinner, having just returned from Persia the other day, from Dmitry.[78] We went to the Alexandrovskaya at 12 1/2. Got home at 1.20. The weather was overcast, in the afternoon was 10°, in the evening 14°.

21 February. Tuesday. Gatchina. In the morning ran in the garden. At 12 o'cl Natasha, J[ohnson] and I went to Petrograd and had breakfast in the train. From the station we went directly to the control office to visit Lavrinovsky. After that I received A. Arapov, Colonel Gulkevich, Yuzefovich and Wrangel. Then Gulkevich showed us his very own American tractor with two machine guns and a new cannon. From the control office Alyosha and I went to his apartment with a stop at a shop, but lost a lot of time as the motor did not work well. Lidval was at Alyosha's, and I had a fitting. At 5 o'cl I went to Countess O. A. Tolstaya's on Mokhovaya, where I met up with Natasha. Both daughters and Klyuke were there. We returned to Gatchina on the 6 o'cl train, Praskovia I traveled with us. After dinner we went to the 'Modern' cinema (for *The Secret of the Bolshoi Theater*). The weather was overcast, 20°, in the evening 16°. - The nights are occasionally moonlit.

22 February. Wednesday. Gatchina. In the morning took a walk in the garden. At 12 o'cl J[ohnson] and I went to Tsarskoe [Selo]. J[ohnson] went to see Boris, then to Petrograd, while I had breakfast with Nicky and Alix.

---

[78] A plaintive letter from Grand Duke Dmitry to Natalia that survives in the Russian archives (GARF, f. 622, op. 1. d. 28. ll. 27-28ob.) describes his loneliness and regret at being so far from home, "My health is now very good, but when I first arrived...for days I was sick, staying of course, on my feet. It is difficult not to catch a cold here because the climate in Persia is strange ... I repeat that I am now used to it, but sometimes one hopes for current news of friends, and after all letters take 3 weeks by mail! ... Be happy. Give Misha a big hug."

At 2 o'cl Nicky left for Mogilev, and I took the extra train to Gatchina at 2 ½.[79] At 4 o'cl Natasha saw off Praskovia Ivan[ovna] in a sleigh to the Baltic Station. Later Margarita Aleksandrovna Derfeldnen, whom we had not seen for many years, came over. Then I played the guitar with Domenici before dinner. Mrs. Bennett had dinner with us. The weather was sunny, in the afternoon 10°, in the evening 16°.

23 February. Thursday. Gatchina. In the morning took a walk in the garden, then the dogs with sleighs came over and Baby rode around in them. (The sleigh with five dogs came from my former corps, they were trained there, they served in transportation there; the other day came over here with my horses.) N. D. Lyarskaya came to breakfast. In the afternoon Natasha and I took a walk in Priorat, then climbed into a sleigh and rode to the Black Gates, then past the farm and home. M. M. Lazarev came over to tea; he currently commands the 3rd Baltic Dragoon Regiment in Abo. In the evening we went to the 'Modern' cinema for *Heart of Ice*. The weather was sunny 3°, in the evening 7°.

24 February. Gatchina. At 12 o'cl I had breakfast, and at 1 o'cl rode horseback to Tsarskoeslavyansky Forest, where we hunted wolf, - Dietz rode in a sleigh, - the circle was past the railroad, to the left of the road, in all the same locations where we hunted previously. A wolf tore through the people and went to surround him, but despite the fact that he was chased by horse riders, they were not able to enclose him because he would not stop. On the way back, I changed to a red Kabardian [horse], while Malinin took Vityaz. Arrived home at 6.10. Did a total of 40 *versts* on horseback. Rested before dinner. In the evening Natasha, J[ohnson] and I went to the city cinema (*Adventures of Miss Holmes*). The weather was sunny, 3°, in the evening, 7°.

25 February. Saturday. Gatchina. At 10 o'cl we went to Petrograd. I received visitors at the control until 11/4, then had breakfast at Alyosha's. In the afternoon Natasha went to run errands and I received Wrangel, then Klopov, then Yuzefovich. After tea got a haircut, then played the guitar

---

[79] Spiridovich notes that at this parting, the Empress broke out in red spots, wept, and retreated to pray for the Emperor in private (Spiridovich, *Velikaya voina I Fevral'skaya revolutsiya*. New York: 1960-62 pp. 488-489.)

with Domenici, but not for very long. At 7 o'cl we all went to have dinner at the Kapnists,' where Olga P and Prince Urusov were. At 8 1/2 N, O P and J[ohnson] went to the Mikhailovsky theater, and Alyosha and I went to his apartment at 9 1/2, where we studied until 12 o'cl. Then with Natasha and J[ohnson], I went to the train station and to Gatchina - Miss Neame was also traveling with us. The weather was overcast, around 5 deg. Today there were disorders on Nevsky Prospect. Workers walked around with red flags, threw hand grenades and bottles at police, the troops had to shoot. The main reason for the disorders - absence of flour.[80]

26 February. Sunday. Gatchina. Got up late. At 2 o'cl J[ohnson] and I went to Petrograd on an extra train. Had breakfast on the train. I went directly to Xenia's; with her to the Cathedral of Sts. Peter and Paul for a *panikhida*[81] - no one else was there except us. Then we returned to her place. At 3 1/2 I went to princess Putyatina's, where J and Mme Donich were. There we had tea, then J and I went to the train station and at 4.25 went to Gatchina. At our arrival home Donich came over and stayed until 12 o'cl. The weather was sunny, around 5 deg, [everything] melted in the sun. The disorders in Petrograd have intensified, around 200 people were killed on Suvorovsky Prospect and Znamenskaya.

27 February, Monday, beginning of anarchy in Gatchina and Petrograd. At 5 o'cl J[ohnson] and I went to Petrograd in an extra train.[82] At the Mariinsky palace, [I] conferred with M. V. Rodzyanko, Nekrasov, Savich,

---

[80] An encrypted military telegram, No. 179, 25 February 1917, describes that rumors in Petrograd began to fly that bread rationing was about to begin caused a rush on bread purchases by the public. Because bread was being held in reserve, prices shot up. On this basis, a strike broke out, accompanied by street rioting. The first day, 90,000 workers went on strike, the second, 160,000 and the third 200,000. Red flags appeared, and shops were destroyed. Tram traffic was halted, and by afternoon, more serious rioting was reported by the Emperor Alexander III monument. It was noted that "vigorous measures" were being taken against the "anti-government" excesses. (Khrustalëv, quoting Interior Minister Protopopov, GARF, op. 1, d. 74, ll. 29-29c6)
[81] *"Panikhida"* A Russian Orthodox liturgical service for the dead.
[82] B. V. Nikitin recalled in his memoirs that the early morning call for Grand Duke Michael to come to Petrograd came from Rodzyanko, who insisted that he attend the meeting of the Council of Ministers, following which Rodzyanko went on to speak with the Emperor on a direct line to Stavka. (Khrustalëv, n. 287, p. 608, citing B. V. Nikitin, *Rokovye gody: Novye pokazaniya uchastnika*, p. 167)

Dmitrukov. Then Prince Galitzine, Gen[eral] Belyaev and Kryzhanovsky arrived. When we got to Petrograd, it was relatively quiet, by 9 o'cl the shooting started in the streets and almost all troops became revolutionary, the old power no longer existed, - because of this a provisional executive committee was created, which started to give orders and decrees. This committee consisted of a few members of the State Duma under the chairmanship of Rodzyanko. At 9 o'cl I went to the Moika[83] to the War Minister and transmitted via a radio device to Gen[eral] Alexeyev (in Mogilev) to pass on to Nicky the steps that needed to be taken immediately to calm this brewing revolution, specifically the resignation of the entire cabinet, then to entrust Prince Lvov to choose a new cabinet according to his own discretion. I added that the response needed to be given immediately, as time does not wait, every hour is precious. The response was as follows: do not make any changes until my arrival. Departure from Stavka was scheduled for tomorrow at 2.30 in the afternoon. Alas, after this unsuccessful attempt to help things I was planning to go back to Gatchina, but it was impossible to leave, there was a lot of shooting, from machine guns, as well as hand grenade explosions. At 3 o'cl Gen[eral] Belyaev was advised to move to the Winter Palace, where Gen[eral] Khabalov, who commanded the Petrograd military region, was located. By this time, it quieted down. J[ohnson] and I drove along Gorokhovaya in our motorcar, along the embankment on horseback to Nikolaevsky Bridge, then to the left, expecting to drive to the train station past Nikola the Seafarer, but suddenly we realized that to go any farther would be more than risky, - everywhere we came across revolutionary detachments and patrols, - near the Annunciation Church they yelled at us to stop. We passed through successfully, but our convoy automobile was detained. We were unable to go farther, and we turned left and decided to go to [the] Winter [Palace]. Gen[erals] Belyaev and Khabalov were there, with 1,000 men under their command, part of the battalion of the Preobrazhensky regiment, 1st Company of the Guard Equipage, and the 1st Don Cossack regiment. I was able to convince the generals to defend the palace, as they

---

[83] **"Moika"** is one of the central rivers in the official section of downtown St. Petersburg. It flows past the semi-circular neoclassical General Staff ensemble building that also faces Palace Square, home to Imperial Russia's War Ministry.

decided, and evacuate the people from the Winter Palace before dawn and thus avoid the inevitable destruction of the palace by revolutionary troops. Poor Gen[eral] Komarov was very grateful to me for such assistance. At 5 o'cl J[ohnson] and I decided to leave the Winter Palace and moved to Millionnaya, 12, Princess Putyatina's place, where we lay down on the sofas in prince's study.

28 February. Tuesday. At 8 1/2 we were awakened by the loud sound of automobiles, passenger [cars] and trucks full of soldiers who were shooting mostly into air, - loud explosions from hand grenades could be heard, too. Soldiers shouted hurrah, all the automobiles drove around sporting red flags, and everyone had red ribbons or bows on their chests or in their lapels. The day passed peacefully for us, and no one bothered us.[84]

March 1917

1 March. In the morning Preobrazhensky soldiers were going around to the apartments of the building, did not come into ours. Prince Putyatin was very nervous. At 12 1/2 a deputation arrived consisting of several officers and a barrister called Ivanov. They asked me to sign a manifesto, which already had the signatures of Uncle Pavel and Kirill.[85] In this manifesto

---

[84] The situation in Petrograd continued to disintegrate rapidly. Conflicting reports to the Emperor from Rodzyanko (which were desperate) and General Khabalov (which were sanguine) prompted the Emperor to wait to respond until he had more information. Because the Emperor gave no orders in the face of the disturbances, on 28 February there was a gathering of Duma factions at that body's meeting place at the Tauride Palace called by Rodzyanko. Rodzyanko was insistent that a new government be formed with a "responsible ministry" enjoying public confidence. Fearful of an internal coup in the Duma, the Prime Minister, Prince Golytsin, preempted the move. Inside the Duma, the Senate, and within the armed forces, however, the revolution had officially begun.

[85] **"manifesto"** Generally known as "The Manifesto of the Grand Dukes." This document was intended to preserve the throne for Nicholas, while appeasing the revolutionary forces. The Grand Dukes, sensing that there was only a very small window in which to preserve the throne, produced this document, which was sent by Grand Duke Pavel Aleksandrovich from his residence at Tsarskoe Selo to Grand Duke Kirill's palace on Glinka Street, from whence it was sent in Ivanov's care to the Grand Duke Michael. Ivanov dutifully took the manifesto to the Duma politician Pavel Miliukov, who signed for its receipt. Scholar Tsuyoshi Hasegawa notes that despite

the Sovereign granted a full constitution. In the afternoon the Vorontsovs and Wrangel came over. In the evening Klopov was here and stayed until 3 1/2 in the morning. I wrote a letter to Rodzyanko. On the streets it continued same as yesterday, the same loud automobiles, shooting. Preobrazhensky soldiers passed by with music. We heard about several killings nearby, done by the soldiers of Count Stackelberg, by the way. Nicky was supposed to return from Stavka today, but never arrived, and it was unknown where his train was, rumors had it that it was outside of Bologov. All power was concentrated in the hands of the Provisional Committee,[86] which finds it very difficult in light of strong pressure on them from the [Soviet] of Workers' and Soldiers' Deputies. Rodzyanko was supposed to come see me but was unable to do so.[87] Alyosha dropped by around 2 o'cl and stayed the night. In the evening N M [Grand Duke Nikolai Mikhailovich, who had also been at the Duma on 1 March][88] came over.

---

the close communication and collaborative effort between Rodzyanko and the Grand Dukes, Ivanov did not submit the document to Rodzyanko, Chairman of the Duma, but to Miliukov, who never passed it on to anyone. The mutual antipathy between Rodzyanko and Miliukov was one of the most serious fissures which faced the incipient Provisional Government. Rodzyanko held the most power and influence in February, but by March, power had shifted to Miliukov, now Foreign Minister, who was at best apathetic towards the dynasty. (cf. Tsuyoshi Hasegawa, "Rodzyanko and the Grand Dukes' Manifesto of 1 March 1917," *Canadian Slavonic Papers*, 18: 2 (1976), 154-67.)

[86] Grand Duke Andrei, then in Kislovodsk with his mother Grand Duchess Maria Pavlovna, noted that he had received telegrams from both his brothers. Kirill wrote "the situation is serious" and his brother Boris noted "everything goes badly." (Khrustalëv, p. 613, citing *Iz dnevnika velikogo knyazya Andreya Vladimirovicha*, Istochnik: 1998, No. 3, p. 47)

[87] It was on this night that a detachment of soldiers was sent to guard Grand Duke Michael at the Putyatins' apartment, and that Grand Duke Michael learned that Prince D. L. Vyazamski had been killed by a stray shell during the fighting. During this time, Duma politician Aleksandr Guchkov and his associates negotiated with the military units in Petrograd and on the morning of 1 March issued orders to the remaining loyal Tsarist troops, who were expected to suppress the uprising and bring order to the capital. (Khrustalëv, p. 610.)

[88] "**NM**" Grand Duke Nikolai Mikhailovich (b. 1859 – d. 1919) had been exiled to his country estates by Nicholas II, but had returned to the capital when he heard of the developments in Petrograd. Likely unaware of the internal shift of power within the Duma and that the Manifesto of the Grand Dukes had been sidelined, and responding

The Manifesto of the Grand Dukes

Note at the top of the page:

The grand dukes [have] decided to present this act or one quite similar to His Majesty the Emperor for his signature. This act will be sent to the Provisional
Committee of the State Duma by the barrister, Nikolai Ivanov.

By the Grace of God
We, Nicholas the Second,
Emperor and Autocrat of all Russia
Tsar of Poland, Grand Duke of Finland, et cetera,
Proclaim to all our faithful subjects:

Seriously attempting to transform the State Administration in the EMPIRE on the basis of wide, popular representation, WE intended to introduce a new state structure by the end of the war.

OUR previous Government, considering it undesirable to institute a responsible Ministry to the Fatherland, [composed] of the persons of the legislative assemblies, found it possible to postpone this act for an indefinite period of time.

The events of the last days, however, showed that the government which did not rely on the majority in the legislative assemblies could neither foresee the rising disturbances nor prevent them

---

to the orders Guchkov had issued that morning requesting that all loyal troops come to Petrograd to establish order in the capital, at approximately 4:14pm on 1 March, Grand Duke Kirill arrived with his Naval Guard at the Tauride Palace. Kirill noted in his memoirs, "The military authorities in the capital gave contradictory orders. One day they were to the effect that certain streets were to be occupied, on other occasions, some equally useless measures were to be taken." (Grand Duke Kirill, p. 206). He also notes Guchkov's order of 1 March: "the Government [Ed note: it is important to note that it was the Imperial Government Kirill went to support, and not the Provisional Government, which was not formed until the evening of 2 March, after the abdication of the Emperor] issued an appeal to all troops and their commanders to show their allegiance to the Government by marching to the Douma [sic] and declaring their loyalty." Kirill, who had less than 24 hours earlier signed a document which Rodzyanko had promised would be signed by the Emperor, no doubt hoped to arrive to a grateful Duma, recently endowed with full constitutional rights. Instead, he "found the place in absolute pandemonium ... a state of chaos and confusion ... I spent the whole of the afternoon and evening in this painful atmosphere, guarded by my men." Kirill was unaware that as he sat at the Tauride Palace, having made an open declaration of loyalty to the Imperial Government and attempting to restore order by guarding the Provisional Committee of the Duma, its leaders were behind closed doors deciding that the Emperor's abdication was imperative.

by force.

Great is OUR sorrow that in the days when the fate of
Russia is being determined on the battlefield, an internal disturbance
had befallen the capital and has disrupted the work of
defense, which is vitally necessary for the victorious end of the war.
It is not without the intrigues of the perfidious enemy that the
Disturbances were created, and that such a difficult trial has befallen
Russia, but strongly hoping in the assistance of God's Providence,
WE firmly believe that the Russian people will eradicate
the disturbances in the name of the good for their native land,
and will not give the enemies' intrigues a chance to triumph.

With the sign of the cross, WE grant the Russian State a constitutional
system and enjoin to continue the sessions of the State
Duma and the State Council, which were interrupted by OUR
Decree. WE entrust the Chairman of the State Duma with the
immediate formation of a temporary cabinet which relies on the
confidence of the country and which in agreement with US will
concern itself with the convocation of a legislative assembly, which
will be necessary for the urgent reexamination of the new fundamental
laws of the Russian Empire, which will be introduced by
the Government.

May the new Governmental system serve for the greater success,
glory, and happiness of OUR beloved Russia.

Given at Tsarskoe Selo, March, First Day in the year one
thousand nine hundred seventeenth from the Birth of Christ, [and in] our
Reign the twenty-third.[89]

[Signed each in their own hand]

Grand Duke Mikhail
Grand Duke Pavel
Grand Duke Kirill

Letter to Natasha:

1 March, 1917

My dear Natasha, heartfelt thanks for your letter. Events are progressing with horrifying speed. I must be here during this time and be completely

---

[89] Hasegawa, "Rodzyanko and the Grand Dukes' Manifesto," pp. 154-167, quoting "*Manifest Velikikh Kniazei*," *Ogonek*, no. 1, 1923.

easy about me. Recently a deputation came, which included the military. This deputation was introduced to me by the director-steward of the public metallurgical factories. I signed a manifesto, which is supposed to be signed by the Sovereign. On it were already the signatures of Pavel A[leksandrovich] and Kirill and now mine as the senior of Grand Dukes. With this manifesto begins Russia's new existence. It's possible that I will go to the State Duma today, or maybe tomorrow.[90] In general, it expects that we will see each other if not today, then tomorrow. Today Alyosha and the Vorontsovs came over. I'm awfully sad that we are not together, love you with all my heart.

May God keep you, my delicate Natasha.

All yours,

Misha.

Grand Dukes at the State Duma. *Russkoe slovo*, 2 March 1917.

On the 1st of March [March 14 - approx. DR], at 4.14 in the afternoon Grand Duke Kirill Vladimirovich arrived at the Tavrichesky Palace. He was accompanied by a naval guard, commanding the Guards regiment and an escort from the lower ranks of the crew.

The Grand Duke arrived at the Catherine Hall and was immediately announced by the representative of the State Duma, M. V. Rodzyanko. Turning to M. V. Rodzyanko, the Grand Duke said:

"I have the honor to stand before Your Excellency. I am in your command, like all the people. I wish the good of Russia. This morning, I spoke to all the soldiers of the Guards regiment, explained to them the importance of the events that were taking place, and now I can say that the entire Naval guard is at the full disposal of the Imperial Duma."

The words of the Grand Duke were covered with shouts of "Hurrah!"

---

[90] It is interesting to note that Michael also planned to go to the Duma on 1 or 2 March. With events moving quickly, and poor communication the norm, it appears that the only member of the three authors of the manifesto to arrive there was Grand Duke Kirill – and by then the situation regarding the Manifesto had already changed.

M. V. Rodzyanko thanked the Grand Duke and, turning to the soldiers around the guards, said: "I am very glad, gentlemen, to hear the words of the Grand Duke. I believe that the Guards, as well as all the rest of the troops, will fulfill their duty in full order and will help to deal with our common enemy and will lead Russia on the path of victory."

The words of the presenter of the State Duma were also greeted with cheers of "Hurrah."

Then Rodzyanko turned to the Grand Duke with the question of whether he would prefer to remain in the State Duma.

The Grand Duke replied that the full force of the Guards' regiments would be arriving at the State Duma crew in full force, and that he wished to meet his reinforcements for The Duma.

"In such a case," Rodzyanko said, "when you need me, you will call me." After this M. V. Rodzyanko returned to his office.

In the face of the fact that all the assistant members of the national Duma were busy, representatives of the committee of Petrograd journalists invited the Grand Duke to enter their room.

The admiral of the guards crew and the Grand Duke's adjutant passed into the room of the journalists together with the Grand Duke.

At six o'clock in the evening Grand Duke Nikolai Mikhailovich arrived in the State Duma, and a little later Grand Duchess Elizabeth Mavrikievna arrived.[91]

---

[91] This contemporary article, related correspondence, and military orders contradict a prevailing narrative that Grand Duke Kirill spontaneously decided to take his troops to the Duma and "swore loyalty" to the Provisional Government, allegedly while wearing a red ribbon and marching under a red banner. The Grand Duke followed Guchkov's orders to bring loyal troops to protect the Duma Committee in the Tauride palace. There are no contemporary reports of a red ribbon or banner. Grand Duke Kirill did not recognize the new Provisional Government until 2 March, after the Emperor's abdication. Perhaps most importantly, other members of the Imperial Family were expected at the Tauride Palace, and others arrived at the same time. Michael notes he was expected there on 1 or 2 March, and we see that Grand Duke Nikolai Mikhailovich and Grand Duchess Elizaveta Mavrikievna were there with Grand Duke Kirill. For further evidence of Kirill's loyalty to the Emperor, see M.

2 March. Got a reply letter from Rodzyanko in the morning.[92] No one bothered us all day. Driving of the automobiles continued, the shooting stopped, soldiers filled all the streets, ignoring officers,[93] - in general I must add that during the last few days complete anarchy reigned. Yuzefovich came in from Tsarskoe [Selo] around 5 o'cl, also Kapnist dropped by. N. M.[94] was here in the evening, he is wearing civilian clothes exclusively, and galoshes instead of boots. Princess Putyatina noticed that the galoshes were most likely worn on bare feet.[95]

Koenig, "In Favour of Grand Duke Kirill," *Royalty Digest Quarterly*, Vol. 1, 2018, pp. 6-9).

[92] The letter noted the failure of the Manifesto and the Duma Committee's change of direction. The lawyer Ivanov quoted his statement to the Grand Duke regarding the failure of the Manifesto: "The Manifesto of the Grand Dukes already belongs to history. The mood in the Tauride Palace is dictated no longer by those who are considered leaders of the movement, but to a large extent by the street and by some behind-the-scenes forces. The role of the Provisional Committee of the State Duma is not increasing but is faltering. Rodzyanko and Kerensky and those with them are forced to [go with the current] and ratify everything the mob brings them." (Khrustalëv, p. 611, quoting V. V. Ivanov, *Vospominanie.*) Rodzyanko later wrote, in 1932, that the arrival of Grand Duke Kirill made the situation even more difficult. (cf. "Lettre du Président de la Douma Rodzianko au Grand-duc Cyrille après sa proclamation, 1932" excerpted in French translation from the original Russian text in the catalogue "Collection du Prince et de la Princesse Youssoupoff," 13-14 November 2014, Couteau-Bergerie, Paris, Lot 123.

[93] The morning of 2 March revealed the final shift within the Duma. At this meeting, the Duma officially announced its rejection of Rodzyanko's policies and instead sought the Emperor's abdication in favor of his son Alexei, under Grand Duke Michael's regency. Grand Duke Michael had been stripped of his right to act as regent in October 1912 as part of his punishment for marrying Natalia Brasova, though this appeared to have no relevance for the committee. The Provisional Committee decided to send Guchkov and his colleague Vasily Shulgin to negotiate with the Emperor at Pskov, where his train had been diverted. Rodzyanko's famous final discussions with General Ruzsky via telegram revealed his waning influence and desperation to maintain some authority. Ruzsky asked if the manifesto establishing a responsible ministry (which he had finally gotten Nicholas II to accept) should be issued by the committee. Rodzyanko replied: "Really, I don't know how to answer you; everything depends on the events, which happen with extraordinary rapidity." (Hasegawa, p. 167)

[94] Grand Duke Nikolai Mikhailovich and Grand Duchess Elizaveta Mavrikievna had also been at the Duma on 1 March, and the Grand Duke no doubt shared his impressions of the day with Grand Duke Michael and the Putyatins.

[95] Nicholas II had abdicated the throne in favor of his son at 3pm on the Imperial train at Pskov but changed the abdication in favor of his brother at 11.20 pm. The act was later predated to 3pm.

3 March. At 6 o'cl in the morning went were awakened by a telephone call. The new Justice Minister [Aleksandr] Kerensky[96] had a message for me that the Soviet of Ministers in its full composition will come over to see me in an hour. In reality they came only at 9 1/2 [the rest of page is blank][97]

Letter to Natasha:

3 March 1917.[98] Dear Natasha, just a few words. Thank you for the letter. I hope to depart tonight or tomorrow morning. Awfully busy and extremely tired. A lot of interesting things to tell. I kiss you affectionately. All yours, Misha.

Olga P., Alyosha and J[ohnson] send you heartfelt regards and think about you a lot. Try to delay M.'s husband for a bit until my return, I send him my regards. I hug and cross you many times.

---

[96] **Aleksandr Kerensky** (b. 1881 – d. 1970) a radical lawyer, member of the Socialist Revolutionary Party and Duma, vice chairman of the Petrograd Soviet, Minister of Justice in the Provisional Government, then Minister of War and Prime Minister. Fled after the Bolshevik coup d'état and emigrated to the United States, where he became a professor of political science at Stanford University.

[97] The meeting lasted all morning. Rodzyanko, Prince Georgy Lvov (the new Prime Minister), Pavel Miliukov, and Aleksandr Kerensky were among those joined by the attorneys Baron Boris Nolde and Vladimir Nabokov to construct a manifesto to be issued by the de facto Emperor-presumptive "Michael II." The legal issues were manifold. Were the acts of the Provisional Committee legitimate? Could Nicholas II remove his son from the succession? Was Michael even legally able to accept the throne? Multiple drafts yielded a document which stood as a conditional acceptance or "deferral" of the throne to the will of the people, with power firmly in the hands of what would become the Provisional Government.

[98] Nicholas II's diary 3 March 1917: "Alexeyev arrived with the latest news from Rodzyanko. It appears Misha has abdicated. His manifesto finishes with something about elections for a Constituent Assembly. God knows who advised him to sign something so vile!" The answer to that question was the team led by Rodzyanko, Lvov, Miliukov and Kerensky.

The Act of Grand Duke Michael Alexandrovich

A heavy burden has been placed on me by the will of my brother, who has transferred to me the imperial Throne of all the Russias at this time of unprecedented hostilities and civil disturbances.

Inspired, in common with the whole people, by the belief that the welfare of our country must be set above everything else, I have taken the firm decision to assume the supreme power only if and when our great people, having elected by universal suffrage a Constituent Assembly to determine the form of government and lay down the fundamental law of the new Russian State, invest me with such power.

Calling upon them the blessing of God, I therefore request all the citizens of the Russian Empire to submit to the Provisional Government, established and invested with full authority by the Duma, until such time as the Constituent Assembly, elected within the shortest possible time by universal, direct, equal and secret suffrage, shall manifest the will of the people by deciding upon the new form of government.

Michael

4 March. Saturday. Petrograd and Gatchina. At 11 o'cl J[ohnson] and I went to the Baltic Station. Two officers accompanied us, and two Junkers [military cadets] with rifles drove in another motorcar. On the way Yuzefovich joined us. The station was crowded with the lower ranks, everywhere were machine guns and boxes with ammunition. We arrived on the extra train, - Yuzefovich and J[ohnson] traveled with me. By the train stood a company, whom I greeted. At the train's departure, the crowd that gathered cheered me. Around 1 1/2 we arrived at Gatchina.[99] I sighed with relief when, finally, got home. George M[100] has been staying with us since Tuesday (he arrived from the front and decided to stay here for now). George's adjutants - Princes Eristov and Naryshkin, came to breakfast as well, they live in a train at the Warsaw Station. In the afternoon and the rest of the day we stayed home and talked the whole

---

[99] Michael was at this point not permitted to leave the Petrograd area or return to his military command.
[100] Grand Duke Georgiy Mikhailovich

time, there were a lot of topics. Eristov and Naryshkin came again to dinner. The weather was sunny in the afternoon, snowstorm in the morning, around 7°. Order is gradually reestablishing.

5 March. Sunday. Gatchina. At 11 o'cl Natasha, George, Tata[101] and I went to church at the palace.[102] Before breakfast took a walk in the garden. In the afternoon Natasha and I went sleigh riding, rode through the Zoo on to Yegerskaya, where we left Volchok at Furazhkin's. Then took a bit of a walk in Priorat. Ran into the lower ranks, many did not salute. After tea read the newspapers, *Novoe Vremya* [*The New Times*], and *Rech* [*Speech*], which appeared again today for the first time after a week's break. Dietz was here and told us how they arrested and took him to the State Duma on Wednesday. In the evening wrote in the diary, in which did not write for a few days. The weather was sunny, [snow] melted a bit in the sun, 6° in the shade, and lot more snow piled up. George has been living here since Tuesday.

6 March. Monday. Gatchina. Got up late. Sergei A[leksandrovich] came from Moscow and described the mood over there, - in Moscow everything went peacefully and without any bloodshed at all. Stayed home all day and talked endlessly. Around 6 o'cl Alyosha and Yuzefovich came over. Also, George's adjutants came to dinner. At 9 1/2 Alyosha and Yuzefovich left, and Sergei also, and we dispersed at 11 1/2. The weather was overcast, it was snowing, 10°. In Petrograd the mood is improving, and order is being

---

[101] In her memoirs, Natalia wrote: "He returned soon after to Gatchina looking exhausted and ill, and I remember his saying; 'Well, that's that, thank God I can now retire into private life.' He was ill most of that spring as I believe that any emotional worry or strain aggravated his trouble, ulcers; and I remember his spending a good deal of his days lying down in his study on the chesterfield and being on a strict diet." (cf. Nathalie Majolier, *Step-daughter of Imperial Russia*, Kindle edition, Sept 18, 2018, Chapter "Menshevik Russia.")

[102] In the early days of March 1917, many bishops of the Russian Orthodox Church called upon subjects of the Empire to submit to the Provisional Government as a legitimate temporary authority. The Archbishop of Perm called the period an "interregnum" and wrote "Let us beg the Almighty to bring his power and his peace to our land, may he not leave us for a long time without a Tsar, as children without a mother. May he help us as he did our ancestors 300 years ago to receive a Russian Tsar from him in unity and enthusiasm." (Khrustalëv, p. 625, citing RGIA f. 797, op. 86, 1917.)

reestablished, cabs appeared, trams will start running tomorrow, but there is still almost no discipline in the army, which is more than sad.

7 March. Tuesday. Gatchina. Sat in the study with George in the morning. Natasha, Naryshkin and I rode in a sleigh to Yegerskaya. Dietz approached us and we visited Volchok and the Furazhkins, then walked across the entire Yegerskaya, at the gates climbed into a sleigh and returned home. Princess Ekaterina Putyatina came over for tea, and a little later Mikhail P, who was chosen by the soldiers according to the new rule as a company commander. He was very anxious about everything that has happened in the past few days. They left at 6 3/4. After dinner we read newspapers. The weather was sunny, around 8-10° in the afternoon, and 20° in the evening.

8 March. Wednesday. Gatchina. In the morning took a walk in the garden with Georgiy. Inna A[103] came over in the afternoon. Natasha and I took a ride in a sleigh, through Marienburg and Yegerskaya. The Vyazemskys came over for tea from the country. Also, Maikhrovsky was here, the director of George's office. Before dinner, Vyazemsky read aloud, the newspapers are rather interesting.[104] The weather was sunny, but it remains cold, 9° in the afternoon, 15° in the evening. Each day is calmer.

9 March. Thursday. Gatchina. At 11 o'cl Yuzefovich arrived. At 2.40 he left together with the Vyazemskys. In the afternoon Natasha and I took a sleigh ride. After tea we read newspapers. In the evening we read and talked. The weather was sunny, 6°. Today Nicky arrived from Mogilev.

---

[103] **"Inna A"** Inna Aleksandrovna Erivanskaya.

[104] On 8 March the newspapers all contained news of Michael's deferral of the throne, describing it as an abdication. The article in *Russkoe slovo* (*Russian Word*) gave details from Kerensky's report of the meeting on 3 March, stating that each member of the Provisional Committee presented his opinion of the situation and made recommendations to the Grand Duke on what should happen next, with only one unidentified late-arriving man pressing vigorously for the "Regent" not to abandon the throne. Michael requested a private discussion with Prince Lvov and Rodzyanko. Rodzyanko refused to speak in private. After a talk with Prince Lvov, however, Michael agreed to sign the deferral, submitting to the majority recommendation. Other newspapers celebrated the fall of the dynasty in abusive and crude language. (Khrustalëv, p. 627-628, quoting *Russkoe slovo*, 8 March 1917.)

They brought him to Tsarskoe [Selo] and to the Alexander Palace, where he is under arrest with his family.[105]

10 March. Friday. Gatchina. At 11 1/2 I went to the Admiralty and cross country skied on the lake, which is still covered with ice. Sheffer came to see George here for breakfast. In the afternoon George, Natasha and I took a sleigh ride, rode through Marienburg and back on Yegerskaya. Read after tea. At 7 o'cl Vyazemskys arrived.

11 March. Saturday. Gatchina. In the morning took a walk with Vyazemsky and J[ohnson], also went to Priorat. After breakfast the Vyazemskys left and Naryshkin with them. He had come to breakfast. The Vyazemskys went to Popelevo, and from there he will go to the corps. Around 2 1/2 Maria V and Fanny M arrived from the Riga front, they stayed with us until 4 o'cl, they plan to leave for Moscow from Petrograd in the evening. Read newspapers before dinner.[106] Colonel Reier[107] came for dinner. He received a warrant from the Provisional Government to take the position of director of Gatchina palace control. Spent the evening as usual, talking. The weather was overcast, 2°. From 6 until 7, Maslennikov was here, told us a lot of interesting things.

12 March. Sunday. Gatchina. At 11 o'cl Natasha, Tata and I went to church. On the palace tower a disgusting red flag was fluttering, they said that the residents demanded it. The double-headed eagle was taken down from the cupola, but it was defended. Maikhrovsky came to breakfast. In

---

[105] Nicholas returned to the Alexander Palace from Stavka to note the change in attitude of the guards, but reported with relief that the family was all healthy and well, save Grand Duchess Maria, who was still recovering from the measles.

[106] The newspapers that day were full of concern over the fate of the former Emperor and his family. *Izvestiia* reported rumors that Nicholas and his family were to be sent abroad, and strongly urged the Provisional Government not to follow through with this plan, arguing that the Imperial family had vast financial resources abroad which could be used to mount a counterrevolution and restore the Romanovs to power. In fact, the Romanovs had repatriated their wealth at the beginning of World War I. (Khrustalëv, p. 627-628).

[107] **"Colonel Reier"** Armii Karlovich Reier (b. 1876 – d. 1938) Director of the Gatchina Palace Administration, member of the white movement, veteran of Gallipoli, lived in France and Germany in exile. Reier was responsible for overseeing the collections at Gatchina Palace after the February Revolution, maintaining inventories, and managing the organization of the Imperial property.

the afternoon Dietz dropped by. Then Natasha, Praskovia I. (who also came to breakfast) and I took a sleigh ride in Priorat. At 5 1/4 came over - Oboloshev and Alyosha. They left at 9 1/2. The weather was overcast, 1°. During all these days they were shooting at the poor deer at the Zoo, they were killed in colossal amounts. Soldiers of various units had shot [them]. The bullets even reached town. Yesterday they rounded them up, i.e. these hunters, and fortunately stopped this carnage and hooliganism.

13 March. Monday. Gatchina. Read in the morning. Mogilyansky came to see George for breakfast. In the afternoon Natasha and I took a sleigh ride, rode around Priorat, then dropped by the palace at Krestyanov's; he is so dejected, the poor chap, Olga N was in Petrograd. After tea read the newspapers.[108] J[ohnson] spent the entire day in Petrograd. The weather was overcast, 3°.

14 March. Tuesday. Gatchina. Read in the morning. Prince Eristov came to breakfast. At 3 o'cl Makarov came to see me. He looked through the palace, - with him came over the newly appointed commandant in Gatchina, Svistunov. Then the daughter of A. V. Chatoriysky was here and told us of the death of her father, who was killed on 1 March by drunk sailors of the Baltic Fleet. Before tea George and I took a walk around the garden. Then Kurnakov arrived, and Alyosha arrived little later. Wrote letters before dinner, then received Colonel Reier. In the evening Krestyanovs came over. The weather was overcast, 2°.

15 March. Wednesday. Gatchina. In the morning Colonel Panteleyev came to see me. From 11 1/2 until 1 o'cl I rode on horseback with Bennett, - from the cemetery we turned left to the Great Over-bridge, then to the Small Over-bridge (near the bison) and rode back home. Kakhovsky came to breakfast. In the afternoon Natasha and I took a sleigh ride. Got out by the palace and walked toward Yegerskaya to Furazhkin's, where we picked up Volchok. There we climbed into a sleigh and returned home. At

---

[108] Michael tried to follow the news assiduously, but the Provisional Government was far less forthcoming with information about the war to the press than the Imperial Government had been. The newspapers were largely concerned with assuaging local fears about the stability of the new government, rather than reports of how the abdication and Michael's deferral were received by the troops in the field. (Khrustalëv, p. 632-633)

5 1/4 arrived - Maria V and Oboloshev. From 6 1/2 until dinner I played the guitar with Domenici. At 9 1/2 Oboloshev left. The weather was wonderful, sunny, 5° in the sun, 5° in the shade.

16 March. Thursday. Gatchina. At 11 o'cl I went horseback riding on Vityaz. From the cemetery I rode to the left and followed yesterday's ride. In the afternoon Natasha, Maria V, Naryshkin and I took a walk in Priorat, then in a sleigh in Marienburg and Yegerskaya. After tea Naryshkin left, and we read. Alyosha came over at 7 1/4. The weather was sunny, 2° in the shade, 4° in the sun.

17 March. Friday. Gatchina. At 10 1/4 I took a horseback ride with Bennett, I rode Vityaz, - we rode around the Zoo on the outside. Alyosha, who stayed the night at J[ohnson]'s, came over at around 12 1/2. Before breakfast I sat on the steps in the garden and warmed up in the sun. In the afternoon, Natasha, Maria V and I took a sleigh ride, - for the first time in entire winter we rode via Tsagov and at the end of the road went past the gate to the left to Priorat, there walked on foot. After tea I rested for a bit, and then studied with Alyosha. At 9 1/2 Alyosha left. The weather was sunny, 6° in the sun, in the shade 2° in the afternoon.

18 March. Saturday. Gatchina. At 2 o'cl Natasha, Miss Neame, J[ohnson] and I went to Petrograd via the Warsaw line, - the parade rooms are no longer opened and they do not give a separate car.[109] Forgot to mention that Maria V also traveled with us. N first went to the bank. Had breakfast at Alyosha's, and besides us there were the Shleifers and Oboloshev. In the afternoon I went to Xenia's.[110] Everyone gathered at Alyosha's for tea. Oboloshev is leaving for the front, Maria V also. We returned to Gatchina on the 6 o'cl train. I took a walk from the Baggovutskaya platform. The weather was overcast, 2°. All the streets in Petrograd are full of soldiers.

19 March. Sunday. Gatchina. At 11 o'cl we went to the palace for liturgy with the children. In the afternoon Natasha and I took a sleigh ride, -

---

[109] **Parade Rooms** The rooms at the station at Gatchina formerly reserved for the Imperial Family. **"Separate car"** refers to the train car previously reserved for members of the Imperial House.

[110] **"Xenia's"** Grand Duchess Xenia Aleksandrovna's palace in St. Petersburg on the Moika Embankment, originally built for Princess Vorontsova.

Priorat, Yegerskaya, Marienburg and the Zoo. After tea J[ohnson] and I took a walk. We walked to the closest grove in the direction of the bridge, then to the right via Tosnenskaya branch, past the cemetery home, about 10-12 versts. The Donichis came over to visit us. They left at 9 1/2. The weather was sunny, 12° in the sun, 5° in the shade.

20 March. Monday. Gatchina. In the morning I received Cornet Baranov and Ensign Paths, both from the 2nd Reserve Cavalry Regiment. In the afternoon Natasha and I took a sleigh ride, rode through the Zoo, and in Priorat walked on the circumferential road. At 5 o'cl the veterinarian came over [blank space] for Volchok. Read before dinner. The weather was somewhat sunny in the morning, 4°.

21 March. Wednesday [sic]. Gatchina. At 10 o'cl Natasha, George, J[ohnson] and I went to Petrograd. I went to see Buchanan [the British ambassador]. At 12 o'cl I went to Alyosha's. Natasha came over at breakfast, J[ohnson] too. Then I received Wrangel, and after that I went to Xenia's, where I stayed until 4 1/2. From her I went to Princess Putyatina's with J[ohnson]. Natasha arrived later, - Baron Rosen was there, Colonel of the Preobrazhensky Regiment. At 6 o'cl we went to Gatchina, George also. The weather was snowy, 1°. After dinner we sat in the bedroom, Natasha went to bed early, as she was not feeling well (nettle fever).[111] The weather was dark, from 3 o'cl thick, wet snow.

22 March. Wednesday. Gatchina. All morning George and I sat in the garden by the house and warmed ourselves in the sun, - I was wearing only a tunic, and it was truly warm, 26 deg. In the afternoon M. Y. Tolstoy came over (from Abo), and at 3 1/4 we took a ride with him, rode through the Zoo, and I dropped him off at the Baltic Station. After tea I played the guitar with Domenici. Mrs. Bennett came to dinner. The weather was sunny, 26 deg., 6° in the shade.

23 March. Thursday. Gatchina. Princes Eristov and Naryshkin came to breakfast. In the afternoon Natasha, both of them, and I took a sleigh ride, rode through Marienburg and Yegerskaya, and walked on foot in Priorat. They left at 5 1/4. Read before dinner, then wrote a letter. The

---

[111] **"nettle fever"** Allergies

weather was sunny during the day, 4° in the shade. The other day Aunt Miechen was arrested in Kislovodsk (house arrest), and Boris in Mogilev.[112]

24 March. Friday. Gatchina. At 9 1/2 Natasha, George and I went to the station but the train was 35 min. late, and we waited at J[ohnson]'s house, - Mrs. Bennett went with us. I went directly to Xenia's, where I had breakfast, there were: Andrusha, Fedor, Nikita, Sofia Dm. and Sonia D. At 1 1/2 I went to Alyosha's, where Natasha and J[ohnson] had breakfast. Then they went to run errands, and I studied with Alyosha, - wrote a letter to Prince Bagration. Dvorzhitsky dropped by, we brought him to Millionnaya, and then J[ohnson], George and I went to the train station, where Natasha also arrived with Shleifer. Our train was so full that we had to take the next one at 4.45. We got off at Baggovutskaya. After tea we went to the palace for an all-night vigil. Today we rode in a sleigh as the roads are in terrible shape and it is hard for a motor to drive. The weather was sunny occasionally, 2°. In Petrograd the streets are in terrible shape, no one really cleans them.

25 March. Saturday. Gatchina. At 11 o'cl we all went to the palace for liturgy with the children. In the afternoon J[ohnson] and I took a walk in the grove, the one past the train tracks. Before tea I rested. At 6 o'cl we went to an all-night vigil. Having returned home in played the guitar with

---

[112] The arrests of Grand Duke Boris and Grand Duchess Maria Pavlovna were among the first of members of the "former" imperial family by the Provisional Government. Nicholas II and his family had been placed under House arrest on 7 March. In the case of Grand Duke Boris and his mother, an intercepted telegram (the contents of which are unknown) was sent to the Provisional Government, precipitating a search of the residence of Grand Duchess Maria Pavlovna the Elder at Kislovodsk. In property belonging to her staff, papers formerly the property of Princess Maria Vasilchikova were discovered. In 1915 Vasilchikova had been accused of acting as a "back-channel" to arrange a separate peace with Germany, and Empress Alexandra had been falsely implicated (cf. Buxhoeveden, New York, 1929, pp. 225-226.) Rodzyanko notes that Vasilchikova had sent letters to Grand Duchess Maria Pavlovna the Elder, as well as to Grand Duchess Elizabeth Fedorovna, I. I. Samarin, and Prince Galitzine, among others (cf. Rodzyanko, London, 1927 pp. 168-170). For the Provisional Government, these papers revived the xenophobic specter of Romanov collaboration with the Germans, and the Grand Duchess and her son were placed under house arrest by Chief of Staff, General Alekseev.

Domenici, after dinner continued playing until 9 1/2. The weather was dark, 3°. It is still fully winter, a lot of snow. Today Mama, Olga and Sandro were supposed to leave for Ai-Todor, and Xenia planned on leaving there from Petrograd, if they ended up giving her a railcar.

26 March. Sunday. Gatchina. At 11 o'cl we went to church, where we rode in a sleigh together, as it was hard to drive in a motor. At 12 1/4 Princess Putyatina, Mme Donich, Tata and Oleg, and also Eristov came over. The latter left at 2 1/2, and we went out to take a walk, made a circle around the streets. Maria Sergeievna Romashova, who had returned from Kronstadt,[113] came to tea, and told us of the horrors that were going on there and continue to go on, and also E. K. Gavriluk[114] was here. Before dinner we sat in the bedroom. At 9 1/2, Natasha and I saw the guests off in a sleigh to the Warsaw Station. The weather was damp, foggy, 2°.

27 March. Monday. Gatchina. At 9 3/4 Natasha, George, J[ohnson] and I went to Petrograd. J[ohnson] and I went to Knop's, then to Denis from Italy, from there to Alyosha's, where we had breakfast, at 1 o'cl Natasha came over too. In the afternoon Prince Shervashidze came over, having arrived from Kiev. Natasha came to tea, after which we went to Fabergé. There George joined us, and we all went to Gatchina on a 6 o'cl train. The weather was foggy, 2°.

28 March. Tuesday. Gatchina. Read in the morning. Natasha stayed in bed as she is not feeling well. In the afternoon George and I walked to Mme Derfelden, but she was not home. After tea J[ohnson] and I headed to Kurakin gates in a cab and walked from there to the Farm, where we ordered butter and cream for Easter. The returned home through the Black Gates and Priorat. George and I had dinner together and then sat in the bedroom. J[ohnson] had dinner at his place, his sister and niece came to visit him. The weather was dark, 5°.

29 March. Wednesday. Gatchina. At 11 o'cl George and I went to church at the palace. Natasha was still in bed with nettle fever. Though it is

---

[113] **"Kronstadt"** An island naval base close to Petrograd.
[114] Elena Konstaniovna Gavriluk was the wife of a naval officer and a friend of Natalia's, and a neighbor of the couple in Gatchina.

weaker, it still has not passed. In the afternoon George and I went to M. A. Derfelden, having stayed there around an hour. At 5 o'cl arrived veterinarian came over for Volchok, who has been ill for a month already. At 6 o'cl George and I went to an all-night vigil. Nowadays we must ride in a carriage. Before dinner and before 9 1/2 I played the guitar with Domenici. In the evening sat in the bedroom. The weather was sunny before 3 o'cl.

30 March. Thursday. Gatchina. At 9 o'cl George and I went to church at the palace. Natasha went to Petrograd with Tata, Miss Neame and J[ohnson]. Having returned home, we read. After breakfast Father Strakhov was here and notified us that for now services at the palace church must cease, i.e. during the holidays. Alyosha came over at 2 1/4. At 3 1/4 Alyosha, Baranov and I walked to the palace to my rooms, where I got part of the old letters, - worked about an hour and a half, returned in a sleigh. Natasha with Tata and Miss Neame returned at the same time and she went to church at the *Realnoe* School. I read the 12 Evangelists before dinner. Natasha was late for dinner. George and I dined alone. The weather was sunny, windy, 6°.

31 March. Friday. Gatchina. Read in the morning. At 2 1/4 Natasha, Tata, Miss Neame and I went by car to the church at the *Realnoe* School. After the service, we returned home, and then we took a walk to Priorat, made a small circle there, on the way back dropped by J[ohnson]'s, but he was not home. At 6 o'cl Princess Olga P came over, as did M. G. Donich and her daughters. We sorted through Easter eggs from the former Imperial Porcelain Factory. At 11 1/2 the ladies went to sleep at J[ohnson]'s, also Mlle Marie. The weather was sunny but windy, 6° in the shade.

April 1917

1 April. Saturday. Gatchina. At 11 o'cl I went to [get] J[ohnson] and with them, that is with Olga P, Mme Donich and J[ohnson], we took a walk in Priorat and walked home. The children had breakfast with us. In the afternoon Natasha, Olga P and I took a walk, rode to Priorat and took a long walk there. After tea I rested. Alyosha arrived at dinner time. At 11

1/2 we all went in automobiles to Realnoye school for matins (entrance was ticketed so not too many people were there). We left after the Gospel, Father Kolachev did the service very well and quickly. We broke our fast deliciously and with spirit. Dispersed around 3 o'cl. The weather was overcast, around 6 deg.

2 April. Sunday. Easter. Gatchina. Got up at 10 o'cl. I sat with the children in the garden in front of the house, and we basked in the sun which was finally warm. Before breakfast the cathedral choir singers came over to glorify Christ. In the afternoon I exchanged triple kisses with the people and horse grooms. Then our guess started to arrive. Baroness Taube arrived first, then Klevzel's eldest son, a little later the Romashevs, Dietz with Velikanov, Kavtarze and Mme Barley. Everyone left after 5 o'cl. Then Donich arrived, but Natasha stayed with him, and J[ohnson], the Princess [Putyatina] and I went to Priorat and the took a walk there, it was very pleasant after [having] all the guests. Donich left at 9 1/2. At this time the Krestyanovs arrived. Around 11 o'cl we dispersed. The weather was wonderful, 7° in the shade, the snow is melting fast, though in Priorat only one road was cleaned while in town the snow is almost all gone.

3 April. Monday. Gatchina. Sat in the garden all morning and enjoyed the wonderful weather. At 11 3/4 Mme Donich went to Petrograd with Tata [,] Putyatina, Olet[115] and Mlle Marie. At breakfast: Tatiana Pavlovna with children and Dvorzhitsky, who was freed from house arrest the other day, like many others who were arrested by their very own soldiers. In the afternoon Father Vladimir was here, then A. I. Arapov, who stayed until 4 o'cl. After tea we all went to take a walk in Priorat, and then dropped by J[ohnson's], where we stayed until 7 o'cl. Having returned home in a motor, I rested. At 9 1/2 Olga P, Tatiana P with the children and Alyosha went to Petrograd. The weather was wonderful and sunny until 4 o'cl, 8° in the shade. Mrs. Bennett arrived at 12 o'cl with her 6-month-old baby girl. She left in the afternoon.

4 April. Tuesday. Gatchina. All morning sat on the terrace and basked in the sun, it was simply hot -- like summer. After breakfast I worked with

---

[115] **"Olet"** A family known to the Grand Duke Michael

Vasily[116] in the garden, the janitor Felix helped, too. We cleaned out the snow from ditches and rerouted a flood of water that was flowing from the former cemetery into our large alley. We were able to reroute the water to Nikolaevskaya Street, or else it would have started to flow into our cellar. At 3 3/4 Natasha and I made a circle around Priorat, then dropped by J[ohnson]'s, where the Kotons were. After tea I went out into the garden again. At 6 o'cl Stepan Andreyevsky (a hussar from Chernigov) came over and stayed until 7 o'cl. The weather was wonderful, sunny, 13° in the shade, and 10° in the evening. The air is completely warm, I worked in the garden in only a shirt.

5 April. Wednesday. Gatchina. In the morning went to the garden with the children. Kakhovsky came to breakfast, and later the Vorontsovs and Inna A. After tea I played the billiards with Larka. They left at 6 3/4. Natasha left to take a walk with J[ohnson], and I played the guitar with Domenici. The weather was overcast, cold, 6°. Today I was retired from uniformed military service.

6 April. Thursday. Gatchina. At 12 1/4 Eristov and Naryshkin arrived and stayed until 2 1/2. In the afternoon Natasha and I took a walk through Priorat, walked along the outside path, almost all roads were cleared of snow. After tea I played the guitar, and at 7 o'cl received Cornet Taryshkin, a guardsman who brought a letter from Koka[117] in Gagry. After dinner, as usual, read and talked. The weather was overcast, cold, 5°.

7 April. Friday. Gatchina. In the morning read *Novoe Vremya*. In the afternoon Natasha, George, J[ohnson] and I went to the Kurakin Gates, and from there walked around the lake and to the greenhouse, where we bought flowers and strawberries. After tea, to

---

[116] **"Vasily"** Vasily Feodorovich Chelyshev (b. 1884 – d. 1918) Valet to Grand Duke Michael Alexandrovich, who voluntarily followed him into exile. After the "kidnapping" of the Grand Duke, he was arrested by the Soviet secret police and shot in Perm in September 1918.

[117] **"Koka"** Nikolai Nikolaevich Abakanovich (b. - d. Finland 1936) Served as a Staff-Captain under Grand Duke Michael during World War I on the Southwestern Front while serving in the Caucasian Calvary Division of the 2nd Cavalry Corps. From 1916, he was a member of the Grand Duke Michael's office staff at 38 Galernaya Street. In the Civil War he fought for the Whites, emigrated, and died in Finland in 1936.

which L. V. Khitrovo came with Rita[118] and their youngest son, I received the warrant officer of the Ingush Cavalry Regiment, Popov. In the evening we read and talked. The weather was overcast in the morning and partly cloudy in the afternoon, 7°. Old Mme Ekse also was here for tea.

8 April. Saturday. Gatchina. Spent the morning on the terrace. George read a newspaper. At 12 o'cl Sonia D and Vera Orbeliani came over. In the afternoon we all went to the Kurakin Gates, and from there walked around the lake and got into an automobile by the greenhouses. The guests left at 5 1/2, and I practiced with Domenici, played the new guitar with four base strings and very good tone. Alyosha arrived at dinner time (stayed the night). The weather was sunny, warm, 11° in the shade. The snow is almost all gone, a bit left in the woods. Mlle Valvin spent the day today with her children.

9 April. Sunday. Gatchina. At 10 1/2 Alyosha and I drove to the Kurakin gates, there got out and took a walk, at first around the Zoo, then walked to the palace and we were in our very own little garden. On the large stone bridge, we met with Natasha, Olga P, Mme Donich and J[ohnson]. Both ladies came directly from the Baltic Station at 12. We all walked to the Berezovye Gates, and returned home from there. In the afternoon we all, except George, went to the Zoo by the river and walked on foot to the edge of the park, got into an automobile there and returned home at 4 3/4. Before dinner we sat in the living room, then J[ohnson] and I played the billiards. N. A. Shilov, who came from Minsk for a few days, arrived at 7 1/2. At 9 3/4 all the guests left. The weather was sunny until 3 o'cl, warm, 14°.

10 April. Monday. Gatchina. At 9 3/4 we went to Petrograd. Once there we went directly to Anichkov [Palace] to my rooms, which Natasha had not yet seen. All the things will be moved to our house on the Embankment. Then N[atasha] went to run errands, and I looked over my clothes with J[ohnson], after which we went to Alyosha's on foot, where we had breakfast at 1 o'cl, N. A. Shilov was there and Natasha came over,

---

[118] **"Rita"** Margarita Sergeievna Khitrovo (later Mme. Erdeli, b. Oryol 1895 – d. New York 1952) served as a Sister of Mercy with the Grand Duke's nieces at the Tsarskoe Selo Service Hospital during the war.

too. Then I got a haircut, after that Alyosha and I went to Lavrinovsky, where Bantle was. From there Alyosha, J[ohnson] and I went to Princess Putyatina's for tea. M. G. Donich was there. The princess is going to her husband at Bologoe for a few days, if she can find a ticket. We also dropped by Fokin, from there to Alyosha's, where Natasha was already. Went to Gatchina on the 6 o'cl train. George and I walked home from the station. The weather was sunny from 3 o'cl, around 3 deg.

11 April. Tuesday. Gatchina. At 11 o'cl J[ohnson] and I went to the Berezovye Gates, from there walked to the lake, sat on a bench, then went to the Baltic Station for Countess Tolstaya and Sonechka. In the afternoon we took a walk with them by the lake. The Kolomeitsevs came to tea. All guests left around 6 1/4. Before dinner I played the guitar. The weather was partly cloudy, 12°.

12 April. Wednesday. Gatchina. In the morning we read newspapers and stayed at home. At 2 o'cl George and J[ohnson] drove in the Packard[119] - the former to Pavlovsk to Aunt Olga's, the latter to Tsarskoe [Selo]. The director of *Realnoe* School Genzel came to see us. At 3 o'cl Natasha and I went to the Zoo and took a walk there. Mr. Stewart, who left Xenia's children, came to tea. He left at 6 3/4, and I played with Domenici at 7 1/. The weather was sunny, cold, 4 deg.

13 April. Thursday. Gatchina at 11 o'cl went to the Black Gates, got on horseback and rode around the Zoo, [I] on Vityaz. Nadezhda Dm[itrevna] Lyarskaya came to breakfast. In the afternoon we stayed home, I did gymnastics. Three young officers from the Apsheron Regiment came to tea. They came to see George, - goodlooking young men. Natasha and I took a walk before dinner. J[ohnson] was in Petrograd all day. The weather was cold, it snowed a little during the night, but it melted quickly, 2°.

14 April. Friday. Gatchina. At 9 3/4 George, Natasha and I went to Petrograd, but the train was 25 minutes late, and we waited at J[ohnson]'s apartment. In the city I went directly to Lidval's, where I met up with Alyosha and J[ohnson]. Then we went to two shops, then to Esipovich's (shoemaker) and by 1 o'cl arrived at Alyosha's, where we had

---

[119] One of Grand Duke Michael's American automobiles.

breakfast, Sergei A[leksandrovich] and A. N. Shleifer were there. In the afternoon Natasha went to run errands, Sergei A[leksandrovich] also left, and we discussed the Derugin and Brasov business, - I forgot to mention that Bantle also had breakfast and stayed until 5 o'cl. Then Shervashidze arrived and stayed until 6 o'cl. Natasha, George and Shleifer went to Gatchina on the 6 o'cl train, and I drove the Rolls-Royce with J[ohnson]. We drove 1 hr. 20 min. After dinner Shleifer left. The weather was appalling, it was snowing with wind, 1°.

15 April. Saturday. Gatchina. Read in the morning, and then did gymnastics. Read in the afternoon, Natasha wrote. At 5 1/2 Natasha and I went to M.A. Derfelden, who is leaving with her daughters to America in a few days via Tokyo. Returned home at 7 1/4. The weather was overcast, 4 deg.

16 April. Sunday. Gatchina. At 11 1/2 Staff Captain Nevyadomsky, who is at the General Staff Academy, came over. Naryshkin also came to breakfast. The latter left with George in a motorcar to Pavlovsk at 2 1/2. At this time M. S. Khitrovo arrived. At 4 o'cl N[atasha] and I drove the guests to Baltic Station, after which we went to the Venus Pavillion. It turns out that the soldiers who constantly walk around the park got inside and ruined the interior. M. A. Derfelden came here for tea. Then I practiced with Domenici. After dinner I played a little more. The weather was wintery, overcast, it was snowing in the morning, 2°.

17 April. Monday. Gatchina. At 10 1/4 I drove to the Farm, and from there rode on horseback through the military field, the tea house, black lake, Korpikovo. Drove home from the farm in an automobile. In the afternoon Natasha and I went to M. A. Derfelden, said goodbye and gave her the letters for D. I. Abrikosov, - she is leaving today. Then N[atasha] and I drove to the palace park, where we took a walk. After tea I read, then did gymnastics. The weather was sunny, cold, 2°. Mogilyansky was at lunch.

18 April. Tuesday. Gatchina. At 10 1/2 I took a ride on horseback, got on the horse by Priorat (near the Warsaw Station) and rode beyond Pizhma, - the fields are still wet, very swampy. In light of 1 May [Labor Day] abroad there are celebrations and rallies everywhere. In the afternoon I napped for a bit, then wrote letters. Around 6 1/2 Natasha, J[ohnson] and I went to

our house on Baggovutskaya and looked around the building. Before dinner I did gymnastics. The weather was sunny almost the entire time, strong icy wind, from 2 to 4 deg.

19 April. Wednesday. Gatchina. At 9 3/4 Natasha, George, J[ohnson], Miss Neame and I went to Petrograd. [On the train] an ensign sat with us and talked [about] interesting things. In Petrograd I went to Lidval's with J[ohnson], Alyosha also came there, then we walked along Nevsky, then rode to Alyosha's. J[ohnson] went to Minister of [Justice] Kerensky, while I wrote several letters. After breakfast Natasha went to run errands, and Alyosha and I to the dentist, Dr Totven, then met with Natasha at Marseru, after which we went to Alyosha's, where we saw B. I. Abrikosov, and for tea we went to Olga P's, where the prince was in. At 6 o'cl we went to the train station and to Gatchina. From Baggovutskaya platform I walked home. Before and after dinner I played the guitar with Domenici. The weather was sunny, in the afternoon it snowed a little, 4 deg. George is spending the night in Petrograd. Yesterday the day passed peacefully in Petrograd, despite the 1 May holiday.

20 April. Thursday. Gatchina. At 10 1/2 I drove to the Farm, there got on horseback and took a ride in the Zoo, - all these last days I rode Vityaz. At 12 o'cl George arrived from Petrograd. He was planning on going to Finland today, but postponed departure for some time.[120] In the afternoon I read, then wrote. After tea Natasha and I drove to the Zoo and took a long walk there. Before dinner I did gymnastics. The weather was overcast, the sun rarely peeked out, strong cold wind, 3°.

21 April. Friday. Gatchina. At 10 o'cl I rode on horseback, got on at the Farm and rode through Yegerskaya, through Salezi to Pedlino, from there passed the black lake and returned to the Farm through Remiz, - rode Vityaz. After breakfast N. D. Lyarskaya came to see us, and after her

---

[120] Grand Duke George tried repeatedly to leave the capital, and in June 1917 he became the first Romanov to leave Russia for Finland, where he rented a villa at Retierve. In the winter of 1917, he moved to Helsingfors (Helsinki). In January 1918 he returned to Russia, now ruled by the Bolsheviks, to attempt to rescue his family. After he asked for a new passport and permission to leave, he was arrested and imprisoned. In January 1919 he and three other Grand Dukes were executed in the Peter and Paul Fortress.

departure Natasha and I went to the palace park, where we took a walk along the lake, went inside the Venus Pavillion, where we fixed the window glass broken by the soldiers. Got into an automobile at Sylvia Gate. After tea I played the guitar, then did gymnastics. I put on a tuxedo for dinner. In the evening O. N. Krestyanova came over, - N. N. is in Petrograd for a few days already, where they will soon move. The weather was sunny, cold wind, 6°.

22 April. Saturday. Gatchina. At 9 3/4 I drove to the Farm, got on horses and took a ride on horseback with Bennett; we rode to Gorvitsy and through Remiz and returned home by the same route. I rode Dalai. In the afternoon Natasha, George and I rode in the Rolls-Royce past the Tea house on Korpikovo, then Marienburg and to the Zoo, where we took a walk. After tea I played with Domenici until 7 o'cl, then wrote letters- to Toria and Simpson, on the 26th M. N. Lavrinovsky is going to London. After dinner continued writing. The weather was wonderful finally, 11° in the shade. Today the commissariat drove over several hundred (over 1000) heads [of livestock] to the edge of the Zoo, and settled the livestock between the Farm and Sylvia [Gate]. Strange choice, why in the park of all places[?]

23 April. Sunday. Gatchina. At 10 1/2 Tata and I went to the Farm, got on horses and rode around the Zoo. Then I took photographs of Tata on Kotik by Sylvia [Gate], where at 12 o'cl Olga P, M. G. Donich, Alyosha and J[ohnson] came from the Baltic Station. We all drove home. After breakfast we sat on the terrace. Around 3 o'cl we went for a drive in two automobiles - I drove three ladies in the Rolls-Royce, and in the closed [automobile] rode: Natasha, Alyosha, J[ohnson] and Dvorzhitsky (who also came to breakfast). We drove around the Zoo, then through Salezi and Pedlino drove to the Motchinsky ravine, where we took a walk. From there drove by the black lake and Lisya-Bugry towards home. Dietz and Donich came to tea. At 7 o'cl we went to our house on Baggovutskaya, showed it to the ladies. After dinner we all went to J[ohnson]'s, where we had tea. The guests left via the Warsaw [Station] at 11 o'cl 17 min. George, Natasha and I sat at J[ohnson]'s until 12 1/4. The weather was occasionally sunny, strong wind, but warm, 13° in the shade. The blue

coppices appeared about 10 days ago, but no grass yet. It is just starting to open up.

24 April. Monday. Gatchina. In the morning I sat at George's. In the afternoon I wrote a letter to Rosenbach, who is leaving Brasovo any day now (regrettably) because the servants are causing him a lot of grief. After tea Tata and I drove to the Farm, and from there took a ride on horseback to the Zoo. Before dinner I did gymnastics. In the afternoon George went to Pavlovsk to Aunt Olga's, and returned by dinner. The weather was cold, it snowed in the morning, from 2 to 4 deg.

25 April. Tuesday. Gatchina. At 9 1/4 Tata and I went to the Farm, rode from there on horseback through Remiz past the tea house. Farther along we crossed the railroad and rode past Paritz, Kolpano and to Priorat. By the guard house near Warsaw Station we got into an automobile and went home. Read before breakfast. In the afternoon Natasha and I went to the palace park and there walked around the lake. After tea I played the guitar, then did gymnastics. In the evening Koton was here. The weather was appalling, it snowed often, strongest wind, 2 deg.

26 April. Wednesday. Gatchina. At 10 o'cl Natasha, George, Tata, Miss Neame, J[ohnson] and I went to Petrograd. I walked from Fabergé house to Alyosha's, - the look of the streets had returned closer to normal. I studied with Alyosha until breakfast. Then Shleifers arrived. Tata was at Putyatins.' In the afternoon I studied with Alyosha. At 4 1/2 we went to Olga P's, where we had tea, and at 5 3/4 we went to the train station to Gatchina. (Olga P and Donichi are leaving to Odessa tomorrow, and Tata P is going to Bologoe today with the Bologov Putyatins.) Upon arriving home, I practiced with Domenici, after dinner also until 9 1/2. In the evening Koton came over. The weather was overcast until 5 o'cl, 3 deg.

27 April. Thursday. Gatchina. At 10 1/2 I went to the Priorat gates near the Warsaw Station, got on horse and took a ride through the fields, rose by the Tyaglino village, then past the tea house and through Remiz, - by Galitzine's house I got into a motor. At 2 1/2 George and I drove in the Packard to Pavlovsk to Aunt Olga's. We had tea with her and stayed until 5 1/2. On the way back passed by the Alexander Palace where the poor prisoners [Ed.: Nicholas II and his family] are being held. Before dinner I

did gymnastics. Natasha did not feel well and she went to bed before dinner. The weather was sunny occasionally, 7° in the morning, 4° in the afternoon. Koton was here in the evening. Today I saw my former cuirassier Brundukov, who is in the regiment again.

28 April. Friday. Gatchina. Read in the morning. At 12 o'cl the Shleifers came over. In the afternoon we took a drive with them in the Rolls-Royce - drove through Yegerskaya, Pedlino, the Black lake, Gorvitsy, Tyaglino, the Warsaw highway and Priorat. Got home at 5 o'cl. After tea I played the billiards with A. N. Shleifer, and then we all went to show the house on Baggovutskaya. Before dinner I did gymnastics, received Ensign Popov (from the Ingush Regiment). During dinner and all evening Fedya Ramsh played the accordion. The weather was sunny, cold wind, 5-6 deg.

29 April. Saturday. Gatchina. At 10 o'cl Natasha, George and J[ohnson] went to Petrograd. Shleifer came over and we read newspapers. At 12 o'cl the head Kukhnov arrived, whom I blessed with an icon, his wedding is tomorrow. Then we had breakfast with the children. At 1 o'cl I got on horse by Remiz and took a short ride, - rode through Ilkino and the woods, from there through Sivortzy, Suida and Pizhma to Priorat, where got into an automobile and went to pick up Natasha and company, whom returned from Petrograd at 7 o'cl., and Koka was with them, he returned from Gagry the other day. His health is much better, and he looks good. Before dinner Koton massaged my arm. In the evening we took a short walk in the streets. I forgot to mention that Praskovia Ivanovna also came over for the night with the others. The weather was bright, fresh, around 6°. I rode with two horses, one of them held by the lead, - Vityaz and Kabardinets.

30 April. Sunday. Gatchina. At 11 o'cl Natasha and Praskovia Iv. went to church at the *Realnoe* School, and George, J[ohnson], Koka and I drove in the Rolls-Royce to the palace park, where we sat near the lake and basked in the sun. Then Natasha came with P. I. and Tata. We took a short walk. After breakfast we sat on the terrace, wheels it was finally warm. Alyosha arrived at 3 1/2 and we all drove in two automobiles to Remiz, where we took a walk in the right clearing. When we returned home at 5 o'cl, Dietz and his wife were already sitting there, - the latter was here for the first time. Later I played the guitar with Domenici. Before dinner I did

gymnastics. At 8 o'cl Maria V arrived from the front, where she liquidated her detachment, - she said that it was impossible to stay there any longer. At 11 o'cl Alyosha left, Koka left at 9 1/2, and Maria V drove off to Petrograd in a hired automobile at 11 3/4. The weather was wonderful, around 10°.

May 1917

1 May. Monday. Gatchina. At 10 o'cl we went to Petrograd. There I went to Alyosha's, and before that dropped Praskovia Iv. at her apartment. I wrote a letter to Xenia and Yuzefovich. Maria V and Alexander N. Shleifer came to breakfast. Around 2 o'cl Miss Neame and Tata arrived. Domenici came over, and I played the guitar until 3 o'cl, and then went to [see] Buchanan, [and went] from him to Prince Shervashidze on the Fontanka. At 5 o'cl we had tea at Alyosha's. Krestyanov and Koka were there. We went to Gatchina at 6 o'cl 10 min. George went to Pavlovsk in the afternoon. The weather was sunny, 12°.

2 May. Tuesday. Gatchina. At 10 1/2 Tata and I drove to the Farm, and from there took a ride on horseback around the Zoo. Then I gave the children, Miss Neame and Mme Barle a ride around the park, then along Priorat, in the Rolls-Royce. In the afternoon Natasha, J[ohnson] and I drove in the Rolls-Royce to Chirikinskaya guard station where we walked. At the guard station they gave Bogdanov four soldiers as an escort to guard the hunting. After tea I played the guitar, then did gymnastics. The weather was overcast, 12°. Yesterday Guchkov, the Minister of War and the Navy, resigned.

3 May. Wednesday. Gatchina. At 9 1/2 George and J[ohnson] went to Petrograd. I read all morning. Brundukov (cuirassier), with whom I had a long conversation, was here to see me. Read in the afternoon; before tea did gymnastics. At 4 o'cl Mrs. Bennett came over, had tea with us at 5 o'cl. Then I played the guitar with Domenici. At 7 1/2 George returned, and Alyosha also came with him, who will spend the night here. Until 6 o'cl it rained, 7°.

4 May. Thursday. Gatchina. At 9 1/2 Natasha, Alyosha and J[ohnson] went to Petrograd. At 10 ½ Tata and I drove to the Farm, where we got on

horses and took a ride first along the military field, then through the Pheasant [enclosure] and back via Remiz. At 12 1/2 we, i.e. George and I, had breakfast with the children, then read a newspaper, and at 2 o'cl in drove with the children and Miss Neame in the Rolls-Royce to Zarechye. Drove all the way to Zarechye, but did not stop at the house and drove back; having driven about 1/2 of verst past the mill, we stopped at the right clearance, where we had tea, which we brought in thermoses. Then we took a walk to the Black River on foot, there got into and drove back home, where we arrived at 6 1/2 (a tire went flat on the way back). At 7 o'cl George left for Petrograd. Natasha arrived at 7 1/2. Wrangel had dinner with us and left at 9 1/2. Koton was here in the evening. The weather was sunny, strong cold wind, 6°. George left because his valet Lebedev, who departed from here three days ago, got sick with typhus and the rooms will need to be disinfected. Poor thing, he is very upset.

5 May. Friday. Gatchina. At 10 1/2 I drove to the Zoo, by the Farm got on horse and took a ride (Lisyi-Bugry, Korpikovo, Black lake, again Lisyi Bugry and Remiz). Having returned home at 12 o'cl, I read, after breakfast, too, and then Natasha and I went to the garden at our new house, - in a few days the fence that separates our gardens will be taken down, - then we went to see the house on Kseninskaya street right by the Priorat. The house is two stories, nice, - we are thinking of leasing it for our servants. After tea Natasha and I drove to the Zoo, where we took a long walk on foot and got into a motorcar by Sylvia Gate. Before dinner I did gymnastics. The weather was occasionally sunny, 6°. Kerensky was appointed Minister of War. Milyukov resigned [as Foreign Minister] the other day. Tereschenko has been appointed to replace him.[121]

6 May. Saturday. Gatchina. At 10 o'cl Natasha and I went to Petrograd. There I went to the office, where I received a deputation of eight men (serving) Brasovo and Derugino. They presented their requests and

---

[121] On 20 April 1917 Pavel Miliukov had sent Britain and France a diplomatic note recommitting Russia to its original war aims, which controversially included annexation of foreign territory. Its revelation precipitated the the Provisional Government's first major political crisis. After the subsequent resignations of Guchkov and Miliukov on the 2 and 4 May, Kerensky became the Minister of War and dominant figure in the newly formed cabinet.

wishes. Then Natasha and Koka came to get Alyosha and me, and we went to Surov's, then Kodak, from there to Alyosha's. After breakfast Larka came over. From 4 o'cl until 5 o'cl I played the guitar with Domenici. After tea, where Larka and Dvorzhitsky were present, - J[ohnson] and I went to Abakanoviches,' where Natasha was, and went to the train with her. There were four others traveling in our compartment, and we talked with them. In the evening we sat in the schoolroom, Natasha was putting post cards into an album, and Miss Neame massaged my head. The weather was sunny in the morning, it rained a bit in the evening, 7°.

7 May. Sunday. Gatchina. Read in the morning. In the afternoon Natasha, J[ohnson] and I went to the house on Baggovutskaya, where my furniture from Petrograd was delivered. At 3 3/4 Natasha and I drove to the Zoo, where we took a walk on foot. At the park's edge we got into an automobile and returned home. After tea I read, then did gymnastics. After dinner I played the guitar. The weather was awful, although the sun did peek out rarely, - it was very cold, and it snowed from time to time since last night, 2° in the afternoon, 1° in the evening.

8 May. Monday. Gatchina. At 9 3/4 Natasha, Tata, Miss Neame, J[ohnson] and I went to Petrograd, E. K. Gavriluk and two others travelled with us in the compartment. I, Tata and Miss Neame went directly to Alyosha's, where Koka was. N[atasha] came to breakfast, also Sergei A[leksandrovich] and Shleifer were there. The we discussed one matter with Sergei A[leksandrovich]. Had tea at 5 o'cl. Then we, with Gatchintzy, went to the train station. Shleifer came with us. With him we walked from Baggovutskaya platform home. After dinner, Natasha, Shleifer and I went to the house on Baggovutskaya, where their rooms were being prepared. Then, having returned home, we sat in the schoolroom. Shleifer left at 11 o'cl. The weather was sunny until 12 o'cl, in the morning everything was covered in snow. All day it stayed from 2 to 4 deg. in the shade.

9 May. Tuesday. Gatchina. At 9 3/4 I drove to the Farm with Baby and Miss Neame, [and] took a ride from there on horseback - Remiz and palace park. I got off near the stone bridge, where Baby and Miss Neame were

waiting for me. At 12 o'cl Sergei A[leksandrovich]¹²² and Alyosha, who arrived from Petrograd, drove by. We drove home and before breakfast sat on the balcony. In the afternoon Natasha, S.A. Sh., Alyosha and I went to the Zoo, where we took a walk. Got into an automobile on the edge of Tsagov and returned home at 5 o'cl. Then Alyosha read a newspaper before dinner. At 9 1/2 S.A. Sh. and Alyosha left. The weather was sunny all day, 12 deg. finally. After breakfast we showed the house on Baggovutskaya.

10 May. Wednesday. Gatchina. At 9 3/4 I went to the Farm with the children and Miss Neame. From there they walked to the palace park to pick flowers, and I rode a horse, through Remiz I rode to the Tea house, then back through Pheasant [enclosure] and the military field. We met up at Sylvia [Gate] and went home. Before breakfast Ensign Kvasny came to see me. In the afternoon Natasha and I drove to the Zoo, where we took a walk. After tea I played the guitar with Domenici until 7 o'cl. At 7 o'cl 50 min. I drove the Rolls-Royce through Remiz, where Dietz joined me, towards the Motchinsky ravine to the capercaillie current. We drove off two capercaillies, while we were going to the current, heard only one call, very far away, no sound of movement, the birds sang little, the evening was wonderful, quiet and warm, first evening during entire spring. At 11 o'cl I returned home. Had tea in the school-room. The weather was sunny all day, 12 deg, 8° in the evening.

12 May. Friday. Gatchina. At 10 1/4 I drove, as usual on horseback, while the children with Miss Neame picked flowers in the palace park; I rode at the Zoo. At 11 3/4 I drove the Packard down Tsarskoselsky highway and, having driven about 7 versts, ran into Marie (M. P.) She switched to my [automobile], and we drove home. After breakfast we sat on the terrace, then took a drive in the automobile across the Zoo, then walked along the lake and stopped by the Birch House and Venus Pavillion, both of which were much ruined by the soldiers. After tea we saw Marie off almost to Tsarskoe [Selo] and returned home at 6 o'cl. Before dinner I

---

[122] **"Sergei A[leksandrovich]"** Sergei Aleksandrovich Sheremetevsky, lawyer and father of Natalia. Grand Duke Michael's father-in-law.

read, and in the evening Colonel Reier came to see me. The weather was sunny until 2 o'cl, 12°.

13 May. Saturday. Gatchina. At 10 o'cl J and I went to Alyosha's in Petrograd. There I tried on [clothes], then studied. Shleifer came to breakfast. In the afternoon I went to Prince Shervashidze's with Alyosha, from who I found out the details of the search at Mama's in Ai-Todor.[123] From there we went to the Vorontsovs,' where Arsenyev and Koka were also. J[ohnson] and I took the 6 o'cl train to Gatchina, traveling us in the compartment was Gen[eral] Filipovsky. From Baggovutskaya platform we walked, and before dinner I practiced with Domenici. At 9 o'cl Colonel Kavtarze came to see me with his son, they stayed for an hour, - he and his family are leaving Gatchina tomorrow. The weather was sunny, 12°. Natasha did not feel very well, therefore did not go to Petrograd. Received a postcard from Mama from Ai-Todor.

14 May. Sunday. Gatchina. In the morning I read in the garden. At 12 o'cl Vasily brought over from Kavtaradze a collie named Reit. Before breakfast Natasha and I stopped by the house on Baggovutskaya, also today they delivered the furniture there, in a few days all will be ready. At 3 o'cl Natasha, the children, Miss Neame, J[ohnson] and I drove in the Rolls-Royce to the Tsarskoslavyanskaya dacha in the woods. The Packard followed us. We stopped at the first current and walked down to its edge, saw one capercaillie. Having returned to the automobile, we drove on and, one verst from the Chirikinsky house, stopped and set up to the right of the road on a clearing, where we had tea, - Natasha read, the children cut deadwood and started a campfire, J[ohnson] and I took a walk, - I showed him the spot where I killed a bear in 1908, on 8 May. At 6 1/2 we drove home, and before dinner I read on the terrace. In the

---

[123] **"the search at Mama's in Ai-Todor"** Like her sister-in-law Grand Duchess Maria Pavlovna before her, the Dowager Empress was subjected to an insulting and frightening search of her property and belongings at her residence in the Crimea. On the 26 April 1917, the Sevastopol Soviet, afraid of "counter-revolutionary conspiracy" had ordered searches of three local estates of the Romanov family, Ai-Todor, Dulber, and Chair. Grand Duke Alexander Mikhailovich described the search as by turns farcical and terrifying. (Cf. Grand Duke Alexander Mikhailovich, pp. 284-287)

evening Natasha, Miss Neame, J[ohnson] and I went to the town cinema (*For the Sins of the Mother*). The weather was sunny, warm, 16°.

15 May. Monday. Gatchina. At 10 1/4 the children, Miss Neame and I drove to the palace park. The children picked flowers near Berezovy house, and I read on the grass. Then we took a walk to the sailors and returned home. In the afternoon Natasha and I went to the Zoo and took a walk there. After tea I read, then we went to the house on Baggovutskaya. Before dinner I did gymnastics. (I made a mistake: before breakfast Natasha, Koton and I went to the house on Baggovutskaya, and after tea Natasha and I picked the buds of black currants for vodka.) In the evening we went to the said house again. Then I wrote a letter to Kerim, which Kvasny took [to him], - I sent him this morning. The weather was sunny, then semi-overcast, around 18°.

16 May. Tuesday. Gatchina. At 10 1/2 I drove to the palace park with the children and Miss Neame; we stopped near Sylvia, - I stayed in the motor and read a newspaper. In the afternoon Natasha, the children, Miss Neame and I drove in the Rolls-Royce to the Tuganitsky ravine, - behind us drove the small Opel with Vedikhov and Borunov. We set up to the right of the road. We started a campfire and baked potatoes, and also boiled water for tea. Natasha reads. At 5 3/4 we took a walk on a forest path along the ravine to the Motchinsky road, - there got into an automobile and drove home through the Black lake, Remiz and the Zoo. Having returned home at 6 3/4, I rested. After dinner we went to the house where the work is almost done. The weather was wonderful, sunny, 18°. Today Reit jumped out of the moving Rolls-Royce, fortunately all was fine. The trees are blooming fast. At 5 1/2 Tanya and Marina came over - they are staying in the house on Baggovutskaya.

17 May. Wednesday. Gatchina. Read in the morning. George came over and stayed until 2 1/2. After that Natasha, the children, Tanya, Marina, Sophie, Miss Neame, J[ohnson] and I drove in two automobiles through Remiz to the Tuganitsky ravine, - there we had tea, started a campfire and baked potatoes. Then everyone took a walk through the woods along the ravine, and I drove around it with Borunov and met them. At 6 1/4 came home. Before dinner I practiced with Domenici. After dinner J[ohnson]

and I went to the garden at the new house, - the husband of the janitor woman approached me, and complained that his family is being moved. The weather was wonderful, 22° in the shade, around 10° in the evening a minor rainstorm passed. Bird cherry is blooming.

18 May. Thursday. Gatchina. At 9 1/2 Natasha, Tata, Miss Neame, J[ohnson] and I went to Petrograd, there is went to Alyosha's and studied with him. After breakfast, where Shleifer was too, I wrote a letter to Sergei A[leksandrovich]. Then I went to George's with Alyosha, where we stayed 1/2 hour, after which returned and had tea, and at this time everyone arrived. We went to Gatchina on the 6 o'cl train. J[ohnson] stayed until evening (Naumov was here for tea). After dinner Natasha, Shleifer and I went to the Berezovy house, from there walked around the lake, also went by the Echo and the little garden, where the electric railroad is. The weather was wonderful, 17°. These last few days I once again have pains in the stomach, and for this reason saw doctor Rogachevsky today, homeopath, who came to Alyosha's before breakfast.

19 May. Friday. Gatchina. Read in the morning. In the afternoon laid on the sofa. Almost no pains in the stomach today. After tea Natasha, Koka and I drove to the Zoo and walked there, - returned home at 6 3/4. Before dinner I lay down in the study. In the evening went to visit the Shleifer children at the other house. Having returned to his home, Alexander N played the piano. The weather was bright, 15°. I played billiards with Koka. Margarita V arrived at 10 3/4. (Koka arrived at 2 o'cl) at 7 o'cl in the evening Tatiana P went to Petrograd until Sunday.

20 May. Saturday. Gatchina. In the morning Margarita V, Koka and I sat in the garden and read. At 12 o'cl A. I. Arapov arrived. After breakfast we walked around the garden and showed the Baggovutskaya house. He resigned the other day and was in civilian clothes. At 2 1/2 he left. Alexander N read a newspaper to me, and I fell asleep, despite an interesting article by Gofshteter. At 3 o'cl Margarita V left, she is going to Finland for two days. Natasha, A. N., Koka and I drove in the Packard to Remiz, there stopped at the circle, sat and read. After tea I practiced with Domenici. J[ohnson] came to dinner from Petrograd, Alyosha too. The

weather was wonderful, 16°. Koka is staying with us downstairs, and Alyosha on Baggovutskaya.

21 May. Sunday. Gatchina. In the morning read in the garden. At 11 o'cl Natasha, the children, Miss Neame Alyosha and I went to *Realnoe* school for liturgy. To breakfast came- Colonel Gorshkov (head of the Gatchina pilot school) and his adjutant Knox. Then Reier arrived, - we walked around the garden, and at 3 1/2 they left, and we all with the children drove in two automobiles to Remiz, where the circle is, we set up and had tea, - it was very pleasant; we read and laid on pillows. By 6 3/4 we returned home, and I rested before dinner. After dinner we all went to E. K. Gavriluk's, where they treated us to tea, and before our departure the lady of the house demonstrated her excellent dog training - English bulldog, fox [terrier] and 16-year old husky named Belun. We returned home at 11 o'cl. The weather was wonderful, 18°.

22 May. Monday. Day of the Holy Spirit. Gatchina. In the morning I read, played the guitar. Before breakfast Aparin, Colonel of the Ingush Cavalry Regiment, came to see me. Dvorzhitsky came to breakfast. Before tea we sat on the terrace, where we had tea, and at 5 o'cl Natasha, Praskovia I, Dvorzhitsky, J[ohnson], Koka and I drove in the Packard across Remiz and Black lake to the Motchinsky ravine. There we walked all the way around the ravine on forest paths, walked around an hour and a half, it was really nice in the woods and marvelous air. Returned home for dinner. In the evening the Shleifers came over from the Baggovutskaya house with their guests: Merchanskaya and the Captain of 2nd Artillery Brigade, Pavlov. At 11 o'cl all our guests left. The weather was overcast, quiet, pleasant, around 16°.

23 May. Tuesday. Gatchina. Read in the morning. In the afternoon Natasha read on the terrace, and Shleifer and Koka played *kosti*. I was playing the guitar in the study. After tea we, i.e. Natasha, Koka and I, drove to the Somersky guard station and from there walked another verst on the Novgorodskaya road. I did not have a rifle, and while the hunters were standing, I took a walk and picked *boutons d'or*.[124] At 10 o'cl we went

---

[124] **"boutons d'or"** Buttercups.

back to the motor. A.N. [Schleifer] shot twice in vain, - Koka killed one and a cuckoo. Got home at 11 o'cl. The weather was overcast, quiet, from 5 o'cl cleared up, 15°, 10° in the evening. Gen[eral] Alexeyev resigned [as commander-in-chief], Gen[eral] Brusilov was appointed, to replace him.

24 May. Wednesday. Gatchina. Read in the morning. Koka went to Petrograd. Before breakfast Filippov came to see me with Kuku, who is 10 years old, totally healthy and very affectionate. Mrs. Bennett had breakfast. She stayed until 5 o'cl with her eight months old daughter. In the afternoon we dropped by the Shleifers with her, but except the children no one was home. Before tea I read. Before dinner I played with Domenici. Read in the evening. The weather was overcast, raining occasionally, 13°. In the afternoon M. S. Romasheva came to tea, she also brought her daughter. Today she left for Helsingfors[125] to join her husband.

25 May. Thursday. Gatchina. Read in the morning. Filippov brought Sharik to show us, who went to a bear hunt. In the afternoon I took a nap, and after tea Natasha and I drove to the Zoo in three Packard, made a stop near the river at the edge of the park, there we read in the automobile- I took a walk with the dogs. Then we moved to between Tsagov and the Farm, where we also parked and read for some time. At 7 1/2 returned home. After dinner we dropped by Shleifer, - Tatiana P is returning from Petrograd tomorrow. Read in the evening. It was raining from time to time, from 5 o'cl the weather cleared up, 12°. At 5 o'cl Mlle Valvin arrived to spend the summer with us.

26 May. Friday. Gatchina. In the morning I read in the corner room. In the afternoon we sat on the terrace and read. After tea, i.e. at 5 o'cl, Natasha, J[ohnson] and I drove in an automobile across Remiz on the way to Gorvitsy, - a little after we passed the black lake, we got out and went to the ravine, which is in the upper part of lake. Natasha read on the bank, and we went to the red sand cave, where there is also a spring. Then we all went back to the automobile and stayed there a bit longer and read. Returned home by 7 1/2. Praskovia Iv. came to dinner. The weather was ideal, 18°. Before dinner J[ohnson] received a deputation from the Soviet

---

[125] Helsinki

of Soldiers' and Peasants' Deputies from Tsarskoe [Selo]. They came in order to confirm the exact quantity of my automobiles.

27 May. Saturday. Gatchina. Read in the morning. At 3 o'cl Natasha, Praskovia I., J[ohnson], Baby and I drove in the Rolls-Royce to Remiz, from the circle we took the right-side road, until the first shooter line, there we left the motors and took a walk on foot. Forgot to mention that in the other motor rode Miss Neame, Mlle Valvin and Tata. (Strange that I was in this spot for the first time.) After the walk we had tea. There was a little table set up at the crossroad. By 6 o'cl we returned home, and I played with Domenici before dinner. E. K. Gavriluk came to dinner. In the evening Reier came to see me. The weather was ideal, 18°.

28 May. Sunday. Gatchina. Read in the morning. At 11 1/2 Gippius and Nevyadomsky arrived, - they are both returning to the 2nd Cavalry Corps. They stayed until 12 1/4. To breakfast came: N. D. Kolomeitsev with his daughter, and Alyosha. Then we showed them the house on Baggovutskaya and the garden, after which they left. We all sat on the terrace and read. After tea Natasha, Shleifers, Alyosha, J[ohnson] and I drove in the "Packard" to Gorvitsy, walked the latter part of the way; there we walked through an estate, that is the garden, and sat in a field. At 6 3/4 we drove back and fixed a bridge on the way, just before Lisyi-Bugry. Got home at 7 3/4. After dinner the British officer Springfield came to see me, he is an instructor and artillerist. The weather was ideal, 16°, all these last days the sky was cloudless.

At 10 1/4 Natasha, Praskovia I, J[ohnson] and I drove the old Delon to Petrograd, traveled for 1 hr. 35 min. At Alyosha's, who was at the office, I tried on an outift and got a haircut. Everyone gathered for breakfast. In the afternoon two servants from Abas-Tuman and Trachtenberg came to see me, and later [blank]. Around 4 o'cl Ossovetsky arrived. Natasha came to pick up me and Alyosha at 5 o'cl, and we went to Abakanoviches on Petrovsky, who live in a large house. The young Zinovievs and Mr. Brey were there. At 7 1/2 drove to Gatchina in the new Packard, which met us seven versts from Pulkovo at 9 1/2. In 1/2 hour were home, and Borunov and Vedikhov, having fixed the car, arrived a 1/2 hour after us. Shleifers spent the evening with us. The weather was wonderful, 18°. Found out from Larka about the death of Irina Vas[ilevna] Dolgorukova.

30 May. Tuesday. Zelentsov came to see me in the morning, talked about George's things, which are at the palace. Then staff captain Repnin was here, he is an artillerist and is going to the front soon. Read in the afternoon, and at 4 1/2 Natasha and I drove in the new Packard to the Motchinsky ravine, there we took a walk on the forest path, and then on the current. In the way back, we brought over some pebbles for the bridge, the one across the small river. Got home at 7 3/4. The weather was nice, the sun occasionally peeked out, and from 5 o'cl it cleared up completely, 14°.

31 May. Wednesday. Gatchina. Read in the morning. In the afternoon Natasha, Tatiana P, her children, Tata, Baby, Sophie L, three governesses and I drove in two automobiles past the tea house and, one verst before the black lake, made a stop and set up for tea time on the left of the road, started a campfire and boiled water. Natasha in the shade, sitting on a blanket, was vigorously reading a whole pile of newspapers. In the way back, we stopped by the river to fix the road and were home at 6 o'cl. Before dinner I played with Domenici. Read in the evening. Tatiana P left to Petrograd at 7 o'cl for duty at the infirmary. The weather was wonderful, 15°. Tino abdicated the throne in favor of son Alexander.[126]

June 1917

1 June. Thursday. Gatchina. At 9 1/4 Natasha, J[ohnson] and I went to Petrograd via railroad. First, I went with Natasha to an English bookstore, then I went to Alyosha's and we occupied ourselves, and also in the afternoon. At 4 1/4 we, i.e. Natasha, Alyosha and I, went to Abakanoviches on Petrovsky, there we had tea and planned to go to Gatchina afterwards, but they asked us to stay. Walked around the garden, then had to study a little. At 7 1/2 had dinner; there were:

---

[126] **"Tino"** H.M. King Constantine I of the Hellenes' (b. 1868 – d. 1923) disagreed with Greek Prime Minister Eleftherios Venizelos over whether Greece should enter World War I. In 1917 Constantine I was forced to leave Greece, and his second son, Alexander, became king.

Frebelius, Zinoviev and Captain of the First Rank [blank]. After dinner Koka showed us his three-wheel German automobile. At 9 1/4 Natasha and I drove to Gatchina in the Delon, arriving at 10.55. The weather was wonderful, 18°.

2 June. Friday. Gatchina. Read in the morning, and also Colonel Velikanov came to see me. In the afternoon we all, i.e. all the Shleifers, all of us and Sophie, drove in two Packards across Remiz to the Tuganitsky ravine, there we had tea, having set up to the left of the road. Then we took a walk on the other side of the ravine. During the walk we stumbled upon a large campfire, which the shepherd lads started, the closest trees already started to smolder, we put them out. The entire company stayed in the Motchinsky ravine, and I returned to the automobiles through the other side of the ravine and brought the automobile there. At 7 o'cl we returned home. I bathed before dinner, and in the evening, we went to Tsarskoe. There in the park Praskovia I. and Alexander N got out, and Natasha, Tatiana P, J[ohnson] and I went to Boris's, who was removed from arrest, but for the time being still has no permission to leave his residence.[127] We walked with him around the garden and at 10 3/4 we went to Gatchina. The weather was wonderful, 22°. (Tata's birthday)

3 June. Saturday. Gatchina. In the morning Dietz was here, then I played the guitar with Domenici until 12 o'cl. After tea at 4 o'cl Tata and I drove

---

[127] **"Boris"** H.I.H. Grand Duke Boris had built himself a fashionable English house in a Tudor revival style at Tsarskoe Selo. The British Architects Sherborne & Scott were engaged in construction work together with staff of the Maple & Co. firm in London. Boris's dacha was completely built from English materials by foreign craftsmen. On the 25 May, a letter from Grand Duke Andrei to the Minister of Justice was published in the newspaper *Russkaya Volya* [*Russian Will*] – "she [ed.: Grand Duchess Maria Pavlovna] has not been charged in any way and has not been told that there are any reasons to do so. Mr. Minister, is there any possible reason for this that you can find? .... On behalf of my mother and myself, I ask you, Mr. Minister, for the results of any investigation in order to seek a defense against the vile and offensive articles which have appeared in the press, and which disgrace my mother's name. [signed] Grand Duke Andrei Vladimirovich." The response came: "The Minister of Justice has declared that he finds no obstacles to the release from House Arrest of G[rand] D[uchess] Maria Pavlovna. In exchange for [freedom from] house arrest, Maria Pavlovna must be placed under an non-exit Order." (Khrustalëv, p. 293-294). All of the Vladimirovichi were subsequently released from all restrictions of movement on 6 June but were denied permission to leave the country to Sylvia.

to Sylvia, from where we took a ride on horseback (military field, Kolpano, Paritsy to the railroad overpass, tea house and Remiz), there we dismounted, - Tata rode home in an automobile. Natasha came there with Alyosha and Praskovia Iv. And we drove on the road towards the tea house but stopped not far from Remiz to fix the road, laid down pebbles and sand. Came home at 7 o'cl. In the evening Alyosha and I studied. (Alyosha came from Petrograd at 4 o'cl) The weather was wonderful, 20°.

4 June. Sunday. Gatchina. Read in the morning. At 12 1/4 E. A. Barkov and Dvorzhitsky arrived. At 1 1/4 the Vorontsovs arrived. In the afternoon we walked around the garden, and at 4 1/2 drove in two automobiles across Remiz on the road to Gorvitsy. Having passed the black lake and bit, we stopped and set up on the right side of the road on the edge of the woods, where we had tea. Then took a walk to the pastor's house. Returned home at 7 3/4, drove by Gorvitsy and Voiskovitsa station, then Ilkino and Tea house. At 9 1/2 the Vorontsovs, Birukov and Dvorzhitsky left, - Alyosha and Praskovia Iv. are leaving tomorrow. Before evening tea, we sat in the garden. The weather was ideal, 23°, 15° in the evening.

5 June. Monday. Gatchina. In the morning I wrote to Olga Pavlovna, M. G. Donich and George (the last of whom is living in Finland.) Alyosha and Praskovia I. left at 12 o'cl. A. I. Arapov came to breakfast, then we showed him the upstairs rooms. At 3 1/4 he left. I cut down two chestnut trees, which dried up, in the garden near the house. After tea Natasha and I drove in the new Packard across Remiz past the tea house. Stopped by the river, and I fixed the highway with Vedikhov on both sides of the bridge. Returned home at 7 3/4. In the evening Natasha, the Shleifers, J[ohnson] and I went to a cinema town theater (for the drama *Horrors of the Night*). The weather was wonderful, 22°, warm night.

6 June. Tuesday. Gatchina. At 10 1/2 Natasha, Tatiana P, J[ohnson] and I drove to Petrograd in the new Packard. Natasha went to run errands, and I to Alyosha's, where I occupied myself with Sergei A[leksandrovich] and Alyosha. Sergei Aleksandrovich Sheremetevsky recently returned from Brasovo, where he went on my orders; the atmosphere there is very tense. After breakfast we kept studying until 4 o'cl. After tea I received A.

Kulomzin, who most likely will be going to Ai-Todor shortly. At 6 1/4 we drove to Gatchina. In the evening I read. The weather was wonderful, as all these last few days, around 20°.

7 June. Wednesday. Gatchina. From 10 1/4 to 11 3/4 I practiced with Domenici. Then received Sister Lukom. Read in the afternoon. Around 3 o'cl E. K. Gavriluk came over with Kostya, who played tennis with Tata and Miss Neame. After tea Natasha, E. K., T. P., A. N. and I drove across Remiz and past the black lake to the Motchinsky ravine. There, we sat on grass, read, and in took a walk, walked around the ravine and returned through the current. Then we all walked a little and returned home only by 8 o'cl. Everyone had dinner with us, in the evening sat in the garden. The weather was African, 26° in the shade, 34° in the sun.

8 June. Thursday. Gatchina. In the morning read, and before breakfast Baby, Shleifer, Miss Neame and I sawed down up to six dead trees. Read in the afternoon. At 5 1/4 Natasha, J[ohnson] and I drove to the Zoo, there at the edge of the park we got out, Natasha and J[ohnson] read on the grass, while I took a walk on foot. At 7 1/4 we returned home. In the evening we sat in the garden and read, newspapers of course. The weather is African again, 27° in the shade, 34° in the sun.

9 June. Friday. Gatchina. At 10 1/4 Natasha, Shleifer, J[ohnson] went to Petrograd in the new Packard, and I read before breakfast, also in the afternoon, and rested a little before tea. At 4 1/4 I rode in a carriage to the Dietz's, they were alone and served tea in the garden. V. P. showed me a pool house in Remiz and offered me to come over to swim. Having returned home, I dropped by Tatiana P's, was having dinner with the children, and then I rode out towards Natasha, but already met up on the second verst and returned home. In the evening Natasha, Shleifer and I went to their house and there, right by the house cut down sawed up three large trees (bird-cherries), as they were too close to the house and wherein they completely bent towards the ground. We worked until 11 o'cl, it was so hot that I even took off my shirt. The weather was African, 26 1/2 in the shade.

10 June. Saturday. Gatchina. In the morning I played the guitar with Domenici. At 12 o'cl doctor Westfalen arrived for Natasha. He had

breakfast with us and left at 2 1/2. At 3 3/4 Shleifer, Alyosha and I went to Remiz. She. and I swam at the pool house there, - Dietz came over. In the water it was 15 deg., which I did not like too much, as I find that it is not warm enough. From there Dietz saw us off, in Remiz along the river it is very pretty, - I was never there before. Returned home at 5 1/4, and Boris had tea with us, he came to see J[ohnson] for entire day. At 7 o'cl he left. I read before dinner. In the evening, like yesterday, we went to Shleifers,' where we sawed down another bird-cherry tree, - Miss Neame and Alyosha also helped. Worked until 10 3/4. At 11 o'cl Maria Vasilievna Sh. arrived and stayed overnight. The weather was African, 25°. Alyosha came over at 1 1/2 o'cl and is staying the night.

11 June. Sunday. Gatchina. In the morning Alexander N read *Novoe Vremya* to me on the terrace, - Alyosha went to the cathedral. Boris came over for breakfast in our motor from Tsarskoe [Selo]. In the afternoon we sat on the terrace, then went to Shleifers. At 4 1/2 had tea at home, after which Boris left to Tsarskoe [Selo], and Natasha, Maria V, Guzhon and I drove in a motor across the Zoo to Remiz. There we stopped by the barge and took a walk along the river, - part of the time sat on a bench. The path was very pretty. We got into an automobile by the guard house, the one in the Peasant building, and returned home at 7 o'cl. After dinner everyone was busy with various business. Alyosha left at 11 o'cl. The weather was wonderful, 22°, - the first fresh wind. Yu. P. Guzhon arrived to breakfast. He and M. V. [Shelaputin] are spending the night here.

12 June. Monday. Gatchina. At 11 3/4 Shleifer and I drove the Rolls-Royce to the village Daimische, which is two versts from the village Gryaznaya (the one on the way to Zarechye). He will stay there with friends, - the Ivanovs. I returned home at 1 o'cl 35 min. In the afternoon I played the guitar, and after tea Natasha, Maria V, J and I drove the Rolls-Royce first to the Admiralty, then to the palace, where the lilac is, the bushes there are majorly ruined, because everyone who was not feeling lazy was tearing off the lilac branches. They also completely ruined the electric railroad. From there we drove past the Farm, across Remiz to Korpikovo, where Natasha made a bouquet from white violets, after which we drove past the Black lake, turned toward Lisyi-Bugry and drove home. Before dinner I cut down two small trees with Baby near the tennis court.

In the evening I played the guitar in the study, and Natasha and Maria V read. At 10 o'cl went to Johnson's for a cup of tea. I was really sleepy, and we returned home at 11 1/4. The weather was wonderful, 22°, from 7 to 9 3/4 it rained and a minor thunderstorm passed. The lilac has almost completely finished blooming.

13 June. Tuesday. Gatchina at 10 o'cl I drove to Petrograd in the Delon with Maria V, Miss Neame, Mlle Valvin and J[ohnson]. I spent entire day at Alyosha's, where I studied, - before breakfast Brandorf came over. I brought Volchok who had to be shown to a doctor, as he is still unwell. Doctor came at dinner time for Natasha. He is the assistant of Doc[tor] Westfalen; will stay here until tomorrow. In the evening we all sat on the terrace. The Shleifers came over. The weather was wonderful, although occasionally cloudy, 22°, and the evening was refreshing.

14 June. Wednesday. Gatchina. Read in the morning, while doctor Koppe was with Natasha, he left at 12 o'cl. In the afternoon Natasha, the children, Alexander N with his children, the governesses and I drove in two automobiles to the tea house, from there walked a little on the road to Korpikovo and picked white violets, then, having returned to the [tea] house had tea in the garden, and drove home at 5 1/2. I played the guitar with Domenici before dinner. In the evening we went to the town cinema with the Shleifers and J[ohnson], for *Lady Mary*, Polish drama. The weather was wonderful, 20°.

15 June. Thursday. Gatchina. At 10 1/4 Natasha, Shleifer, J[ohnson] and I drove to Petrograd in the new Packard. The car worked badly, and we traveled for 2 1/2 hours. I went to see the Ministerial Chairman [Prime Minister] Prince Lvov about some business (on Teatralnaya), and from there to Alyosha's. Had breakfast the same way - Maria V and Shleifer. Then everyone went to run some errands, and I studied with Alyosha, and I also received Gen[eral] Markov. From 4 to 5 we were at the dentist Kazarnovsky. For tea at Alyosha's were: Yuly Petrovich and a those who were at breakfast. At 8 1/2 we all went to Kontana, where we had dinner

in separate room. At the end of dinner Gulesko[128] played. At 10 1/2 Natasha, J[ohnson], Shleifer and I went to Gatchina, - arrived at 12 o'cl. The weather was sunny, 22°. (Margarita Vasilievna was at breakfast and tea.)

16 June. Friday. Gatchina. Read in the morning. At 2.20 the Shleifers and I drove in the Rolls-Royce to Lisino, drove through Tsarskoe [Selo], from there on Moscow Highway and through Tosno. Arrived in Lisino at 4.20. A little old man, D. M. Kravchinsky, was in the garden with his 8-year-old grandson and was very happy with my unexpected appearance. Then his wife came, and also his son's wife with her elder son and Krieger. They served us tea and white wine, - sat on the balcony. Before departure I took a few photographs, in the garden, as well as in the house. At 6.10 we drove to Gatchina through Kaushta, Vyritsa, Suida, and Pizhma. Arrived home at 8.20. The road was pretty acceptable. In the evening we all went to the town theater (for the drama *The Poison of Jealousy*). The weather was wonderful, though there were occasional storm clouds, nevertheless the sun was shining constantly, 22°. In Lisino, we did not go into the big house, as it was boarded up by the peasants, - they want to turn it into a school. Kravchinsky, most likely, will leave service in the autumn.

17 June. Saturday. Gatchina. Read in the morning and Colonel Reier came over. After breakfast I received Kartsev, who was appointed Master of the Hunt. (Prince Galitzine had retired long ago, and V. R. Dietz just recently, but will stay in his house until autumn.) At 2 3/4 we all drove in two automobiles with the Shleifers and Captain Pavlov, across Remiz to the Tuganitsky ravine, where we had tea. Returned home via the same route at 6 o'cl, and I played the guitar with Domenici before dinner. Alyosha arrived from the city with J[ohnson] at 8 3/4. In the evening we took a walk in the garden and dropped in on the Shleifers, who then came over our place with Captain Pavlov and had tea with us. The weather was African, 26° in the shade, around 9.10 in the evening a light rain passed.

---

[128] **"Gulesko"** Jean Gulesco (b. 1877 – d. 1953) was a Romanian *tzigani* (gypsy) violinist and conductor. Gulesco worked in Petrograd until the revolution and returned to Romania, leaving a large group of recordings.

18 June. Sunday. Gatchina. Read in the morning and afternoon. At 6 o'cl Natasha, Alyosha, J[ohnson] and went to the Tsarskoslavyanskaya dacha, where we walked around and picked strawberries. By the sand path we got into an automobile and returned home. After dinner we with the Shleifers and Captain Pavlov went to the town cinema, for *Cleansing Fire*. The weather was wonderful, sunny and light, 15°. In Petrograd today, there was a demonstration by the Bolsheviks,[129] it seems like all ended well.

19 June. Monday. Gatchina. At 11 1/2 Shleifer and I took Alyosha to J[ohnson]'s, and at 12 o'cl he went to Petrograd. Shleifer and I went into the park by the palace and walked around the lake, - got into an automobile by Kurakin Gates. In the afternoon Shleifer and I cut down dead apple trees, - Natasha and Baby were present. After tea Natasha, J[ohnson] and I drove Rolls-Royce past the Somersky guard station. There we walked and picked white violets. Bogdanov now has 9 soldiers for guard, - the senior one is Boiko, a handsome lad. On the way back, we enjoyed observing an elk, which was eating grass on the clearance about 200 steps away, - I walked over to him about 50 steps away, but despite this he continued eating. His antlers were large, about 12 points. After dinner Natasha and I took a walk in the garden, then the Shleifers came over. The weather was wonderful, 18°. Good news from the front, - we started a successful offensive on the Southwestern Front.[130] Took 9 thousand prisoners. First offensive since the Revolution.

---

[129] **"demonstration by the Bolsheviks"** In her diaries Madame E. A. Naryshkina, formely lady-in-waiting to the Empress, wrote about this day: "18 June/1 July -- ...There is a large demonstration in Petrograd today: posters inscribed 'Down with the Government!' and 'Down with the War!' are being carried. The same thing here: to the sounds of the *Marseillaise* they marched through the courtyard to the graves of the 'victims of the revolution.' Here, this demonstration was expressed only through idiotic orations." (Khrustalëv, p. 642, citing GARF: f. 501, op. 1, d. 595, l. 14ob.)

[130] **"successful offensive"** At the request of Russia's Western Allies, an offensive was launched on 18 June. After two days of intense engagement, the Russian troops had advanced impressively into Austrian territory. Ultimately, the offensive stalled on 30 June, but both Michael and Nicholas II reacted positively to its brief flash of success. Nicholas II wrote in his diary: "Just before lunch came the good news of the beginning of the offensive on the Southwestern Front. In the direction of Solochovsk, after two days of artillery fire our troops broke through enemy positions and caputured about

20 June. Tuesday. Gatchina. At 10 o'cl 20 min. Natasha, the Shleifers, J[ohnson] and I drove to Petrograd with Vedikhov in the old Packard. I went directly to Alyosha's. After breakfast N[atasha] and J[ohnson] went again to run errands, and I to the dentist with Alyosha (Kazarnovsky on Sergeyevskaya). Returned on foot. At 6 o'cl N[atasha], J[ohnson] and I went to Gatchina and changed a tire on the way. The weather was fresh, around 14°, from 4 o'cl it rained.

21 June. Wednesday. Gatchina. In the morning read and played the guitar. At 3 o'cl J[ohnson] and I drove to Kurakin Gates, and took a long walk in the Zoo, and got into an automobile in the palace park, and returned home at 4 3/4. After tea Natasha and I did a trial drive in the new Packard, i.e. the 12-cylinder of last year's model. Lately it has been capricious. We got to Taits and back. At 6 o'cl returned home, and I played the guitar with Domenici before dinner. In the evening we all went to the cinema, - *Under Cover of the Night*, a French drama. The weather was overcast until 5 o'cl, 14°.

22 June. Thursday. Gatchina. At 10 1/4 the mechanic Mr. Casey came over, a very respectable young man. To check the 12-cylinder Packard we took a ride with him on the Pulkovsky highway, then returned home across Krasnoe and were home at 1 o'cl. Shleifer and Kozlovsky drove with him. In the afternoon Mr. Casey was giving us certain information regarding the automobile. He speaks like a real American and it is rather difficult to understand him. At 4 1/2 he left. At 6 o'cl Natasha and I drove to the Zoo, there we stopped in a meadow, and N[atasha] read, sitting on grass, while I took a walk. In the evening we read. The weather was sunny, very pleasant, 15°.

23 June. Friday. Gatchina. At 10 3/4 Natasha, Tatiana P and J[ohnson] drove to Petrograd in an automobile, and Tata and I went to ride, got on horses by Konnetable and rode across the railroad overpass and through forest along a ditch got and rode around the grove, where once in winter

---

170 officers and 10,000 troops ... Thank God! ... I feel very different after this joyful news." Khrustalëv notes that this response is strange (Khrustalëv, p. 642) as the offensive was defeated. It appears that Nicholas and Michael had the same early misinformation from the newspapers.

we did the round ups, and by the gun powder cellar we got into an automobile and returned home at 12 1/2. At 2 o'cl Alexander N and I drove to the Rolls-Royce to Peterhof. Rode past the Yegerskaya settlement, then Salezi, Repuzi, Kipen, Ropsha. (The palace is occupied by some charity organization.) From the village Nastolovo we turned left across Babigon. Belvedere is boarded up and guarded. Then we rode through the English park and palace, where the soldiers are staying. By our dacha everything has been trampled by livestock (for slaughter), the lower park of Sergeevka[131] is filled with horses, as is Oldenburg's park.[132] The entire lower park from Marly to Alexandria, as far we noticed, is in good shape. Alexandria was shut, regrettably. The Grand palace is not occupied. The ladies-in-waiting house and others are occupied by the Soviet of Workers' and Peasants' Deputies and automobile repair. A club of socialist soldiers is located in the house of Sonia D. We also drove through the Alexander Park, where we made a stop and had tea from thermoses. Near Kipen, we got caught in the rain and it occasionally made us rather soaked until 5 1/2, but after that time the weather cleared up completely. After Alexander Park we rode by Znamenka (the palace is not occupied), Mikhailovka (the suite house is occupied by soldiers) and Strelna, where we drove around the entire park. A big meadow below the house was turned into a horse pasture, and the palace was given over to a school. From there we drove through Krasnoe to Gatchina, to which we returned at 7 1/2, Natasha arrived from Petrograd a little after me. The weather was sunny in the morning and evening, and it rained occasionally in the afternoon, there was no rain in Gatchina, 12°. We drove 115 versts in total.

24 June. Saturday. Gatchina. In the morning I played the guitar, then read. After breakfast, which included Mrs. Bennett, I drove to the Farm, and from there took a ride on horseback (Tsagov, Big Rezino, Salezky forest, direct clearing to the Pedlinsky current, village Pedlino, through the forest to Korpikovo and the tea house). From the tea house I returned home in a motor at 5 o'cl. Before dinner I played the guitar with Domenici.

---

[131] **"Sergeevka"** an estate of the Duke and Duchess of Leuchtenberg, Prince and Princess Romanovsky -- not far from Peterhof.

[132] **"Oldenburg's park"** grounds on the estate of the Duke of Oldenburg, the former father-in-law of Grand Duchess Olga Aleksandrovna, sister of Nicholas II.

After 9 o'cl Natasha, Tatiana P, Miss Neame, Mlle Valvin, J[ohnson] and I drove in the Packard to Krasnoe Selo. We stopped on Strelinskaya mountain and enjoyed the view, then drove on to Volkonsky highway, where we turned around and drove back. The automobile drove uphill wonderfully. Changed a tire past Krasnoe, and at this time a gypsy woman was walking by, she read J[ohnson]'s fortune, all sorts of nonsense. The weather was rainy until 3 o'cl, 8 deg., from 5 o'cl it cleared up.

25 June. Sunday. Gatchina. From 10 1/2 to 12 1/2 I rode [horses] with Tata. We got on at Konnetable and rode on the highway, then turned right and through the fields rode almost to Tyaglino, rode across the railroad overpass, the made a circle to the left in the woods, from there rode to the Tea house, where we got off and drove home in a motor. Dvorzhitsky came to breakfast. At 2 1/2 Praskovia Iv left, and we stayed home until 5 o'cl, and then Natasha, Dvorzhitsky and I drove in an automobile on the Ropshina Road until Repuzi, then drove through Salezi to Pedlino, got off there and walked to the direct road that leads to Lisyi-Bugry. After dinner we went to the town cinema for *Forgotten Worries of Past Days of Youth* and *Jealous man from Alaska*. Dvorzhitsky left at 11 o'cl from the cinema. Between the shows one actor sang and whistled wonderfully. Returned home late. The weather was sunny in the morning, then a bunch of rain passed, and it cleared up from 4 o'cl, 9 deg.

26 June. Monday. Gatchina. (Natasha's birthday) Natasha came downstairs only at 12 1/2. On the terrace was the table with gifts. All the Shleifers, Tatiana Mikhailovskaya and Mrs. Bennett came to breakfast. At 3 1/4 we all drove in three automobiles to Chirikinkaya guard station. Before tea took a short walk, then I played in the hay with the children. Returned home at 6 1/2. Raush (general) came to dinner. He left at 11 o'cl. The weather was cloudy, around 16°.

28 June.[133] Wednesday. Gatchina. In the morning Tata and I rode on horseback, started the ride by the Pheasant building, - ended by the tea house. Itinerary: Pheasant building, tea house, Korpikovo, through the forest past Ryakhkilevo, direct route to Gorvitsy, before reaching

---

[133] Natalia Brasova's birthday.

Gorvitsy, turned left and through clearings came out on the road to the Black lake, through the forest to the right to the tea house. Got home at 12 3/4. At 3 1/4 Natasha and I went to the Zoo and took a walk. By the Farm got into an automobile. After tea and before dinner I played with Domenici. In the evening we went to the town cinema for *Song of Freedom*. The weather was overcast, 13°, got fussy towards the evening. In the evening Colonel Reier came over and brought from the palace cigars and Turkish cigarettes, which had belonged to Papa.

29 June. Thursday. Gatchina. At 10 1/4 Tata and I drove to the Tea house, there got on horseback and rode across Korpikovo to Pedlino through the woods, from there by clearing across Pedlinsky and Salezky forests to the village of Maloe Rezino and the Zoo, where an automobile was awaiting us on Tsugov. In the afternoon I went to the garage construction site, then we cut dead branches around the house. After tea Natasha and I drove the Rolls-Royce across Pizhma, Suida to Sivortsy, from there on the highway to Gatchina, where we arrived at 7 1/4. Bologov Putyatins came to dinner. We walked in the garden and showed them the house on Baggovutskaya. They left at 11 o'cl. Spent the evening on the terrace, then the living room. The weather was sunny, wonderful, 20°. Received a letter from Xenia in Ai-Todor.

30 June. Friday. Gatchina. At 10 1/4 Tata and I rode on horseback, got on at the overpass to the cemetery. Halfway to the bison we turned right at the clearing, crossed the shooting range and rode by Pustoska through the copses, then turned left into the forest and by Volasniki walked [horses] across the river. Returned home through Pizhma and got off by Priorat. After breakfast Natasha, J[ohnson] and I drove to Petrograd in the Rolls-Royce. While Natasha was at the beauty salon, Alyosha and I stopped by St. Isaac's Cathedral. Then we all had tea at Alyosha's, where Tatiana P was, after which Natasha, Tatiana P and I took a walk on the embankment, along Kamennoostrovsky, to Strelna and returned to Alyosha's only at 7 1/2, where I had a haircut, after which we all went to dinner at Kontana and sat in a gazebo, - the whole garden was filled with people. Then we went to the 'Piccadilly' cinema for *For Another's Sin*. At 12 o'cl Natasha, Tatiana P, J[ohnson] and I, from Alyosha's, drove back

to Gatchina in the Rolls-Royce! And we traveled for exactly 1 hr. 4 min. The weather was hot, around 20°, sunny.

July 1917

1 July. Saturday. Gatchina. In the morning Tata and I rode on horseback, got on in Priorat by the Warsaw Station and rode along Priorat, then through the Baltic Station, Kolpano, across the Pheasant building to Remiz and got off at Sylvia. In the afternoon we went to the Shleifers (birthday of A. N.). The birthday boy played the piano, then they served tea on the terrace. From 5 1/2 until 7 3/4 I played the guitar with Domenici. After dinner, to which Alyosha came, we went to the Shleifers, where the husband and wife Ivanov were (timber merchant). I played [guitar] with Domenici until 10 3/4, and the rest played *zhelëzka*. Alexander N and I smeared each other's heads with burnt cork, both ended up with the most impossible look. We dispersed only at 2 o'cl. The weather was wonderful, 20°. Today (to economize) the clock was turned one hour forward, following the European example.

2 July. Sunday. Gatchina. Got up late. N. D. Kolomeitseva and Obukh (he commands the Polish Uhlan Regiment) came to breakfast. The former left soon, and we went to the Shleifers. When we were leaving, there was a horrible fight in the garden between my two dogs and the Shleifers' [dogs], while separating them I got slightly bitten by Reit but of course not on purpose. Obukh left at 4 o'cl. After tea Natasha, J[ohnson] and I drove in the Rolls-Royce to Elizavetino, drove through Pizhma, Suida, Sivoritsy, and from there via fields to Elizavetino. The house has tenants, therefore we just walked around the outside, walked by the church to the park. J[ohnson] has not been there for 19 years. N[atasha] and I were in Elizavetino for the first time. At 7 o'cl 40 min we drove to Gatchina via Tuganitsky road, before reaching Tuganits, we turned right and passed across our ravine, then past the black lake and through Remiz. At 8 3/4 arrived home. In the evening we went to the town cinema for *The Roses Withered*, *The Dreams Disappeared* and *Bridegroom in the Pocket*. Returned home late. The weather was hot, thick clouds, 20°.

3 July. Monday. Gatchina. From 11 o'cl and until breakfast, I took a drive in the Rolls-Royce with the children, Miss Neame and Mlle Valvin (the Zoo, Kipensky highway, Kozlevsky forest to the Motchinsky ravine, Gorvitsy, across Remiz, home). After breakfast I rested for a bit. After tea and before dinner Natasha, Shleifer, Baby and I cut dead branches in both gardens. After dinner, we, with Shleifer and J[ohnson] drove the Rolls-Royce to Petrograd through the Zoo, Yegerskaya, Salezi, Pedlino, then before reaching Tuganitsky ravine, turned left and returned home across the black lake, Paritsy, Kolpano and the Baltic Station. The weather was hot, 20°, almost no sun, it rained many times, but after 6 o'cl in the evening it stopped. In Petrograd at 8 o'cl in the evening, disorder started, there was shooting in the streets.[134]

4 July. Tuesday. Gatchina. At 11 o'cl Alexander N and I drove to the Kurakin gates, from there we walked to the palace park, walked around the lake, got into an automobile at Sylvia. In the afternoon Natasha, Alexander N, Baby and I cut dead branches around the tennis court, worked until tea time, and at 5 o'cl Natasha, J[ohnson] and I drove the Rolls-Royce across Pizhma, Volasniki, Kovshovo, Kaushta, Vyritsa, Suida and again Pizhma. It was a wonderful drive, and the places very pretty. Returned home at 8 1/4. After dinner we went to the cinema, for *Her Victims*. The weather was hot, 20°. During the drive, it was raining hard around us, but didn't wet us much. Since yesterday, disorders continue in Petrograd, - a lot of Bolsheviks, more than 6 thousand sailors

---

[134] In the diary of E. A. Naryshkina, who lived in an apartment in the Catherine Palace at Tsarskoe Selo, there is a mention of this event: "July 4/17. It turns out that yesterday in Petrograd there was a speech against the government. Five ministers have resigned. They say there was even gunfire. I have no details: today the newspapers were not published. There was a lot of excitement here, but nothing serious. I am afraid of two possibilities: Kerensky's resignation and the capture of Petrograd by the Germans. In both cases, the life of our poor royal couple will be in immediate danger. [Princess Olga] Paley has just left. She said that a group of young officers had secretly made a crazy plan: to take them at night by car to one of the ports, where they will wait for an English steamer. I'm afraid Varennes [Louis XVI's attempt to escape revolutionary France in 1791] won't happen again. I am in unspeakable anxiety. And where to run when there are mines everywhere?" (Khrustalëv, p. 643 citing GARF, f. 6501, op. 1, d. 595, l. 15).

arrived from Kronstadt,[135] - there some units still on the side of the government, who will stand behind it. A lot are injured, around 500.

5 July. Wednesday. Gatchina. Read in the morning. After breakfast Natasha picked strawberries in the [garden] beds with the others, and I cut the branches near tennis court. At 4 1/2 I got on horse near Konnetable and rode on the major road to Khimozi, from there on the green road to Suida, and there on the birch alley to the left to the edge of the Kovshovsky forest along the river, left the village Pustoshka to the left, and through the meadow to the village Maloe Zamostye, then on the highway toward home, but past the railroad rode on the peat clearing to the right, crossed the Warsaw road at the Tatar crossing, and was home at 7 1/2. Natasha took a ride in the Rolls-Royce with Shleifers and J[ohnson]. They made a circle around Tuganitsky ravine, across Tuganits and via Kipensky highway, home. After dinner we all went to the cinema for *Vampires*. The weather was wonderful, despite light rain in the morning, and playful in the afternoon, around 16°.

In Petrograd order is being reestablished,[136] altogether about 1,000 people were injured, including children and women, and about 20 Cossacks were killed and about 70 injured.

6 July. Thursday. Gatchina. From 11 o'cl to 11 3/4 I rode horseback at the Zoo in Dalai. After breakfast I cut dead branches near tennis court. At 4 o'cl Natasha, the Shleifers and I drove in the Rolls-Royce to Elizavetino, but not reaching the final destination, we ruined our front spring, having driven into a pothole, hence we turned back on the way to

---

[135] In May 1917, the Kronstadt Soviet refused to recognize the authority of the Provisional Government and its officials. Kronstadt sailors appeared in all political demonstrations in Petrograd and were active in October during the overthrow of the Provisional Government.

[136] This refers to the brief calm which followed the "July Crisis" of the Provisional Government. After the dispersal of the demonstrations of 3-4 July, on 9 July, the Provisional Government began investigations into who had instigated the uprisings, and turned to examine the Bolsheviks as a source of the dissent, maintaining that their leader, Lenin, had planned the uprising with the intent of overthrowing the Provisional Government. Despite Michael's later observation that the "success of the Bolsheviks is starting to decrease," the investigations only served to antagonize the Bolsheviks, who coalesced around their leader.

Gorvitsy. On the way we made a stop in the forest and picked wild strawberries. Arrived home at 7 3/4, - drove past the black lake and the tea house. After dinner I was present at the disassembly of the spring and its straightening. The weather was wonderful, 20°. Success of the Bolsheviks is starting to decrease, the masses are starting to realize they are working to the benefit of the Germans and their money.

7 July. Friday. Gatchina. In the morning rode on horseback at the Zoo. At 3 1/2 Natasha and I went to see Nadezhda Dmitrievna Lyarskaya, where they served us tea. There, was N. D. Kolomeitseva and Durova. Having returned home at 5 1/4, Natasha, J[ohnson] and I took a drive in the Rolls-Royce (Kipensky highway to Repuzi, Salezi, Yegerskaya), then drove to Remiz, where we made a stop on the right clearing. Natasha and J[ohnson] took a walk, and I played the guitar while sitting on grass. After dinner we went to the cinema for *The Dream Is Dead*. Forgot to mention that Alyosha arrived at dinner and will stay here until Sunday. The weather was hot, cloudy, 20°. Events of the day: the enemy broke through our front near Brzezhan thanks to one regiment, not wishing to go on offense, had retreated without warning, - instead of the Minister Chairman [Prime Minister] Prince Lvov - Kerensky, who [also] remained the War and Navy [Minister] and also picked up the Ministry of Trade and Industry.

8 July. Saturday. Gatchina. In the morning Tata and I took a ride on horseback to the Zoo, - I, as usual on Vityaz, and she on Dalai. Before breakfast I read, in the afternoon as well in the garden. At 4 o'cl N. D. Kolomeitseva came over with her son the page, we had tea on the terrace. When they left, admiral Kolomeitsev arrived soon after, who came from Petrograd. Then I played with Domenici before dinner. In the evening we went to the town theater, where they had a concert. The weather was hot, 20°, occasionally sunny. Petrograd quiet for now, - on the Southwestern Front the bad luck continues.

9 July. Sunday. Gatchina. In the morning studied with Alyosha. Dvorzhitsky came to breakfast. In the afternoon we sat in the garden, and then I received two Chernigov Hussars: Baumgarten and [blank], who is at the Gatchina pilot school. At 4 1/4 Natasha, Tatiana P, Dvorzhitsky and I drove in the Rolls-Royce, with Alyosha and J[ohnson in the Packard

behind us. We drove through Remiz and the black lake to Elizavetino. At the edge of Kezelevsky forest, across the left clearing we made a stop and had tea. Around 5 1/2 drove on and from Elizavetino to Zarechye through the Fifth Mountain. The road was horrible, country [road], but traveled well. In Zarechye we encountered children, whom we drove to the mill. From the village Gryaznaya we turned right to Daimische and dropped by the Ivanovs to pick up Shleifer, but the latter was at the Chikin factory. Then we returned to Gatchina via major highway. It was very windy and cold, and the ladies moved to the other automobile, and Alyosha to mine. Got home at 9 o'cl. Alyosha and Dvorzhitsky stayed the night. The weather was sunny until 5 o'cl, and then interchangeable, 20°, 13° towards the evening.

10 July. Monday. Gatchina. In the morning Tata and I took a ride on horseback at the Zoo. In the afternoon I read, and after tea Natasha, Tatiana P, all the children and I drove in the Packard to Tsarskoeslavyansky Forest, where we picked wild strawberries in two spots, also in the meadow near the guard station. Having returned home at 6 1/2, I read before dinner. At 9 o'cl J[ohnson] arrived from Petrograd. The weather was overcast almost the entire day, 15°. Events of the day: the poor Shleifers' Petrograd apartment was robbed,[137] - horrible news from the front. Tarnopol has fallen without a shot, 12 regiments deserted, and a majority surrendered.

11 July. Tuesday. Gatchina. Read in the morning. At 8 1/2 Natasha and I went to the cathedral, where there was a memorial service for Olga Sergeevna, Vera Sergeevna and Ekaterina Nikolaevna. Having returned home, we had tea, and then drove to the Kurakin Gate, from there took a walk around the lake, we're near the palace and got into an automobile by Sylvia. Klupfel, the local cuirassier, was here to see me before dinner.

---

[137] The Petersburg papers reported a slew of Petrograd robberies beginning in late April. "The number of robberies now occurring should surprise no one, as today about 20,000 thieves have been released. The brigands received full civil rights and walk freely about the streets of Petrograd." (Khrustalëv, p. 646-647 citing a Petersburg leaflet dated April 24, 1917). Many Petrograd residents who were able had fled the capital for country residences, and their lavish unoccupied town residences were easy targets.

After dinner we went to the cinema for *The Price of Life*. The weather was overcast, cleared up towards the evening, around 15°.

12 July. Wednesday. Gatchina. Read in the morning, played the guitar for a bit. In the afternoon took a ride on horseback from Sylvia and got into an automobile in Remiz. (Rode off at the edge of the Zoo and rode across Large Rezino to Salezsky forest, to the left to the black lake, then past the tea house to Remiz.) After tea I played the guitar with Domenici. After dinner we headed to the town cinema for Secret of the iron door. The weather was overcast, windy and cold, 9°.

13 July. Thursday. Gatchina. In the morning rode on horseback at the Zoo. In the afternoon Natasha, Shleifer and I cut dead branches in the garden. After tea Natasha, the Shleifers and I did the drive on the "Rolls-Royce" to Peterhof through Ropsha. We drove around Babigon, the English park, our dacha, Sergeevka, the Lower Park, Alexander Park, Znamenka, Mikhailovka and Strelna. Returned to Gatchina at 8 o'cl 20 min. J[ohnson] arrived from Petrograd, as usual with interesting news. The weather was overcast, 14°. News from the front is not very comforting, as southwestern front continues to retreat almost exclusively for the reason that entire divisions are voluntarily retreating and do not obey the command. Commander of the Southwestern Front Gen[eral] Kornilov sent a shocking telegram to Kerensky about the shameful conduct of the army and the desperate situation at our front. The government decided to reinstate capital punishment at the front.[138]

14 July. Friday. Gatchina. In the morning rode on horseback at the Zoo. In the afternoon Nadezhda Dmitrievna Lyarskaya dropped by to see us. We took a walk in the garden, and she left after tea. Natasha and I were cutting dead branches and bushes near the Shleifers' house all the way until dinner time. At 8 3/4 Alyosha and J[ohnson] arrived. In the evening, with Shleifer, came Frakman, who arrived from the front outside of Tarnopol

---

[138] Nicholas II also noted the authorization of capital punishment with dismay: "Shame and despair! Today it was announced that the Provisional Government has imposed the death penalty against those convicted of treason." (Khrustalëv, p. 647, citing GARF, op. 1., d. 265., ll. 158-159).

(he is in the Heavy Guard Division) and tells of horrors that are happening there. The weather was overcast, 14°.

15 July. Saturday. Gatchina. In the morning rode horseback at the Zoo. Shleifer and Frakman had breakfast. Around 3 o'cl Natasha, Tatiana P and I drove in the Rolls-Royce to the Tuganitsky ravine, behind us Alyosha and Alexander N drove behind us in the Packard. We took a bit of a walk on the left side of the ravine. Returned home, i.e. past the black lake and the tea house. After tea I played the guitar with Domenici. After dinner we went to the cinema for *And She Took the Secret to Her Grave*. The weather was overcast until 2 o'cl, around 16°.

16 July. Sunday. Gatchina. Stayed home in the morning. At 12 o'cl Dvorzhitsky came over. In the afternoon Natasha, Dvorzhitsky, Shleifer and I cut dead branches and boughs in the garden on Baggovutskaya, worked until 3 3/4. At 4 1/2 Natasha, Tatiana P, Dvorzhitsky and I drove in the Rolls-Royce to Remiz, - behind us drove Shleifer and Alyosha. In Remiz, on the right clearing we had tea, then took a ride in automobiles, - from Gorvits drove by the Swiss graves via sand forest path to the railroad overpass, then straight through the village, through forest, where the roundups happened in 1915, and drove out on to the Dvinsk Highway, returned home across Priorat at 7 1/2. After dinner Dvorzhitsky and I worked in the garden for a bit, then he played *kosti* with A. N. The weather was wonderful, although overcast until 4 1/2, 16°. The Shleifers had dinner with us.

17 July. Monday. Gatchina. Alyosha and Dvorzhitsky left for Petrograd at 9 1/2. Alexander Nikolaevich and I at 11 o'cl drove the Rolls-Royce across the Zoo, Kipen, then via the Narva Highway through Yamburg, Narva, Gungerburg along Narova. There we sat on the beach where it was very foggy. Then drove back through Merekul. Drive was wonderful, only towards the very end near Staroskvoritsy lost 1/2 hour due to gas tank, did not change tires, on average traveled 40 versts an hour, 300 versts in total. Snacked at 1 o'cl, having stopped in the forest for 25 minutes, and on the way back stopped in the same spot for 15 min[utes] and had tea. Starting from Kaskov and all the way to Gatchina everything was covered in smoke from the peat and forest fires, - the smoke was so thick that it burnt one's

eyes, and it was hard to breathe, very unpleasant. The weather was wonderful, around 20 deg., the road in some places was simply good. Returned home at 9 o'cl 20 min and the two of us had dinner. Natasha had Tatiana P and Elena K. Gavriluk over. In the afternoon Natasha went to Remiz with everyone.

18 July. Tuesday. Gatchina. In the morning Tata and I rode horseback at the Zoo - I, as usual on Vityaz, while Tata on Dalai. At 3 3/4 N. E. Kolosova came over to see us, her sister Serekrants with stepdaughter, Andrei and Misha Kolosovs came to see the children. Soon we drove in two motors to Tuganitsky ravine, where we had tea. I drove the Rolls-Royce and was bringing the three ladies listed earlier, and in the Packard followed: Natasha, Tatiana P, Merchanskaya, Alexander N and J[ohnson]. On the way back, we drove across Pedlino, Salezi and Yegerskaya and made a circle along the river in the Zoo. Returned home at 7 1/4, and then the guests left. After dinner we went to the town cinema for *At the Peak of Fame*. The weather was wonderful, 21°.

19 July. Wednesday. Gatchina. From 10 10 1/2 to 12 1/2 Tata and I rode horseback, got on at the Farm, rode through Big Rezino to Salezky forest, then along the edge of the forest to Korpikovo to Remiz and got off by the tea house. After breakfast Maria Vasilievna came over (this time as Mme Guzhon), their wedding took place recently in Moscow. Read in the afternoon. V. N. Lazareva and Dietz came to tea. Then I played with Domenici. After dinner Natasha, M. V., T. P., J[ohnson] and I made a circle in the Packard across Rezino, Salezi and Marienburg. The weather was wonderful, sunny until 2 o'cl, after 9 o'cl it started raining. Kornilov was appointed Supreme [Army] Commander-in-Chief, replacing Brusilov.[139]

20 July. Thursday. Gatchina. In the morning I rode horseback with Tata at the Zoo. In the afternoon Maria V and I cut branches near the Shleifers, and before that there was the usual dog fight. The Shleifers' bulldog bit Reit's tail. After tea the staff captain Plyshevsky came to see me, he serves at Stavka, and told us a lot of interesting things. After dinner we went to

---

[139] **"Kornilov"** General Lavr Georgevich Kornilov (b. 1870 – d. 1918) would serve as Supreme Commander of the Russian Armies from 19 July to 27 August 1917.

the cinema for *At the Last Line*. The weather was wonderful, but rained occasionally, 18°.

21 July. Friday. Gatchina. At 10 1/2 Natasha, Tatiana P, Maria V, J[ohnson] and I drove to Petrograd in an automobile. Before breakfast I saw Staff Captain Plyshevsky at Alyosha's, and at 2 o'cl came over: Shatsky (who is now appointed controller of my estate) and Birukov. Shatsky returned from the estates the other day, and he was forced to calm some tempers, of the servants, as well as the workers and peasants. We discussed various subjects regarding the estates until 5 1/2, then had tea. After which Alyosha and I walked along Nevsky to Morskaya, J[ohnson] also joined us. At 6 3/4 J[ohnson] and I got into an automobile, where Natasha, M. V. and T. P. already were, and drove to Gatchina. (In the morning, our tire burst). After dinner Shleifer and I took a walk in the grove beyond the overpass, the evening was ideal, as was the entire day, which was sunny and very hot, 21°. Natasha, Tatiana P, Maria V and J[ohnson] played *zhelëzka* on the terrace until 3 o'cl. Gen[eral] Erdeli was killed at the front, by a bullet in the back, when he was gathering the cowards who ran from the battle. All the ministers resigned.

22 July. Saturday. Gatchina. From 10 1/2 to 12 1/2 Tata and I took a long ride horseback, - got on at the Vaivolovsky Gate and rode past Pudost Station, crossed the Kipensky highway, and via the fields entered the forest, and rode to Kezelevsky Forest, from there to the left through clearings to Salezky Forest, where we got into an automobile and drove home through the villages of Salezi and Yegerskaya. In the afternoon I read. After tea, which we had on the terrace, Natasha, Maria V, Tatiana P and J[ohnson] took a drive in the Rolls-Royce, while I played the guitar with Domenici until 8 o'cl. Yuly Petrovich Guzhon came to dinner. Had dinner on the terrace, after which Yu. P. and I took a walk in the palace park, where we got into an automobile and returned home. Alyosha arrived at 10 o'cl and traveled an hour and a half, due to large number of passengers he could not get on the first train and lost a lot of time waiting. In the evening Natasha played *zhelëzka* with the guests. The weather was wonderful, 23°.

1. In Grand Duke Michael's hand: "The church in Vienna, where we were married." Circa 1912. Private collection

2. Travelling in Europe. Seated, Irina Nikolaevna Shilova, a friend of Natasha's. Circa 1914. From the private collection of Shilova's great-grandson, Boris Stechkin.

3. Norway: Michael on horseback. Irina Nikolaevna Shilova, third from left. Circa 1914. From the private collection of Shilova's great-grandson, Boris Stechkin.

4. V. N. Shilova at left, Irina Nikolaevna Shilova at Michael's right. Circa 1914. From the private collection of Shilova's great-grandson, Boris Stechkin.

5. Knebworth House. Circa 1914. From the private collection of Boris Stechkin.

6. Michael with singer Feodor Chaliapin and the Shleifers. Circa 1914. From a private collection.

7. Michael with his son George ("Baby") and Mrs Shleifer. Norway. Circa 1914. From a private collection.

8. Michael with his brother, Tsar Nicholas II, nieces and nephew, on the balcony of the Alexander Palace in Tsarskoe Selo. L-R: Grand Duchesses Maria, Olga, Tatiana, and Anastasia, Michael, Nicholas and Tsesarevich Alexei. Circa 1915-16. GARF, f. 640, op. 3, d. 25, l. 66ob. № 979

9. Michael on horseback, prior to 1917. From a private collection.

10. Michael and friends, at Gatchina in winter, prior to 1917. From a private collection.

11. Grand Duke Michael with his brother, Tsar Nicholas II, prior to 1917. From a private collection.

12. Michael and Natasha's house in Gatchina on Baggovutskaya Street. This house no longer exists. Circa 1916. From a private collection.

13. Natalia and Nicholas Johnson. Circa 1914. From a private collection.

14. Michael horsing around for the camera, prior to 1917. From a private collection.

15. Michael with the Russian ballerina Tamara Karsavina (in the foreground). Michael is in his swim suit, holding on to the boat. Circa 1914. From the private collection of Boris Stechkin.

16. Michael posing in front of the Kodak building on Nevsky Prospect in St. Petersburg, prior to 1917. From a private collection.

17. Michael playing the guitar, most likely circa 1916-17. From a private collection.

18. Michael visiting the 2nd Siberian Regiment, circa 1916. From a private collection.

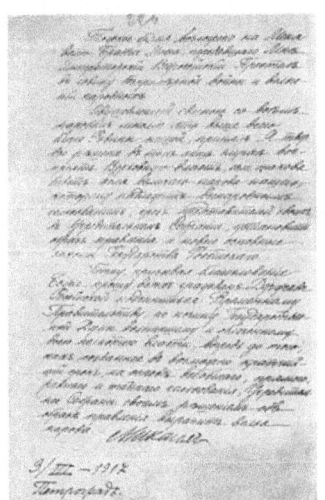

19. Michael's written refusal to accept the Russian throne, signed "Mikhail," issued in Petrograd on 3 March 1917.

20. Likely the last known photo of Michael, taken in Perm in April 1918. With him is Piotr Ludvigovich Znamerovsky, who has often been misidentified here as Nicholas Johnson. At least two copies of this photo exist: one at the State Archives of Russian Federation (GARF, f. P9440, op. 1, d. 1, l. 1991), which presumably belonged to Znamerovsky, as his landlady found it in his apartment after his arrest. The other copy is in the private collection of the Pauline Gray Estate.

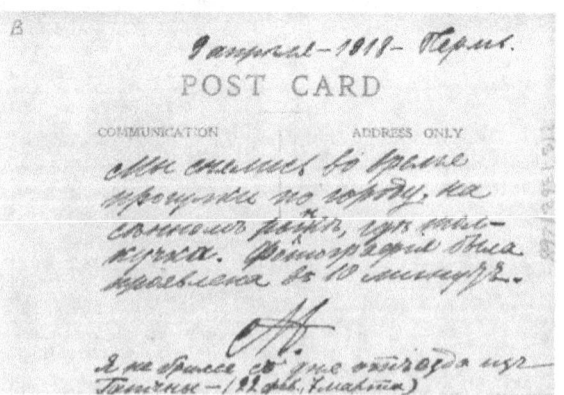

21. On the back of the photo from the Gray collection, Michael wrote: "9 April 1918 – Perm. We were photographed during our walk in town, at the hay market, where the flea market is. The photograph was developed in 10 minutes. M. I had not shaved since the day of departure from Gatchina – (22 February/7 March)." Courtesy of Pauline Gray Estate.

23 July.[140] Monday. Gatchina. In the morning Tata and I drove to the Farm, where we got on horseback (Military field, Pheasant building, Tea house, Remiz and the Farm). At 12 o'cl the Bologov Putyatins came over. They are living in Petrograd for now. After breakfast Baby received gifts in the schoolroom. At 3 o'cl we drove in three covered automobiles to Chirikin, i.e. to the Tsarskoeslavyansky Forest, there we picked wild raspberries, and then had tea in the house, as it was cold and damp. Maria V read the newspaper aloud. At the picnic were: the Shleifers, the Putyatins, the governesses (3), Mlle Barley and Sophie Lyarskaya. We returned home at 6 1/2. Putyatins left at 11 o'cl. The weather was cold and rainy, 11°. They played *zhelëzka* until (I fear to admit) 4 1/2, while I went to bed at my usual time.

25 July. Tuesday. Gatchina. Read in the morning. At 1 1/2 Natasha, Tatiana P, J[ohnson], and I drove to Petrograd in the Packard. On Pulkovsky highway a boy threw a bottle at our automobile. J[ohnson] and I ran after him and chased him across the field for more than a verst. Unfortunately, there was no chance at all of catching him. Fixed a tire before reaching the city. J[ohnson] and I went directly to Lavrinovsky's apartment (Galernaya, 38), where Alyosha was. We looked at all the rooms. Nikolai Pavlovich was cleaning the apartment, and Alyosha is thinking of moving in. Soon Natasha arrived, and we went to have tea at Alyosha's. Then all together we went to the English shop and two others. Returned to Alyosha's at 6 o'cl. Shatsky gave a report about his trip to Brasovo. Around 8 o'cl, went to have dinner at Kontana, the Guzhons invited us, beside us in our group were: Prince Eristov and Naryshkin. After dinner Gulesko played in our room, with his Orchestra, they played wonderfully. At 12 o'cl the whole group went to Alyosha's, where we all dispersed to our respective homes after tea, except the Shleifers, who are spending the night at Alyosha's. The evening was very lovely. At 2 1/2 we got home. The weather was hot, warm evening, around 20°. At Alyosha's we saw Sergei A[leksandrovich] before dinner.

---

[140] "**23 July**" 6 August 1917 (n. s.) -- The sixth birthday of Michael's son, Count George Mikhailovich Brasov.

26 July. Wednesday. Gatchina. Read in the morning, after breakfast as well. At 4 o'cl Tata and I got on horseback in the Priorat near the overpass and rode on the path toward Pizhma, but before reaching the village, we turned left and rode past Pustoshka through the field towards the edge of Tsarskoeslavyansky Forest, then straight across the clearing, and after two versts rode through the clearing to the left and came out on to the road, which leads from Chirikinskaya guard station to Gatchina. A motor was waiting by the little bridge at the first current. Miss Neame was waiting for us. From there we returned home by motorcar. At 6 o'cl we were home, and before dinner I played the guitar with Domenici. In the evening the Shleifers dropped by, and we laughed about that small incident, which happened yesterday with Tatiana P. The weather was wonderful, 23°. In the afternoon Natasha took a ride in a carriage to the tea house with J[ohnson] and Baby. Naryshkin left for his regiment at the front today. The Goujons[141] left for Moscow.

27 July. In the morning Tata and I rode horseback at the Zoo. After breakfast we went to Tatiana Pav.'s. Before tea I read, and are 4 1/4 Natasha, Tatiana P, J[ohnson] and I drove in the Rolls-Royce through Pizhma, Suida, Siverskaya, Vyra, Sivoritsy, and after a few versts turned left on the military road and then rode out to the Bornitsky forest, came out to the village Bornitsy, from there rode to Ilkino, then the tea house and Remiz. Returned home at 7 o'cl 50 min. It was a wonderful ride, and the air was flagrant and marvelous. In the evening J[ohnson] and I took a walk in the field past the railroad and in the grove. The weather was marvelous, in the afternoon some clouds sprinkled the dry earth, but the sun shone constantly, 22°.

28 July. Friday. Gatchina. In the morning Tata and I took a ride horseback. Got on at Vaivolovsky gate and rode through Orlovskaya grove via Krasnoselskaya highway, and after the 7th verst turned left at the clearing, the whole time rode towards the village of Malaya Istinka, on old Krasnoselskaya road through Repuzi, then across the fields past Rezino to the Zoo, where we got into an automobile. Princess Vera Orbeliani came to breakfast, she recently arrived from Ai-Todor. In the afternoon took a

---

[141] **"The Goujons"** Madame Goujon was the former Natalia Shelyaputina.

walk in the garden, and also sat on the terrace. At 7 B. N. Nikitin arrived and told a lot of interesting things. At 9 1/2 Natasha, J[ohnson] and I drove the guests to the train in Tsarskoe in the Rolls-Royce and returned home before 10 3/4. The weather was wonderful, 22°.

29 July. Saturday. Gatchina. In the morning Tata and I rode horseback at the Zoo. Boris and Marie came to breakfast. Boris left at 4 o'cl. Had tea on the balcony, that is the terrace, where we sat until Marie's departure, - at 6 1/2 we drove Marie to Tsarskoe [Selo] in the Rolls-Royce. J[ohnson] and Prince Eristov (who came over around 6 o'cl) also drove with us. We drove back to Gatchina through Krasnoe Selo and were home at 8 o'cl. After dinner the Shleifers came over and Kulikovsky (artillerist), who arrived from outside of Tarnopol, told many interesting things. The weather was hot, sunny, it drizzled occasionally, around 20°. Alyosha came over during breakfast.

30 July. Sunday. Gatchina. From 10 o'cl to 12 1/4 Prince Eristov and I rode on horseback. Got on by the Farm, rode through the Big Rezino to Salezsky Forest, straight down a road to Tuganitsky ravine made a left and rode past village Ryakhkilevo, the black lake, tea house to Remiz, where Natasha was waiting for us, and with her we returned home in an automobile. In the afternoon we sat on the terrace. At 2 1/2 Dvorzhitsky arrived. Around 5 1/2 Natasha, Tatiana P, Eristov, Dvorzhitsky and I drove in the Rolls-Royce to the village of Volasniki, behind us Alyosha, Shleifer, and J[ohnson] rode in the Packard. We chose a place right near the river at a spot where it comes close to the road and within one verst, approximately, from Volasniki. (Initially we couldn't decide for a long time where to stop and lost a lot of time on this). Started a campfire and got busy cooking. Dinner was ready at around 8 o'cl and was very tasty. A little man from Chukhontsy approached, about 45 years old, we talked with him and fed him. The picnic was very merry and successful. Returned home at 10 1/4. Having had tea, Natasha and I drove Dvorzhitsky and Eristov in the Rolls-Royce to Tsarskoe [Selo] Station and returned home at 12 o'cl. The weather is wonderful, sunny, around 21°. In the afternoon it rained from some clouds, but we did not get wet.

31 July. Monday. Gatchina. In the morning took a ride with Tata on horseback at the Zoo (I rode Dalai, she Kotik). After breakfast I slept in the study, was feeling a bit unwell. At 4 o'cl Princess Orbeliani came over. At 6 1/4 Natasha, she, J[ohnson] and I drove to Petrograd in an automobile. Drove J[ohnson] directly to the Winter Palace, where he saw Kerensky, - drove the princess to Moika, and ourselves to Alyosha's, where we had dinner. At 10 o'cl went to Boris's in Tsarskoe [Selo]. At 12 o'cl the palace commandant Kobylinsky came for me, and we drove to the Alexander Palace. Got out by the kitchens and entered the palace through the cellar [by tunnel] to the fourth entrance and to Nicky's reception room, where there were: Count Benckendorf,[142] Kerensky, Valya Dolgorukov and two young officers. From there I walked to the study, where I saw Nicky in the presence of Kerensky and the ensign guard chief. I found that Nicky looked rather well. Stayed with him around 10 minutes and went back to Boris's, and then to Gatchina. Kerensky arranged this meeting for me and it was called for due to the fact that today, completely by accident, I found out this afternoon about Nicky's and family's departure to Tobolsk, which will take place tonight. The way to Gatchina was very foggy with smoke, peat is burning everywhere. - The weather was sunny and hot.

---

[142] **"Count Benckendorf"** Count Pavel Konstantinovich Benckendorf (b. 1853 – d. 1921) had served three emperors as Marshal of the Court and recorded the meeting of the two brothers. "He [Kerensky] told me that the Grand Duke Michael Alexandrovich would be arriving. The Minister had arranged this meeting so that the brothers might say good-bye. I mentioned this to the Emperor, who was touched and surprised. When the Grand Duke arrived, Kerensky and his aid preceded him into His Majesty's office. He sat down at the desk and leafed through some albums. The aid guarded the door. The meeting lasted about 10 minutes. The brothers were wary of speaking in front of others and they found few words. The Grand Duke told me later in tears that he had not even properly looked the Emperor in the face. Kerensky then [left and] sat down in the waiting room. We spoke on different topics. Since he assured me several times that the absence of Their Majesties would not last more than a few months, I asked him when I could expect the Imperial Family to return. He again assured me that after the [meeting of the] Constituent Assembly in November, nothing would prevent the Tsar from either returning to Tsarskoye Selo or going wherever her wanted to go. (Khrustalëv, p. 648, citing *Sevodnya,* Riga, 1928; 18 February.)"

August 1917

1 August. Tuesday. Gatchina. Got up at 10 o'cl, and at 11 1/2 N, T. P., J[ohnson] and I went to Petrograd. Had breakfast at Alyosha's, and Princess Orbeliani was there. In the afternoon N[atasha] went to run errands before tea, and Alyosha and I walked along Nevsky, went into shops, ran into Irina [Yusupova].[143] Went into the Church of the Resurrection. At 4 3/4 returned to Alyosha's, where Enden and Rybarsky were, and had tea. They both told us a lot of interesting things, - the former still commands Zarnitsa, the latter was commissar of Sevastopol the entire time. At 8 1/2 we returned to Gatchina. In the evening Natasha, T. P., Miss Neame and Mlle Valvin went to the cinema, and I wrote in the diary. The weather was wonderful, 21°. In some evening newspapers they already reported Nicky's departure, but instead of Tobolsk, it said Kostroma.

2 August. Wednesday. Gatchina. At 10 o'cl Tata and I got on horses by the Tea house and rode past the black lake, past Gorvitsy to a forest and past the village Bornitsy and the arrow line initially, and then via another road rode out onto Dvinsk Highway on the eighth verst from Gatchina, - a motorcar was waiting for us on the highway across from Kirka. Returned home at 1 o'cl. In the afternoon played the guitar with Domenici. At 6 o'cl Natasha and I drove to the center of Remiz, got out there and took a walk in the right clearing, then to the left along a fence and completed the circle, - in one spot we sat on the grass. On the way back ran into Ditz. After dinner we went to the cinema for *Goodbye Dreams, Farewell Wishes*. After having returned home, Colonel Reier came over to see us.[144] The weather was wonderful, 21°. My poor Volchok's light went out, - he had been at the hospital for around 12 days and had been ill since early March. So sorry for him, such a wonderful dog he was.

---

[143] **"Irina"** Michael's niece, HH Princess Irina Aleksandrovna of Russia (b. 1895 - d. 1970), after her 1914 marriage also Princess Yusupov, Countess Sumarokov-Elston.
[144] Colonel Reier (cf. note. 125) had just completed an inventory of works constituting the personal property of the Dowager Empress remaining at Gatchina on the 28 July. The "Gatchina list" included seven of the famous Imperial Eggs by Fabergé. (cf. Fabergé, Skurlov, et al., *The Imperial Empire Egg of 1902*, Harrison Piper & Co. New York: 2017, p. 16-17.)

3 August. Thursday. Gatchina. In the morning Tata and I rode horseback at the Zoo. Read before breakfast. From 2 to 3 1/2 Krevezal was here to see me, - he arrived from Riga for a few days, from the headquarters of the 12th army. At 5 1/2 Natasha and I drove the Rolls-Royce to the Zoo, where we walked along the river to the end and returned to the motor along Tsagov, and on the way back drove through the palace park. In the evening Shleifer, J[ohnson] and I took a walk along the railroad tracks. The weather was wonderful, around 19°. Poor Volchok's light went out not yesterday but three days before, and the cause of death was starvation. They did an autopsy, and it turned out that he had ulcers in his bowels.

4 August. Friday. Gatchina. In the morning Tata and I rode on horseback, got on at the Farm, finished the ride by the tea house. At 12 o'cl Prince Putyatin arrived (he now filed his resignation). After his departure, i.e. at 2 1/2, N[atasha] and I went to the Shleifers and cleared the dead branches off the bushes near the house. Had tea at their place for Tanya's birthday. Then we took a ride with the Shleifers in the Rolls-Royce (through Priorat to Dvinsk Highway, then to the right past Tyaglino towards Gorvitsy and home past the tea house). Before dinner I dug a grave for Volchok in the garden, near the spot where Jack and Bulka are [buried]. In the evening we went to the cinema for *No Forgiveness*. The weather was wonderful, around 21°.

5 August. Saturday. Gatchina. Read in the morning. During breakfast J[ohnson] and Alyosha arrived. (Forgot to mention that in the morning I buried Volchok with Vasily, he was placed into a zinc box.) In the afternoon played the guitar with Domenici. At 4 o'cl Tata and I got on horses at the Priorat by the Warsaw Station and rode through Pizhma, then on the road towards Volasniki, by the river turned left and rode initially through forest, then by the edge of the woods to the bisons, where we got into an automobile and drove home. Read before dinner. In the evening Natasha, T. P. and J[ohsnon] took a ride in the Rolls-Royce (I drove as usual), we drove through Yegerskaya, Salezi, Pedlino, Ryakhkilevo, Black lake, Paritzy and Priorat. The weather was wonderful, 20°.

6 August. Sunday. Gatchina. Read in the morning, - Alyosha went to the cathedral. In the afternoon Baron Rausch and Natalia Evgenevna dropped

in to see us. After tea Natasha, Alyosha, J[ohnson] and I drove to the Zoo and took a walk along the entire river and along Tsagov reached the Farm, from there returned home in the automobile. Read before dinner. In the evening we went to the cinema for *The Stolen Documents*. The weather was wonderful, 20°. At 12 midnight we suddenly heard four shots in our garden near the house, - turned out that the guard saw two men dressed like soldiers, who crept near the children's house; when he called to them and told them to stop, they ran from him, - he shot three times, and they, running away and climbing over the fence, shot from a revolver.

7 August. Monday. Gatchina. At 10 o'cl Natasha, Tatiana P, Alexander N, Alyosha, J[ohnson] and I drove the Packard to Petrograd. (For approximately 8 versts peat was burning on both sides of the road, - this fire has been burning for a while now, it spread to a very large territory and is giving off a mass of smoke.) In Petrograd I went to the office, and from there walked to the Admiralty Shipbuilding Factory with Rybarsky. There we were met by the shipping engineer, Lieutenant Colonel Eremeev, - at first, we went to the shed to see my old electric boat (today they will transfer it to the River yacht-club), and then walked through the workshop, - a little later Alexander N came over. Then we returned to the office, and from there Alyosha and I took a cab to his apartment, where we had breakfast. Then the two of us went to the shops, and having returned to the apartment, studied until 5 o'cl. By this time N. A. Dobrovolsky arrived, the poor thing was freed from house arrest just the other day, his health is bad, and he is going to the Caucasus for treatment, - he was under arrest for 6 months. At 7 o'cl Natasha, T. P., J[ohnson] and I went to Gatchina. In the evening I wrote. The weather was wonderful, pouring rain passed in spots, 21°.

8 August. Tuesday. Gatchina. From 10 1/2 to 12 1/2 Tata and I rode horseback, - got on at the gates on the Dvinsk Highway and rode through Khimozi and overpass of the railroad directly into the forest and on the clearing, rode out to the Pizhmenskaya road and across the forest to the village Zamostye, where we got into an automobile, and got home at 1 o'cl (Reit ran after us and lagged behind.) By one large ditch Vityaz got capricious and we lost about 15 minutes. In the afternoon I wrote to Mama. At 4 o'cl they brought the horse Koko, which I bought from Maria

Vasilievna, - a lead gelding, 7 years old, 7 versions [4.4cm = vershok], it once belonged to Lilli Gugovna. After tea Natasha, T. P. and I took a ride in the Rolls-Royce. Dropped by Furazhkin's and visited with Boiko, who is almost completely recovered, the weather rode through Salezi, Pedlino, black lake, - walked to the river on foot, returned home at 7 1/2 across Remiz and the Zoo. In the evening we went to the cinema for the *Maharaja's Favorite*. The weather was wonderful, occasionally semi-cloudy, around 18°.

9 August. Wednesday. Gatchina. In the morning Tata and I rode horseback at the Zoo, - I tried Koko, who rode excellently. Before breakfast I wrote to Mama and Xenia. At 2 1/2 Natasha and I drove the Packard to Petrograd, to Alyosha's. At 4 o'cl Princess Orbeliani[145] came over and stayed until 5

---

[145] **"Princess Orbeliani"** (cf. n. 18) Vera Orbeliani met with the Dowager Empress two days later and told her about this meeting, which she mentions in her diary: "August 12.1917 - Saturday: ... At 4:30 in the afternoon Vera Orbeliani was here, and had just arrived from Petersburg ... She had run into Misha on the street and had only just managed to tell him that Nicky was being forced to leave Tsarskoe [Selo] the following night, which he had not suspected. After this, they gave them permission to meet - for the first time during this whole episode. But how did all this take place!? In the room, in addition to the guard officer, was Kerensky so the brothers were unable to speak, yes, and they did not give them more than a quarter of an hour - unheard of, disgraceful, cruel. Is it possible that people can be so heartless - it is beyond my understanding. When Nicky proposed to Misha that he meet with Alix and the children, Kerensky announced in a completely calm voice that this had not been planned and so he would not allow him to see them - that shameless character. According to Paul's [Benckendorff] words three weeks earlier, they made them understand that they would be sending them off to the Crimea, to Livadia, which made them very happy. But when the time had come to depart, they ordered them to take only warm clothing, and only then did they realize that the impending trip for them was not to the south at all. These unconscionable hangmen, moreover, had only told them about this JUST before the departure itself. They only told them that day that they would be traveling that same night! The pigs did not even set a time for departure, so as a result, they were forced to spend the whole night without changing from 12.30am until 4.30 am in the rotunda of the Alexander Palace with their unfortunate children, where, in addition to those wishing to say good-bye, were crowds of soldiers smoking in their presence and who completely carried themselves abominably, not even making the effort to remove their hats. And really, I never could have imagined such vile and disgraceful behavior like this. I hope that, at some time or other, retribution will strike all these bastards ... Vera stayed for tea, after which Xenia and I went off to visit Olga." [Olga Aleksandrovna's son, Tikhon Kulikovsky, was born

o'cl. - she is leaving today for Ai-Todor. Natasha and I drove back at 6 o'cl. I read in the evening. The weather was overcast, although occasionally the sun peeked out, fog with smog, 18°.

10 August. Thursday. Gatchina. From 10 o'cl to 11 1/2 Tata and I rode horseback, - got on at the Farm and rode through Remiz, past the tea house, rode across the Baltic railroad near Ilkino a drive rode through the fields past Matryona-Pine to the Dvinsk Highway, - got into an automobile which was waiting at the 4th verst. Read before breakfast. Natasha and I ordered marble tiles for the dogs' graves. Domenici was here in the afternoon, and we played until 4 1/2. After tea Natasha, the Shleifers, Nina A. Kun and I took a ride in the Rolls-Royce, went to the palace park, then Remiz, black lake, Korpikovo, Yegerskaya. Before dinner Vasiliev and I hammered in insulators from our house at the house on Baggovutskaya. In the evening we went to the cinema. J[ohnson] arrived from Petrograd with news. The weather was overcast, it rained occasionally, 16°.

11 August. Friday. Gatchina. In the morning I read, and also Klevzel was here and took his leave, he is going back to Riga. Read in the afternoon, and at 4 o'cl I got on a horse by the Warsaw Station in Priorat and took a lovely ride: Malaya Zagvozdka, through the fields and woods to Pustosha, then Tsarskoeslavyansky forest, where I took country roads and rode out to the road towards Chirinkinskaya guard station in two versts from the little house and rode on the road to Gatchina. Soon I met up with the Rolls-Royce in which rode: Natasha, T. P. and Yuly Petrovich. Gave the horse to the groom, and went with them. We almost reached the guard station, and on the way back we extinguished the [burning] peat right by the road. Before dinner I received staff captain Sedeler. In the evening we went to our chicken house and gathered the chickens which decided to spend the night outside. As of yesterday, our guard consists of 10 junkers [cadets]. We spent the evening on the terrace. Yuly P left at 11 o'cl. The weather was wonderful, 20°.

12 August. Saturday. Gatchina. From 10 o'cl to 12 1/2 Tata and I rode horseback. Got on at the Farm and rode through the Military field, then

---

that night.] (cf. *Dnevniki Imperatristy Marii Fedorovny*, Bagrius, Moscow: 2006, p. 19)

across the fields to Tyaglino, from there to Khimozky grove rode around the outer clearing, i.e. the shooter line. The automobile was waiting at the edge of the woods on the road to the village. N. D. Lyarskaya came to breakfast. In the afternoon we went to show the chickens and transferred them to the new building with great difficulty. N. D. left at 3 1/4, - I lay down on the sofa to rest before tea. At 5 1/2 Prince Eristov arrived, - Natasha and I took a drive with him in the Rolls-Royce. We drove first across the Zoo, then Sivoritsy, then via a country road through Suida to Pizhma and Gatchina, - after Sivoritsy and before the village Pogost we walked. Got home at 8 1/4. Alyosha arrived. In the evening we sat on the terrace. The weather was ideal, 20°. Today the State Conference in Moscow opened.[146]

13 August. Sunday. Gatchina. Read in the morning. In the afternoon I went to the palace park with Shleifer and Surov (photographer), we made photographic images from the Venus Pavillion to the pontoon bridge. Having returned home, we all had tea (Surov left Tata 5 1/4, had tea separately). At 6 1/ Ekaterina P and Mikhail P arrived, and soon we all drove in two automobiles to the tea house. At first, we took a walk to the river, and having returned home we cooked dinner. Around 8 o'cl and majority thunderstorm started. Sat down to dinner at 8 3/4, the candles were lit, it was very cozy. Tatiana P and I took a short walk before departure which was at 10 o'cl. We headed directly to the cinema for *Secret of a Northern Bank*. Returned home at 12 o'cl. The weather was overcast in the morning, then sunny occasionally, around 16°. The first day of the Moscow Government conference was yesterday, - today is a break.

---

[146] **"State Conference"** The State conference, held from 12-25/15-28 August 1917 was chaired by Kerensky and attended by 2,414 deputies. At the opening, Kerensky announced he would crush any resistance to the Provisional Government with "iron and blood." Speeches from Kornilov, Milyukov, Shulgin, Kaledin, and others promised to eliminate the Soviets, bring the war to a victorious end, and to restore capital punishment not only at the front, but at home to achieve discipline in factories where revolt was present. (see Khrustalëv, note 353, p. 651-652, citing the transcript of the State Meeting printed in 1930.)

14 August. Monday. Gatchina. Read in the morning. Alyosha and Prince Eristov left at 10, that is at 9 1/2. Putyatins spent the night at J[ohnson]'s and also left. In the afternoon we sat on the terrace and read. At 6 1/2 doctor Gordon arrived, who smeared my throat, - it hurts for a third day, but I feel well. Koton was also here. We chatted in the evening. The weather was sunny from 2 o'cl, around 15°, in the morning there was a brief rain.

15 August. Tuesday. Gatchina. Read in the morning. After breakfast played the guitar with Domenici. At 4 o'cl we, all the Shleifers with their children, Sophie L, and J[ohnson] drove in two motors across Remiz to the Tugnitsky ravine, where we had tea, then took a walk through the woods. Having returned home at 6 3/4, I laid out the telephone line with Vasiliev. After dinner Natasha with the others went to the cinema, while I read. J[ohnson] also stayed. The weather was wonderful, sunny, around 17°.

16 August. Wednesday. Gatchina. Read in the morning, also in the afternoon. At 3 3/4 I drove to the 5th verst of the Dvinsk Highway, got on Vityaz there and rode across Khimovskaya Grove, crossed the railroad and through birch woods rode out on to Pizhma and rode in the direction of Volasniky, past the river turned left, left Pustoshka behind on left and came out to Tsarskoslavyansky Forest, rode through clearing for 1 1/2 versts, then, on the left clearing, rode out to the motorcar, which was waiting on the road to Chirkinskaya guard station at the first turn. At 6 1/2 I arrived at home. Was able to finish before dinner laying the telephone line to the house on Baggovutskaya. Read in the evening. The weather was wonderful, around 18°. The government meeting ended in Moscow yesterday.

17 August. Thursday. Gatchina. Read in the morning. At 2 o'cl Dietz arrived. With the gardener from Brasovo. Natasha and I marked the spot in the new garden for a small greenhouse. At 4 1/2 went to the Farm, from there took a ride horseback at the Zoo. Before dinner I laid out the telephone [line] with Alexander N at their house. In the evening went to the cinema for *The Golden Vortex*. The weather was overcast, 16°, from 11 1/2 o'cl it was pouring rain.

18 August. Friday. Gatchina. At 10 3/4 Natasha, Shleifer and I went to Petrograd (J[ohnson] too). Before breakfast at Alyosha's, I had a fitting and a haircut. In the afternoon went to Fabergé with Natasha, and then with Alyosha went to Krikh and bought a Waterman pen. Having returned to Alyosha's, Dvorzhitsky was there, and we took care of the Abas-Tuman business. At 7 1/4 N[atasha], J[ohnson] and I drove back to Gatchina in the new Packard, while the old one is getting fixed up a bit. After dinner we went to the cinema for *The Heart is Torn Up from Mourning and Wounds* ([Eleanora] Duse). The weather was nice, 16°, sunny.

19 August. Saturday. Gatchina. From 12 to 12 o'cl Tata and I rode horseback at the Zoo. After an early tea Natasha, Tatiana P and I took a ride in the Rolls Royce. At first, we brought Boiko to Furazhkin, and then made a circle through Salezi, Pedlino, Black lake, Remiz and the Zoo, where we caught three boys from the Orphan Institute 10-12 years old, who started a fire under the trees. Having put them in the motor, we took them to the institute and gave them over to the teacher. Then we returned to the park and went to see the old birches burning at the Mortyashkin meadow, where we ran into six children, who told us that the arson is mainly done by the soldiers and showed us five more fir trees also felled by fires. Having circled the Zoo, we returned home at 6 1/4. Had dinner at 7 1/2 and went to the town theater, where they had a concert - singing, balalaika (Abaza), operetta in one act and dancing, - in general, it was rather charming. The weather was wonderful, 18°.

20 August. Sunday. Gatchina. In the morning Natasha went to church of the *Realnoe* School with the children, while I stayed home and read. To breakfast came over: Alyosha, Dvorzhitsky and a little later Ekaterina Pav. with the prince. In the afternoon we sat in the garden, - had tea on the terrace and Kotons came over, and at 5 o'cl Baron Rausch came over with his son. When the guests left, that is at 6 1/4, Natasha, E. P., J[ohnson], Dvorzhitsky and I drove in the Rolls Royce to the tea house, from there drove across Korpikovo to the black lake and again to the tea house. Behind us drove: Princess Put[yatina] and Alyosha. Started to cook dinner in the kitchen, which was ready at 8 1/4. Then took a walk to the river; from one side you could still see sunset, from the other - the moon was rising. We left the house at 10 o'cl. Everyone went directly to the town

theatre, while Alyosha and I returned home, as today I still had some pain in the stomach. They returned from the cinema at 11 3/4, and after tea the Putyatins, Alyosha and Dvorzhitsky left for Petrograd in the aerodrome automobile. The weather was wonderful, 18°.

21 August. Monday. Gatchina. At 11 1/2 Natasha, T.P. and J[ohnson] went to Petrograd. Before breakfast Alexander N and I drove the Rolls Royce to Mozino, turned right and drove towards Pavlovsk, - drove on this road for the first time, - then via Volkonskoe Highway drove to Mikhailovka, where we stopped by the sea across from the palace and had tea, which we brought in thermoses. All over the park state owned horses are grazing, the park is very dirty. At 4 3/4 headed to Gatchina, - drove through Strelna, Bezzabotnoe, Ropsha, Kipen and the Zoo and were home by 6 1/2. In 15 minutes our garden and house was surrounded by a large number of soldiers with two officers. Soon the assistant to the Commander-in-Chief of the Petrograd military district Captain Kozmin, accompanied by the Gatchina commander Captain Svistunov and Commissar of the City of Petrograd Lieutenant [blank] and announced to me that by order of the Minister of the Interior and the War Minister, I will be placed under house arrest. Natasha, T. P. and Johnson returned from Petrograd in 1/2 hour. Kozmin presented the same type of arrest paper to Natasha as well, which she had to sign, just as I did,[147] Then he left, but the guards remained with the commander, Lieutenant [blank], assigned to me. The darling Shleifers wished to stay with us, while Mlle Valven left to Petrograd at 11 o'cl in the evening. Had dinner around 8 3/4. The weather was wonderful, around 18°, sunny. Our mood is agitated but cheerful, as our conscience is clear.

---

[147] **"arrest paper"** From the Order of the Head of the War Ministry B. V. Savinkov, the Commander-in-Chief of the Petrograd Military District G .P. Polkovnikov, dated 21 August 1917: "Based on Article 1 of the Provisional Government's decree of 2 August granting exclusive powers to the Ministers of War and the Interior by their mutual agreement, I order you to detain Countess Brasova with this order as an individual whose activities are pre-threatening to the defense of the State, internal security, and freedom won by the Revolution, and she must be maintained under house arrest by guards under special instruction. This order is to detain Countess Brasova and to keep her under arrest until further notice. Manager of the War Ministry Savinkov" (GARF f. 601, op. 1, d. 2472, l. 12). On the original order there is a note of receipt: "Read - N.S. Brasova, August 21, 1917" (cf. Khrustalëv, note 354, pp. 652).

22 August. Tuesday. Gatchina. Read in the morning. In the afternoon Natasha and I went through old letters. After tea we took a walk in the garden with the Shleifers, J[ohnson] and Miss Neame. In the evening we read, played billiards. The weather was rainy until 12 o'cl, 13°, overcast all day. The watch that has been guarding us since yesterday consists of 60-70 men, assigned along the outer garden path and on the other side of the fence. We just finished reading about our arrest in the *Evening Times*. - Uncle Pavel was also arrested in Tsarskoe Selo. Yesterday at my arrest a paper containing the following was presented to me:

> To the Chief Military Commander of the Petrograd region. As per the 1st resolution of the Provisional Government from the 2nd of this August on granting exceptional powers to Ministers of the Military and internal affairs by mutual consent, I order you to detain the former [*sic*] Grand Duke Michael Aleksandrovich on receipt of this order as an individual whose activities are pre-threatening to the defense of the State, internal security, and freedoms won by the Revolution, and he must be maintained under house arrest by guards under special instruction. This order is to detain the former Grand Duke Michael Aleksandrovich, and to keep him under arrest until further notice.
>
> Manager of the War Ministry Savinkov
> 21.VIII, No. 580 Petrograd[148]

23 August. Wednesday. Gatchina. Read in the morning. In the afternoon we all swept the paths. *Novoe Vremya* reported our arrest today. Three days ago, the Germans took Riga. After dinner I wrote a letter to Kerensky. The weather was a bit sunny in the morning, and from 5 o'cl. it started to rain, 12°.

24 August. Thursday. Gatchina. Read in the morning. In the afternoon, Miss Neame and I rubbed petrol with Vaseline into Reit (personal patented technique), as he is very itchy. Around 5 o'cl. Captain Kozmin came to see me, holding my letter to Kerensk. He said that Kerensky asked him to tell me that "the Provisional Government does not doubt my loyalty and that the position of democracy and the Government is such that it became necessary to isolate me from the world." – To the question of leaving abroad, Kozmin responded – "at present time this is completely

---

[148] In the archives there is a receipt for this document reading "Read – G. D. Mikhail Aleksandrovich, 21 August 1917" (cf. GARF f. 601, op. 1, d. 2472, l. 8)

impossible." – Read before dinner. In the evening played the guitar. The weather was rainy, windy, 8°. The plants are still completely green, only some isolated yellow leaves. Our garden is full of flowers, mainly *nicotiana* and sweet peas, not a lot of roses right now.

25 August. Friday. Gatchina. Spent the entire day in the house. It was announced to us that a junior officer will follow us, so we decided not to go out for now. Before dinner I played the guitar. In the evening we read newspapers. The weather was overcast, 8°. These last few days the newspapers wrote a lot about the discovery of a counterrevolutionary conspiracy,[149] the center of which was Margarita Khitrovo, who was arrested. It turned out that our arrest and that of Uncle Pavel occurred due to the discovery of this conspiracy. But apparently there is no such conspiracy.

26 August. Saturday. (Name day of Natasha and Tata. Gatchina. At 12 o'cl. f[ather] Strakhov serviced a prayer service in our dining room, - a deacon and two acolytes were there, the commandant who was assigned to us was present,- Ensign Lavrentev. In the afternoon we sat in the garden by the house and read. In the evening I played billiards with Shleifer. The weather was overcast, 10°. Today [the following] were sent abroad: A. Vyrubova, Badmaev, Manasevich-Manuilov, Glinka-Yanchevsky and Staff Captain Elvengren.

27 August. Sunday. Gatchina. Read in the morning. In the afternoon Koton came to see me, as I had a very strong pain in the stomach, - the commandant was present at this visit. After tea, Shleifer and I took a walk in the garden for exactly an hour, and likely walked about 5 ½ versts. Was lying down before dinner, in a lot of pain, after dinner too. The weather

---

[149] **"Conspiracy"** There was a great deal of indignation surrounding the arrests of members of the Imperial Family, many of whom remained popular and had supporters who rushed to their defense. A certain document began to be circulated which purported to raise funds for Cossacks at the front under the hope of restoring the monarchy. One of these documents was found by a Novgorod official on or near the Khitrovo estate and maintained that the Khitrovo famiy were behind it. Young Margarita was arrested but soon released, as the Provisional Government found no evidence to the rumors. The members of the Imperial Family, however, remained under arrest. (cf. Khrustalëv, n. 364, p. 656.)

was semi-sunny, 12°. Went to be early, in Elizaveta N's room, since I sleep badly and bother Natasha.

28 August. Monday. Gatchina. In the afternoon Miss Neame washed Reit in the garden. For the most part I was lying down on the sofa in the study. Around 5 o'cl. Koton came over, - of course the commandant was present for this. From *The Evening Times* we learned for the first time about Gen[eral] Kornilov's speech.[150] At 11 o'cl. I went upstairs, fell asleep for about an hour. The weather was warm, until 4 o'cl there was a strong downpour, 14°.

29 August. Tuesday. Gatchina (and move to Petrograd). I was awakened at 3 o'cl. The commandant announced that we would depart for Petrograd in an hour and 10 min. At the appointed time we were all ready. Actually we departed only at 5 o'cl. 10 min. because the military drivers could not start our motorcars, and only after Vedikhov was summoned and this was done (we foresaw this and warned the commandant), they drove us towards Tsarskoe [Selo]. A truck with 30 armed soldiers drove in front. We rode in the new Packard. Near the driver sat a soldier – a member of the Soviet. We drove endlessly to Tsarskoe [Selo] (more than 2 hours). There was a stop near the Soviet R. and S. D. Instead of a truck we drove in a sedan motorcar, and they drove us past Pulkovo to Petrograd. Near the Moscow outpost, due to engine malfunctions we were delayed for another ½ hour under awful downpour and hail. On Voskresenskaya we ran into the Preobrazhensky Reserve Regiment, which apparently was moving to guard Petrograd. Finally, at 9 o'cl. we reached the Regional Headquarters, waited in the automobile for a long time, then they took us into the office of the commander, where we were met by the Staff Captain Filonenko. He

---

[150] **"Gen[eral] Kornilov's speech"** General Lavr Kornilov, Commander-in-Chief of the Russian Army from 10 to 13 September 1917 (27 to 30 August old style), attempted a coup d'état against the Russian Provisional Government headed by Aleksander Kerensky and the Petrograd Soviet of Soldiers' and Workers' Deputies. There is enormous confusion around this putsch, but a commonly agreed understanding was that Kornilov had been organizing a force of soldiers in order to move into Petrograd and eliminate the Soviet. He had the backing of the British attaché and various important Russian businessmen, but the coup was a failure, and if anything, served to galvanize support for the Bolsheviks, whom Kerensky armed in response.

asked us to wait until they assign rooms to us. At 11 ½ they announced to us that we were assigned rooms on Morskaya 60, where our caravan headed. It turned out that this was the home of the Minister of the Interior, and its N° is not 60 but 61 (across from Prince Orlov's house). The rooms turned out completely unsuitable to live in, with only three beds and no facilities at all. At 1 o'cl. we had a bite, after which we lay down to rest, while J[ohnson] left to Regional Headquarters to try to get us a transfer to Alyosha's on Fontanka. Round 4 o'cl. he returned with a positive response. They expected to transfer us between 5 and 6 o'cl., but we actually got moved only at 9 o'cl. We saw Alyosha, but he was forced to move, in order not to end up under arrest too. The children soon went to bed, and I around 11 o'cl. Towards the evening my stomach pains got worse. They assigned 65 guards to us, and we continued under the strictest arrest. From *The Evening Times* we learned that Kornilov's speech and movement toward Petrograd is apparently doomed to failure. Everyone had dinner. The weather was sunny from 9 o'cl., 12°, strong wind. Memorable and difficult day.

30 August. Wednesday. Petrograd, Fontanka, 54. Got up very late. Spent the entire day in bed. Alyosha came by before breakfast, - spoke in the presence of the commandant, of course. We all felt extremely tired, with wound up nerves. Events of the day: Gen[eral] Kornilov's offensive against Petrograd halted completely. Gen[erals] Denikin and Markov were arrested by Provisional Government. Kornilov has been dismissed from his post, and it was announced that he will undergo a military-revolutionary trial by jury. The weather was sunny, 12°.

31 August. Thursday. Petrograd. Alyosha stopped by in the morning. I spent part of the day in the armchair, part in bed. The officer on duty is located near the front room, while a pair of guards are standing by the front entrance. Thus they are guarding such dangerous criminals! Events of the day: Kornilov's speech is being eliminated. Kornilov himself is ready to start talks with Provisional Government about his capitulation. Kerensky took over chief command [of the Russian Army], while Gen[eral] Alekseyev is his chief of staff. We cannot get any information about ourselves. We sit here in depression. The weather is rainy, 10 degrees, today, like yesterday Vedikhov is driving the R[olls] R[oyce] to Gatchina

and brings back necessary things and provisions, as wells as flowers. A five-member government was formed: Kerensky, Tereschenko, Nikitin, Verkhovsky and Verderevsky. My pains got worse.

September 1917

1 September. Friday. Petrograd. Spent the entire day in bed. Around 11 1/2 Herman Georgevich Westfalen[151] arrived from Finland and diagnosed a round ulcer in my stomach. Told me to drink only milk with a biscuit every two hours, lie down and apply a hot water-bottle.[152] The cause of illness is from nerves, in this case the effect of the arrest on me. The weather was damp, 8°.

2 September. Saturday. Petrograd. The situation is unchanged. Westfalen was here in the morning. From newspapers we know that Kornilov and his entire staff were arrested in Mogilev and an investigation on him was started. In the newspapers it was mentioned that Gen[eral] Kaledin (Hetman of the Don [Cossack] troops) is planning something on the Don. Provisional Government ordered his arrest, and this was done. The weather is damp and rainy, 9. Towards the evening it got blustry. Today we woke up to hear that Russia has been declared a democratic republic. What difference does it make what type of government, as long as there is order and fairness in the country.

3 September. Sunday. Petrograd. No changes at all. Read Turgenev. The weather is sunny, 9°.

4 September. Monday. Petrograd. At 3 o'cl a consultation took place: Sirotin, Tseidler and Westfalen. They diagnosed a stomach ulcer, which appeared as a result of anxiety about major troubles. Treatment consists of

---

[151] **"Herman Georgievich Westfalen"** (b. 1859- d. ?) State Councilor, Director of the Alexander Men's Hospital, and noted generalist practicioner. Dr. Westfalen diagnosed and treated Michael's ulcers in Petrograd. Retired from Imperial service in 1915, Westfalen returned from Finland to help the Grand Duke.

[152] **"ulcer in my stomach"** For many years, people with peptic ulcers were told to consume plenty of milk and dairy, under the impression it would soothe the stomach and heal the ulcers. While dairy might assuage the pain for a minute, dairy stimulates the stomach to produce hydrochloric acid, which only serves to irritate the ulcers further.

dairy diet, lying down with poultice applications to the stomach, and most importantly emotional tranquility, but where to find that, living here? Mrs. Bennett visited. In the evening J[ohnson] played the piano. After 9 o'cl Grigorev (Kerensky's adjutant) stopped by and advised of our upcoming release. The weather is rainy, got blustery towards the evening, 9°.

5 September. Tuesday. Petrograd. Situation is the same. Around 1 o'cl Zinoviev stopped by, who brought news of Koka's health. At 2 1/2 Westfalen was here, and at 3 o'cl M. Jules cut Baby's long hair, and he now looks much better, he immediately transformed from a girl to a boy. In the afternoon I read Turgenev. The weather was clear in the morning, then rainy, 11.

6 September. Wednesday. Petrograd and Gatchina. Since last evening 9 o'cl I started a complete fast on the advice of Westfalen, since the pains did not stop. Westfalen was here in the afternoon. Between 5 and 6 Kozmin was here. It was decided to leave for Gatchina at around 9 o'cl. We were ready at the appointed time, but Kozmin only came to get us at 10 1/4. He was delayed by a talk, via direct connection with Stavka, where he asked for Kerensky's permission to transfer us to Gatchina. Our cortege consisted of 5 motors, of which two are ours. Natasha, the children and I rode in the Packard. Kozmin rode with us. In front were two automobiles with people and things, in the back rode: Miss Neame, Johnson and the commandant in a closed automobile, finally the last was the Rolls-Royce, with guards. Arrived in Gatchina at 12 1/4 in the morning. The Shleifers met us, who from this moment on were again under arrest with us. Soon everyone had tea in the dining room, - Kozmin and Lavrentev were there and there were interesting conversations. Meanwhile I went to bed immediately after arrival. It was pleasant to finally returned home. The weather was sunny until the evening, 11°, during the night it started raining.

7 September. Thursday. Gatchina. Got up very late. The pains finally stopped. From 12 to 6 o'cl was lying on the sofa in the garden. Alexander N read, and then transferred to the study. Koton visited. In the evening everyone sat with me in the study. The weather was wonderful, but strong

wind, northwesterly, 20° in the sun, 12° in the shade. The greenery is very nice, not much yellowed.

8 September. Friday. Gatchina. At 10 1/2 Dr. Westfalen arrived and allowed me to drink 2 glasses of milk halved with Vichy, for entire day, and until this time I ate nothing for 3 days, did not even drink a drop of milk. I stayed in the study until 1 1/2, and then until 7 o'cl on the terrace. A. N. read to me. In the evening everyone sat in the study. In the afternoon the weather was sunny, in the evening it started raining, 11°. The pains are almost completely gone. I'm envious of those who almost reached eating, while I still have to fast for a while. Gen[eral] Alexeyev resigned as chief of staff to the commander-in-chief [Kerensky], and the entire staff and Stavka will be dismantled. Tomorrow *The New Times* comes out.

9 September. Saturday. Gatchina. Was lying down on the sofa in the study all day. Drank only 4 glasses of milk with Vichy the entire day. The pains are gone. Thinking with envy of those who can eat everything. Koton was here in the afternoon. The weather is rainy, 8°. *The New Times* came out, it was closed since 28 August.

10 September. Sunday. Gatchina. Spent the day like yesterday. At 3 1/2 Captain Kozmin came to visit us. I asked him to let Kerensky know about releasing us from arrest.[153] The weather was rainy occasionally, 9°. During the last 4 day the leaves got really yellow. There is still a lot of flowers in our garden. Drank 4 glasses with 1/2 milk for the day.

11 September. Monday. Gatchina. For now, the pains are completely gone, for several days already. Spent the day on the sofa in the study, and in the evening from 9 to 11 1/2 in the sitting room. In the evening A. N. read to me. The weather was occasionally rainy, 8°. Gen[eral] Dukhonin was appointed the chief of staff to the commander-in-chief.

---

[153] The possibility of restoration was collapsing as even supporters of the monarchy pulled away. On this same day, Vladimir Purishkevich wrote: "I'm a monarchist, but alas, now I am but a monarchist ideologue, because I have no candidates. Who? Nicholas II? A sickly heir and the regency of Alexandra Feodorovna – a woman whose name I cannot hear without wincing? Michael Alexandrovich, the man who openly declared that he is waiting for the decision of the Constituent Assembly? Who? Tell me, for I do not know of anybody suitable."

12 September. Tuesday. Gatchina. Was lying down all day. Between 6 and 7 Dr. Westfalen came to visit with Koton. They found improvement in my health. He asked me to continue lying down and follow the diet until his return, i.e. until Thursday the 21st. A. N. read a lot to me, as usual. From 9 o'cl I moved to the sitting room and was lying down there. A. N. and J[ohnson] played billiards, and N [played] *kosti* with T. P. The weather was overcast, it rained occasionally, 9°.

13 September. Wednesday. Gatchina. Thanks to wonderful weather I was lying down on the terrace with open doors, and from 3 1/2 to 6 3/4 in the garden and enjoyed it as much as possible. Then washed my hair. At 8 1/2 Kozmin arrived with adjutant Domatsiants and on Kerensky's behalf announced our freedom from arrest.[154] They had dinner with us and stayed until 11 1/2. Very interesting conversations were conducted. The Shleifers were also there. From 8 o'cl I was lying down in the sitting room. The weather from 11 o'cl got sunny and warm, 15° in the shade. Why we were placed under arrest is unknown,[155] and, of course, there were no charges presented, and, of course, could not have been. Where is the guarantee that this won't happen again? Kozmin makes a very good impression - idealistic, modest and intelligent.

14 September. Thursday. Gatchina. Thanks to wonderful weather is was lying down in the garden in the morning. A. N. read to me. From 1 o'cl

---

[154] **"freedom from arrest"** The order, signed by Kerensky, read: "To release from arrest the former [*sic*] Grand Duke Michael Alexandrovich Romanov, Grand Duke Pavel Aleksandrovich, Countess Brasova, Princess Paley, and Prince Vladimir Paley." The receipt of Grand Duke Michael Alexandrovich is dated September 13, 1917: "I listened to the decree of the Provisional Government, announced to me through the assistant to the commander-in-chief of the Petrograd Military District, Captain Kozmin, on the lifting of my strict arrest imposed on August 21, 1917, on September 13 of the same year. Thoroughly heard. [signed] Grand Duke Michael Alexandrovich."
[155] **"why we were placed under arrest is unknown"** In a 20 September 1917 interview with *Izvestiia* the Interior Minister of the Provisional Government A. M. Nikitin replied: "The Provisional Government considered it necessary to remove them [The Romanovs] from Petrograd in order to weaken, or, fundamentally, to suppress the idea of easily restoring them to power. Further events showed that the Provisional Government was quite right. Imagine if during the Kornilov Affair [*kornilovskie dni*] the Romanov family had been at Tsarskoe Selo?" The same might be said of the imperial colony at Gatchina.

Father Strakhov came over and performed a prayer service in the dining room on the occasion of removal of our arrest. I was lying down in the study. Batushka and Deacon Krylov stayed for breakfast, besides them, all the Shleifers were there. Then I moved to the sofa in the garden. Batushka stayed for a long time and talked to me, and the deacon with two young and presentable acolytes (the latter breakfasted separately) also sat in the garden. The Shleifers moved to their place in Petrograd in our Packard after tea, and I stayed in the garden until 7 o'cl and read. (Forgot to mention that Koton came over after breakfast and stayed until 5 o'cl). Then I moved to the sitting room; Tata played the piano. I was present at Natasha's dinner. J[ohnson] was not there as he is unwell. Read in the evening. The weather is ideal, sunny, 18° in the shade, but very strong wind (western).

15 September. Friday. Gatchina. Was lying down on the terrace all day and reading. Koton was here after breakfast. Natasha took a ride in the Zoo in a carriage. At 4 1/2 Boris[156] arrived with Kube (the latter brought me a letter from Andrei[157] in Kislovodsk). Boris is leaving to the Caucasus next week. Around 6 o'cl Alyosha arrived with Leonid, and Boris and Kube left. I was present during dinner. At 10 1/2 captain Kozmin arrived completely unexpectedly, who kindly brought the paper with permission and full cooperation for going to the Crimea based on our wishes. He stayed until 12 1/4, - very interesting conversation. He drove Alyosha and Treskin in a motorcar. The weather was sunny, strong western wind, 13°. Baby has been in bed for 3 days, light cold.

16 September. Saturday. Gatchina. Stayed on the terrace all day and reading. For now, I subside only on milk. Kotons, Nadezhda Dm, Mme Ekse came to tea. J[ohnson] came at dinner from Petrograd. The weather is sunny, 11°. The other day found out that Mama had waking pneumonia,[158] and then middle ear infection. Now, thank God, she is

---

[156] **"Boris"** Grand Duke Boris Vladimirovich
[157] **"Andrei"** Grand Duke Andrei Vladimirovich, who was with his mother Grand Duchess Maria Pavlovna the Elder.
[158] **"pneumonia"** Grand Duchess Xenia Aleksandrovna wrote from Ai Todor to Queen Olga of the Hellenes: "Mama has already told you about the search. It was something dreadful and impossible to forget … she was quite shaken emotionally and

better. Because of Kornilov's demonstration, they are now under more strict arrest.

17 September. Sunday. Gatchina. Was lying down in the study all day. Prince P. P. Putyatin came to breakfast and stayed until 7 o'cl. In the afternoon Reier stopped by. At 5 1/2 Alyosha and Leonid N arrived. I was present at dinner, too, in an armchair. Spent the evening in the sitting room as usual. At 10 1/2 Alyosha left, Leonid N stayed the night. The weather was occasionally sunny, 7°.

18 September. Monday. Gatchina. Before breakfast I was lying down in the study, and Leonid N was reading to me. At 1 1/2 Natasha went to Petrograd with him. I read all day. Natasha returned for dinner and brought Kerim with her, whom I hadn't seen since 29 August of last year (we parted in village Gorozhanka in Galicia). Spent the evening in the sitting room. The weather is cold, 6°, got blustery in the afternoon, frosty during the night. Ate biscuits for the first time.

19 September. Tuesday. Gatchina. In the morning Kerim read to me. In the afternoon Natasha took him around the garden and showed the house on Baggovutskaya. Then they took a walk in the span, went to the Zoo, and were in Yegerskaya. Returned for tea. Before dinner Kerim sat with me. Spent the evening in the sitting room. The weather was gray, it rained occasionally, 6°.

20 September. Wednesday. Gatchina. At 11 1/2 Natasha, Kerim and J[ohnson] went to [Petrograd]. I was lying down on the terrace and reading, and at 1 3/4 Father Pospelov arrived, who had breakfast on the terrace, after which we moved to the garden and he read to me, while sitting on my sofa. At 4 o'cl, having had tea with the children, he left. I stayed in the garden until 7 o'cl, then washed my hair. At 9 o'cl Natasha returned, and Margarita V and Leonid N arrived with her. I was present at dinner. The weather is sunny but windy, 16°. For the first time I ate rice porridge and semolina cereal.

---

physically ... she coughed for a long time and felt truly terrible. Now, thank God, she's back." (see Khrustalëv, n. 373, p. 662, citing GARF f. 686, op. 1, d. 198, l. 7)

21 September. Thursday. Gatchina. At 10 1/2 Dr. Westfalen arrived and allowed me to eat jelly, coffee and bread with butter, but he wasn't too pleased, as the last three days and nights I was feeling some pain again. He left at 12 o'cl. After breakfast Margarita V left, - she is going to Koka in Finland. In the afternoon I was lying down on the terrace. Andrei Iv. came over, and a little later Nadezhda Dmitrievna. The guests stayed almost until 6 o'cl. Then I moved to the study. At dinner I ate oatmeal porridge for the first time. Until 2 o'cl was sunny, then it rained occasionally.

22 September. Friday. Gatchina. Read all day. After tea Natasha and J[ohnson] went to Remiz and took a walk there, - then drove to the Tea house and from there walked on foot to the Black lake. Returned home at 6 1/2. From 5 to 7 o'cl I was lying down on the terrace. Before dinner Koton stopped by. At dinner I ate oatmeal. In the evening J[ohnson] read the newspaper aloud, - about the Democratic meeting in Petrograd.[159] The weather was rainy, in the afternoon the sun peeked out, 11°.

23 September. Saturday. Gatchina. Was lying down on the terrace all day, as usual, with open doors into the garden. Before breakfast Natasha, Baby, Miss Neame drove over to the Zoo in Tsagov for mushrooms. After tea Natasha went to the Black lake with Miss Neame, - before reaching the lake they looked for mushrooms. At 7 1/4 Herman Georgevich Westfalen arrived; we sat down to eat at 7 3/4, and Westfalen was able to swallow 3/4 of his dinner in 15 minutes before his departure to the train station. At 9 1/2 Natasha, J[ohnson] and Miss Neame went to the cinema. The weather was rainy, 9°.

24 September. Sunday. Gatchina. From morning was lying down on the terrace. Natasha with the children and Miss Neame went to the cathedral, and after 1/2 hour they returned. At 2 1/2 N.P. Makarov (assistant of Golovin) came over to see us. He gave us an interesting and detailed

---

[159] **"democratic meeting"** Grand Duke Michael is referring to the All-Russian Democratic Conference convened in Petrograd on 14-22 September 1917. The task of this democratic caucus was to determine the principles of the future government before the convention of the Constituent Assembly, which was to be elected in November 1917.

account of Nicky and the family's journey to Tobolsk. After tea, that is at 5 o'cl, he left. He is a nice and kind man. At 5 1/2 Alyosha came over, and we took care of business, while Natasha, J[ohnson], Miss Neame and E. K. Gavriluk went to Remiz and took a walk from the barge to the tea house. After dinner E. K. left, while J[ohnson] headed to N. D. Lyarskaya's with Miss Neame. Alyosha read aloud and left at 11 o'cl. The weather was sunny, around 10 deg. Over these past few days, the trees got very yellow due to cold nights, mornings, some trees are still green, but no bare ones yet.

25 September. Monday. Gatchina. Read all day - I'm reading a history of the French Revolution. In the afternoon Natasha, J[ohnson], Baby and Miss Neame drove towards the black lake, - and prior to reaching it, walked around looking for mushrooms. In the afternoon I sat on the terrace and wrote in my diary, which was very much neglected during my illness, exactly a month that I haven't written. Had dinner with everyone. From 5 3/4 to 6 3/4 Natasha and J[ohnson] took a walk, - initially in town, then in Priorat. In the evening J[ohnson] read to me. The weather was sunny from 2 o'cl, 9 deg.

26 September. Tuesday. Gatchina. Before breakfast Natasha with J[ohnson] walked to meet Praskovia I[vanovna Ab'erino], but the train was late, and they returned home at 1 1/2. Soon P. I. arrived, and we sat down to breakfast. In the afternoon they went for mushrooms, at first, they looked at the Zoo, and then at Bornitsky forest. Returned at 5 1/2. In the afternoon I sat on the terrace and read. Before dinner P. I. read to me. The weather was sunny, 8°. During the night it froze, the flowers in the garden are starting to wither completely.

27 September. Wednesday. Gatchina. In the morning Praskovia Iv. read to me. Westfalen was here in the afternoon and allowed me to take a walk, ride in an automobile, but after meals instructed me to lie down for an hour. In the afternoon everyone rode in a motorcar for mushrooms near black lake. I took a walk around the garden 3/4 hour, it was pleasant to finally walk. Then read on the terrace. Everyone returned for tea. From 6 to 7 o'cl I played with Domenici. He came here for a few days. From 10

o'cl to 11 o'cl I played with him again. The weather was occasionally sunny in the afternoon, 8°.

28 September. Thursday. Gatchina. Natasha, J[ohnson] and Praskovia I. went to Petrograd at 10 3/4. I played with Domenici for an hour before breakfast. Had breakfast all together. After a rest, or rather lying down for an hour, I played the guitar one more time, and then took a walk with Miss Neame around the garden, went to the chickens. Had tea with Domenici, then I was lie down for a nap, and played quite lying, it was very pleasant. Before dinner I wrote in the old diary. At 8 11/2 Domenici and I sat down for dinner, and Natasha and J[ohnson] arrived only at 9 1/2. From 10 to 11 we again played the guitar and the mandolin. The weather was rainy, 8°.

29 September. Friday. Gatchina. After every meal I lie down for an hour, the rest of the time I was on my feet. Before breakfast played with Domenici for an hour. In the afternoon N. D. Lyarskaya was here, she left after tea, - and I took a walk in the garden, while Natasha headed to E. K. Gavriluk before dinner and played the guitar. After dinner J[ohnson] read, then Domenici and I played the guitar. The weather was rainy, but from 4 o'cl the rain stopped, in places blue sky was peeking through, in the morning 5°, in the afternoon 12°.

30 September. Saturday. Gatchina. Before breakfast I played the guitar with Domenici for an hour. After breakfast he left. All these days, Domenici dined with us. At 3 o'cl Natasha and I drove to the Birch Gates, from there walked to Love Island, where we found a broken and toppled marble statue. The weather walked along the bank, past the old greenhouses and to the Zoo, walked past the Aviary. I forgot to mention that during the summer all the birds were sold off. - The cows are starving, no one thought to prepare hay for them all summer. We got into an automobile by the Farm. At 5 1/2 Alexander N arrived. Before dinner we played a game of billiards. In the evening I was lying down, and A. N. read to me. Natasha was pickling mushrooms. The weather was semi-cloudy, pleasant, 10°.

October 1917

1 October. Sunday. Gatchina. Natasha and the children and Miss Neame went to the *Realnoe* School [church] for liturgy. Alexander N read to me. Alyosha and Ekaterina P came to breakfast, as they were late, I already had breakfast earlier on the terrace, where it was rather warm. At 3 o'cl we all drove in the Packard to the edge of the Tsarskoselsky Forest and from there took a walk back to the village, then drove to Remiz and walked to the tea house. Meet up five people with rifles and a dog. These anyone who wishes can hunt, having paid 17 rubles for a ticket. Almost all game has been exterminated. We returned home at 5 1/4 and had tea on the terrace. Then I lay down for an hour, and Praskovia I read to me. Before dinner I played billiards with A.N. in the evening P.I. played the piano, E.P. sang, A.N. with Johnson played the billiards. At 11 o'cl Alyosha and E.P. left. The weather was wonderful, sunny from 2 o'cl and warm, 22°. The other day I received a letter from Xenia.[160]

2 October. Monday. Gatchina. At 12 1/2 everyone had breakfast and went to Petrograd, and I had breakfast at 1 o'cl. At 2 1/2 Koton came to see me, and we drove in the "Rolls-Royce" to the Berezovye gates, from there walked, - Venera pavilion, Admiralty, private garden, old greenhouses, Cascade gate, Tsagov, the turned left and towards the Farm, there got into an automobile and returned home via street and Priorat. Koton left after tea, and lay down and fell asleep, then Baby came over and ate dessert with me. Before dinner I played the guitar. They came from the city at 9 o'cl 10 min, and we sat down to dinner. Tatiana P also came. The weather was sunny until 2 o'cl, from 2 1/2 to 3 1/4 it was raining, the day was very warm and evening too, 12°.

3 October. Tuesday. Gatchina. Read before breakfast. From 2 to 3 o'cl Tatiana Pav. read to me. Then I drove to Berezovye gates and from there

---

[160] **"letter from Xenia"** Xenia mentions she received a letter from Michael in a letter to Nicholas II who was then in Tobolsk on 15 October, 1917. "We had news from Misha through Shervashidze (*Finalement*!), he fortunately is free again, but health not so good, again the old pains have recurred. In my opinion this is strictly nerves. We were also arrested, for the length of three weeks (at the same time), now they let us out again. So barbaric!" (Maria Feodorovna, *Dnevniki,* p. 291)

walked in the palace park. On the long island someone overturned an antique marble vase. At 4 1/2 we met with Natasha at the Farm (she took T.P. to the Baltiysky train station), and we returned home. After tea Natasha went to Elena K., and then to J, who was unwell. A Chechen who was in my convoy back in Lomna came to see me. He found out that I'm in Gatchina, and immediately came to visit me. I rested until 7 o'cl, then played the guitar. Was lying down after dinner, and then played the guitar again. The weather was rainy until 2 o'cl, then semi-cloudy, 8°.

4 October. Wednesday. Gatchina. Read before breakfast. At 3 o'cl Natasha and I went to Remiz where we found two mushrooms, then took a walk up to the tea house and returned home. Father Strakhov came to tea, who then gave a lesson to Tata. From 5 1/2 to 7, I practiced with Domenici. In the evening we read. J[ohnson] has been unwell since yesterday and is lying in bed. The weather was sunny in the morning, then semi-clear, 7°, barometer 768.

5 October. Thursday. Gatchina. Read in the morning. At 2 3/4 Westfalen came to visit me, - he left after 40 minutes. In the afternoon Natasha and I went to the Zoo, where we looked for mushrooms along the Zubrova. There weren't many mushrooms. Then we took a walk along the Tsagov, got into an automobile there and returned home for tea. Before dinner I read and played the guitar. In the evening Natasha and I went to J[ohnson]'s. He is in bed with bad kidneys, today he feels better. At 11 1/2 we returned home. The weather was overcast in the afternoon, 6°. There are still a few flowers in the garden. There was a battle at sea from 3 to 4 [October]- the Germans occupied the entire i[sland of] Oesel.[161]

6 October. Friday. Gatchina. Read in the morning. At 3 o'cl Natasha and I went to get Elena K and then to Remiz for mushrooms. The ladies stayed to look for mushrooms, while I took a walk. Walked across the Pheasant building, through the military field to the Zoo and met them in Tsagov, from there they drove across to Zubrovaya, to which I walked. At 5 o'cl returned home, - Father Strakhov had tea with us, after which he and E. K. left. Read before dinner. In the evening Natasha and I went to visit

---

[161] **"Oesel"** now called Saaremaa, in Estonia, the island was occupied by the German Army in Operation Albion in October 1917.

J[ohnson], whose sister was visiting with her daughter and Miss Neame. The weather was overcast, 6°.

7 October. Saturday. Gatchina. At 11 o'cl Natasha went to Petrograd. I read before breakfast. At 2 1/4 I went to J[ohnson] in a charabanc [a kind of early bus] and navigated Fanza. He had his sister and niece over. Then I drove to the palace, got out there and took a walk to the edge of the park, via Zubrovaya and on Berezovaya to the Kurakin Gates. From there returned home in a charabanc. At 5 1/2 Domenici arrived, and we played until 7 o'cl. Natasha returned at 6 1/4 in and train. In the evening we read. The weather was foggy, 8°. We have evacuated from Dagö Island and have retreated from the Moon islands.[162]

8 October. Sunday. Gatchina. Read in the morning. At 1 1/4 Alyosha arrived in our automobile with K [blank space]. In the afternoon we drove in an automobile to the Tea house, and from there walked to Ryakhkilevo past the Black lake. At 6 1/2 we returned home and drove across Pedlino and Salezi. Before dinner we sat and talked. Had dinner at 8 3/4. The guests left at 11 1/2. The weather was wonderful, from 1 o'cl the sun appeared, 11°, barometer 770. Before breakfast the old Bennett stopped by, who is leaving for England soon. During the walk we picked a small bouquet of field flowers.

9 October. Monday. Gatchina. In the morning read and took a walk in the garden. In the afternoon Natasha and I took a walk from the Berezovye gates, walked on bank of the lake and got into an automobile at the Farm. After tea I played the guitar, then read. In the evening we went to the cinema, (wonderful American film) "Peace of the nations or if you want peace get ready for war." I returned home on foot. The weather was damp, 8°. In the evening I wrote a letter to Olga Pavlovna in Odessa.

10 October. Tuesday. Gatchina. Read in the morning. In the afternoon Natasha and I went to Nadezhda Dmitrievna Lyarskaya, where we also saw her mother, a very energetic little old lady of 75 years. After tea, that

---

[162] **"Dagö" and "Moon' islands"** Two Estonian islands locked in the Estonian conflict of 29 Sept/12 Oct to 7/20 October 1917. These two islands are now referred to by their Estonian names, *Hiiumaa* and *Muhu*.

is at 5 3/4, Natasha and I took a walk along Olginskaya, Alexandrovskaya, and Nikolaevskaya. Before dinner I only had the chance to wash my hair. In the evening J with Miss Neame went to the cinema, while Reier came over to see us and stayed until 11 1/4. The weather was dark, 2°. The first cold day, it started to smell like winter was coming.

11 October. Wednesday. Gatchina. At 11 o'cl Natasha, the children, Miss Neame, J and I went to Petrograd. Before breakfast I got a haircut at Alyosha's. Everyone gathered for breakfast; in the afternoon they went to run errands, while Shatsky came to see me with a report, and before him the tailor Grenfeld was here. Before tea I wrote a letter to Mama. From 5 to 6 o'cl Prince Shervashidze dropped in, who departed to Ai-Todor at 9 o'cl.[163] After his departure, i.e. wrote three postcards - to Xenia, princess Orbeliani and Maria Alexeyevna. Before dinner played with Domenici. At 9 1/4 we went to the Shleifers, who had over: Mme Myasoyedova and Balts. After tea Natasha, J and I went to Gatchina, drove very slowly, but why - Vedikhov never was able to give us the exact answer. I forgot to mention that the children returned to Gatchina for dinner, that is at the 6 o'cl. The weather was sunny, 6°.

12 October. Thursday. Gatchina. Read in the morning and took a walk in the garden. Having returned home, the son of Baranov came to see me, he asked me to be the godfather to his son Andrei. At 4 1/2 Nadezhda Dmitrievna with her mother came over. They left at 6 o'cl. Then I read and

---

[163] **"departed to Ai-Todor"** Prince Shervashidze served as a courier for letters to the Grand Duke's family in the Crimea. On 14 October, the Dowager Empress wrote in her diary: "We were waiting all day for the arrival of dear Prince Shervashidze, but he arrived only at 10pm. It was a great joy to see him again. He brought a letter from my darling Alix [sister, Queen Alexandra of Great Britain]. He talked about everything he saw in Petersburg, about the desperate situation in the country, which is subsumed in pure chaos. The next day, I had breakfast alone with Shervashidze, and was happy to hear all his stories over again. The prince's arrival turns out to be the best medicine.... I am growing dark and gloomy because of the lack of news from my dear ones. Loneliness takes hold of me. Telegrams I have sent are returned... and on the few letters that do reach me, they cross out the title and insert 'Romanova' which only makes me laugh." (See Khrustalëv, n. 381, p. 664, citing GA RF *Dnevniki imperatritsy Marii Feodorovny*, 1914-1920, 20 gg. s. 217-218).

played the guitar. In the evening we sat in my study and read, - J read to me. The weather was rainy and windy, 6°.

13 October. Friday. Gatchina. At 3 o'cl Natasha, J and I drove in the "Rolls-Royce" to Krasnoe, from there to Kipen, and then to Gatchina, where we returned at 5 o'cl. At this time Koka's cousin P.P. Abakanovich came over. He graduated an aviation school in England at the end of June, and the other day the Gatchina aviation school. He stayed with us until 6 1/2. We read before dinner. In the evening went to the cinema- "The holy ideal is broken and insulted." The weather was rainy, 4°, strong wind, disgusting.

14 October. Saturday. Gatchina. In the morning read and took a walk in the garden. After breakfast J read to me, after which Natasha and I took a ride in the "Rolls-Royce" to Gorvitsy, and returned at 4 1/2. At this time Mme Ekse came over, had tea with us and left at 5 3/4. Then I played the guitar with Domenici until 7 o'cl. Read before dinner. Then we sat in the study, - Natasha read, while I played the guitar. The weather was nice until 4 o'cl, when it started raining, but not for long, 3°.

15 October. Sunday. Gatchina. In the morning was in the garden for 1/2 hour with Baby. At 2 1/4 Praskovia I and Alexander N came over. At 3 o'cl we drove in the Rolls-Royce to Kurakin Gates, there A. N. and I got out and took a walk around the palace park, while the ladies drove to Gorvitsy. We took a walk past the Admiralty and the palace. At 4 1/2 we met up with the automobile by the palace and returned home together. At this time Alyosha came over to see us. After tea we took care of some things, then I played a game of billiards with A. N. after dinner we all went to the cinema for *An Episode from the Capture of Erzerum* and *Defeated Eve*. The weather was sunny until 3 o'cl, 7°.

16 October. Monday. (The anniversary of our wedding). Gatchina. In the morning Shleifer and I took a walk in the garden. Had breakfast at 12 1/2, then went to Petrograd. I drove the Packard, - inside: Natasha, Praskovia I and Shleifer, - behind us in the Rolls-Royce rode Miss Neame and J[ohnson] (Alyosha left on a train in the morning). In the city everyone dispersed on different errands. I went to Alyosha's, who soon arrived from the office. At 5 o'cl Natasha arrived, and a little later Sergei Petrovich. At

7 1/2 Natasha, Alyosha and I went to the tailor Grenfeld, returned for dinner at Alyosha's, and these guests arrived as well: the Andreyevs, Praskovia I and Shleifer. The dinner was very lively, followed by interesting conversations at the tea table. A. N. got a bit tipsy. At 1 o'cl 1/4 we left to Gatchina, - behind us in the Rolls-Royce rode Miss Neame and J[ohnson], the night was moonlit, 4°. The weather was dark, 8°. To bed at 3 3/4. Got a letter from Mama, brought by Dehn. Koka also sent a letter.

17 October. Tuesday. Gatchina. Read in the morning. In the afternoon Natasha, J[ohnson] and I drove to Remiz, by the second gate we got out and took a walk past the tea house to the black lake. Shot a Mauser revolver by the river to test it. Before reaching the lake, we got into an automobile and returned home at 5 o'cl. Nadezhda Dmitrievna came over to tea and stayed for dinner. I read and played the guitar. In the evening we went to the cinema for *How They Lie*. Nadezhda Dm went home from the cinema, - it was close by. The weather was sunny from 2 o'cl, 9°.

18 October. Wednesday. Gatchina. Read in the morning and ran around the garden with the children. In the afternoon Natasha, J[ohnson] and I drove the Rolls-Royc to the Birch Gates and from there took a walk, walked past the Admiralty, down the long island to the point, then came out to the Cascade Gate and walked to Sylvia, where we got into an automobile and returned home. From 5 o'cl to 7 o'cl I played the guitar with Domenici. After dinner we read, and at 10 1/4 went to the cinema, as usual to the town theater, for *The Crime, or Was She Able To Do This*. The weather was wonderful, sunny all day, 7°, moonlit night, barometer 773.

19 October. Thursday. Gatchina. At 11 o'cl Natasha, J[ohnson] and I went to Petrograd in the Packard. Leonid N was at Alyosha's. Natasha and J[ohnson] came to breakfast. In the afternoon I studied with Alyosha, and from 3 3/4 to 4 1/2 Alyosha, Leonid and I took a walk on Nevsky. Then I received Shatsky and Bolokhovsky regarding the Derugin question. At 5 1/4 the Shleifers arrived, and a little later Sergei Petrovich as well. Natasha came over later. At 7 3/4 Natasha, J[ohnson] and I drove to Gatchina, - on the way dropped off the Shleifers on Izmailovsky [Avenue] and picked up their children, who chatted charmingly the entire way. Arrived at 9 1/4.

After dinner J[ohnson] read to me. The weather was sunny until 3 o'cl, it froze up a bit during the night, in the afternoon it was 5°. Any day now, we expect the Bolshevik spectacle.[164]

20 October. Friday. Gatchina. Read in the morning. Andrei Ivanovich came to breakfast and stayed until 3 o'cl. Then Ekaterina P Koton came over, with whom Natasha and I drove to the Iron Gates, where we got out and walked around the lake passing by the Admiralty and the palace, and got into the automobile by Sylvia. After tea Ekaterina Petrovna left. Natasha and I read, then I lay down on the sofa. After dinner we went to the cinema for *Slavery in Golden Chains*. The weather was dark, had to turn on electricity at 1 o'cl, 6°.

21 October. Saturday. Gatchina. At 11 o'cl Natasha and J[ohnson] went to Petrograd. I read before breakfast. At 2 o'cl in drove in the automobile with the children, Miss Neame, Tanya, Marina, Sophie. We drove across Yegerskaya, Salezi, Pedlino, then turned left towards the black lake, - from the tea house to Korpikovo and home. Returned home at 3 3/4. From 4 1/2 to 7 o'cl I played the guitar with Domenici, then read. At 7 3/4 Natasha returned together with Praskovia I and Leonid. After dinner we read. The weather was dark, 6°.

22 October. Sunday. Gatchina. At 1 1/4 Natasha with Praskovia I and the children went to church at the *Realnoe* School. Leonid read to me before breakfast. At 3 o'cl Natasha, P .I., Leonid, J[ohnson], and I drove to the Zoo and took a walk along the entire river, - got into an automobile at the end in Tsagov and drove Leonid to the Baltic Station. He is leaving for Moscow tomorrow, and in a few days to the front. After tea P. I. read to me, and I fell asleep, then played the guitar. After dinner we went to the cinema for *Under the Power of a Criminal Brother*. From there we went

---

[164] According to Vladimir Nabokov's diaries, "Until the last moment [Kerensky] was completely unaware of the situation. Four or five days before the Bolshevik uprising, during one of our meetings at the Winter Palace, I asked him directly what he thought about the possibility of a Bolshevik revolt, about which everyone was talking at the time. 'I would serve a prayer service for such a spectacle to happen,' he said. 'Are you sure you can handle it?' – 'I have more strength than I need. They will be utterly crushed.'" (Khrustalëv, n. 382, p. 664, quoting V. D. Nabokov, *Vremennoe pravitel'stvo: Vospominaniya*. p. 37.)

to Johnson's, where we had tea, Koton also came over. At 12 1/2 returned home. The weather was dark, 3°.

23 October. Monday. Gatchina. Got up very late. At 3 1/2 Natasha, Praskovia I, J[ohnson] and I drove to Remiz, - got out by the barge and took a walk past the tea house and farther prior to the turn in the road to the black lake. There we got into an automobile and returned home at 5 1/2. After tea I read, then played the guitar. In the evening we read, then J[ohnson] and I played billiards. The weather was semi-clear in the afternoon, 2-3°.

24 October. Tuesday. Gatchina. In the morning Praskovia I read to me. At 3 o'cl Natasha, P. I., J[ohnson] and I drove to the Kurakin gates, and from there walked along the lake, reached the palace and got into an automobile by the Farm. N. D. Lyarskaya was here for tea, when she left, P. I. read to me. At 7 1/4 Mitya Dehn arrived, - he is returning to Ai-Todor tomorrow. We sat down to dinner at 7 3/4 and at 8 1/4 he left. After 9 o'cl we went to the cinema for *The Sin*. The weather was dark, 2°. In Petrograd all the bridges were raised in preparation for the Bolshevik attack, which is expected at any moment.

25 October. Wednesday. Gatchina. Before breakfast I started to write letters to Mama and Xenia and finished at 3 1/2, then Natasha, Praskovia I, J[ohnson] and I went to walk in our garden. After tea P. I. read aloud to me. From Alyosha and Andreyev in Petrograd we found out that in the morning Kerensky left to the Dno station, according to rumors, they presume after the troops, - the Winter Palace was taken over by the Bolsheviks, where according to rumors, the members of the Provisional Government are located, - the Soviet of the Russian Republic has been disbanded by the Bolsheviks as well, - the country's headquarters is in their hands, in the streets shootings in some places,- the entire Petrograd garrison went over to the Bolsheviks, all schools on the side of the Provisional Government. After dinner we went to the cinema for *The Oath of Revenge*. J[ohnson] is staying the night with us. Tanya and Marina continue to stay with us, while there is unrest in the city. The weather is overcast, 3°.

26 October. Thursday. Gatchina. Read in the morning. Koton was here in the afternoon. At 4 1/4 Natasha and I walked over to Elena Konstantinovna, who now moved to Baggovutskaya, 11-b. We had tea with her. A little later J[ohnson] arrived. At 7 o'cl N and I returned on foot. Nadezhda Dm came to dinner. In the evening Reier stopped by. The guests left at 11 1/2. The weather was semi-clear from 2 o'cl. All power was taken over by the Military-Revolutionary Committee,[165] which took over all banks, ministries, and the Winter Palace, which was exposed to major shootouts, not only with rifles and machine guns, but also artillery (it was protected by the primary battalion, *junkers* [cadets], and the 1st Women's Battalion ["The Women's Death Battalion"], - there were a lot of casualties). All ministers were arrested and taken to Kresty,[166] in other words, the Bolsheviks gained a victory, but for how long?

27 October. Friday. Gatchina. Read in the morning. In the afternoon Natasha, J[ohnson] and I headed on foot, first to J[ohnson]'s apartment, and then to the Priorat, where we saw the march of Don Cossacks, - it seems there were one hundred of them with a machine gun and two cannons. One Cossack recognized me, despite my civilian clothes, and asked if I were the Grand Duke Michael Alexandrovich. I responded to him that I would not name myself. Near the Admiralty Gates we got into an automobile and drove across the Zoo and past the palace and saw how they brought over weapons confiscated from the units that arrived from

---

[165] **"Military-Revolutionary Committee"** – the military organization of revolutionary Petrograd, controlled by the Bolsheviks and led by Lev Trotsky. After seizing power, its agents took immediate steps to isolate and intimidate the Romanovs around the country. In her diary entry of 26 October, the Dowager Empress wrote, "We have been cut off from the outside world again, and they have forbidden anyone from entry here. Prince Shervashidze was at Simeiz, and on returning here suggested that I hide all my papers and things, which, of course, made me furious, although I understand he fears future searches." The next day, she noted "All rumors have been confirmed. The Bolsheviks have toppled the Government and have arrested everyone, so that now all the power is in their hands. 14 Bolsheviks have been selected, among them Lenin, Zinoviev, Trotsky, and others. All of them are Jews under false names. We receive neither letters nor newspapers ... What a disgrace, what a brilliant spectacle these swine are playing out."

[166] **"Kresty"** is the name of a prison on the Vyborg Side of St. Petersburg. Built in 1892 in the form of a cross (hence the nickname), by 1917 it largely held political prisoners.

Petrograd, - the Cossacks also disarmed the sailors who were stationed at the Warsaw Station and besides rifles they had 10 machine guns. After tea I read. At 7 1/4 Alexander N arrived. After dinner we all went to the cinema *Loving Forever Put to Sleep* (Francesca Bertini). Then we stopped by the Lyarskys'. From them we went to J[ohnson]'s, where we saw Sergei Petrovich. Returned home at 1 1/2. The weather was overcast, damp in the afternoon, 3-4°. All bourgeois newspapers have been closed. Today Cossack units with artillery arrived in Gatchina via the Warsaw railway. Gen[eral] Krasnov commands the troops concentrated outside of Petrograd. He and his headquarters are located at the palace, - Kerensky and Kozmin are there as well. We found out that at 2 o'cl in the morning and detachment is marching out on Tsarskoe [Selo], where a battle is expected, and after than will follow to Petrograd.[167] The Bolsheviks it seems are starting to have a bad feeling.

28 October. Saturday. Gatchina. In the morning Alexander N and I walked in the garden. In the afternoon Natasha, A.N., J[ohnson] and I took a walk; by the Tatar overpass we walked along the railroad tracks for about one and a half versts and reached the spot where yesterday the Cossacks took apart the rails. From there we walked to the right through the field to the edge of the grove, closed the circle again to the overpass and walked to Sobornaya and along Alexandrovskaya, and home. After tea I played the guitar. After dinner I played the billiards with A. N. J[ohnson] spent the last three nights at our house. The weather was overcast, 5°. According to rumors, the Tsarskoe Selo Bolsheviks have surrendered without much of a struggle; supposedly there is a detachment of sailors near Taaitsa, expecting to march on Gatchina to arrest Kerensky, who is staying at the palace; according to rumors from Petrograd, the Bolsheviks robbed the Winter Palace and are robbing the State Bank, aside from that they are printing credit slips at Expedition in the amount of 35 million a day for

---

[167] On 28 October, the Dowager Empress had already heard the news: "Rumors have reached us that all the ministers have been arrested and despatched on foot to the fortress, where they are under detention. Only the Prime Minister has escaped. They say he, Kerensky, has headed to Pskov, appointing himself Commandant in Chief [*sic*] and that now, together with his Red Army, is headed to Petersburg, and has already taken Gatchina. What dreadful chaos!" (Khrustalëv, n. 386, p. 665, citing *Dnevniki imperatritsy Marii Feodorovny*, 1914-1920, 20 gg. S. 220).

their own pockets. In the evening we learned that Gatchina has been declared under siege.

29 October. Sunday. Gatchina. At 11 o'cl, Natasha, the children, Alexander N and I went to the *Realnoe School* for liturgy. Then we took a ride in an automobile past the palace, there are weapons set up on parade ground. In the afternoon Natasha, J[ohnson], A. N. and I took a walk, went to Priorat, walked by the house, then the spot where music is playing, turned left and came out near the *Realnoe* School. Returned home via Baggovutskaya at 4 o'cl 40 min. (Natasha was tired and returned in a cab). Before dinner I played the guitar. In the evening Natasha lay down on my sofa, while the men played billiards. After the evening tea J[ohnson] went to the palace for news, which were the following:

Kerensky continues to stay in Gatchina.[168] Tsarskoe [Selo] was taken in a battle, combat continues on Alexandrovskaya, - in Petrograd there is a battle between Pavel Military School and the Bolsheviks. The telephone station again went over to the Bolsheviks - according to rumors, they're smashing the State Bank, - there is partial rift among garrison units. The weather was dark, foggy, 4°. After tea Elena K and Reier came over.

30 October. Monday. Gatchina. In the morning took a walk in the garden. A. N. headed to the housekeeper. After breakfast Natasha took a walk among the new buildings. At 3 o'cl J[ohnson] and I walked on foot around town, walked by the palace, then through Remiz to the tea house, where Natasha with A. N. drove in an automobile. Together we drove a bit farther and then returned home through Priorat. After tea I played the guitar, after which fell asleep on the sofa. In the evening I played the billiards with A. N. At 11 1/2 J arrived from the palace and announced that the situation in Gatchina is threatening us. The detachment of Gen[eral] Krasnov was forced to retreat from the Alexandrovskaya-Pulkovo line, due to its small size and lack of artillery, to the Izhor river line. Krasnov himself with Staff

---

[168] During the early days of the October Revolution, the Bolsheviks focused their attention on harassing and detaining those who were considered counterrevolutionary, and the mention of Grand Duke Michael during the Kornilov affair was more than enough pretext to rearrest him and keep him at Gatchina, now entirely under Bolshevik control.

arrived here. At 12 o'cl A. N. and I went to J[ohnson]'s, where we stayed around 2 hours. Having returned, we found a lively packing of valuable things. Went to bed at 4 1/2. The weather in the afternoon was semi-clear, 5°.

31 October. Tuesday. Gatchina. Got up late. The political horizon is not clearing up, but not getting worse either. Packing continues. Before breakfast A. N. and I took a short walk in the garden. In the afternoon I packed. After tea A. N. took a walk in the streets and heard single rifle shots towards the Zoo and the palace. J[ohnson] did not have dinner with us. At 10 o'cl Natasha, A. N. and I went to J[ohnson]'s]. Sergei Petrovich came in an hour. We returned home at 2 1/2. The weather was wonderful, sunny, 4°. Both sides declared a truce to discuss the composition of future government until 12 o'cl the next day. Gen[eral] Krasnov's detachment (during the battle) consisted only of 1200 artillery men, while the infantry only had 250-300 rifles. The main opposition against them consisted of 5000 sailors and the red guard. The Cossacks losses were about 20 men, while the other side about twenty times more.

November 1917

1 November. Wednesday. Gatchina. Reier dropped by in the morning. Before breakfast A. N. and I took a walk in the garden. The children with Miss Neame, Nadezhda Dm and Sophie went to Vyra, the estate near Rozhdestvenno, which belongs to the Nabokovs. They left at 11 1/2 and will stay there until everything settles down. Koton came by in the afternoon, and at 3 1/2 Natasha, A. N. and I went to the Zoo. Walked along Berezovye and Dubrovaya to the end of Tsagov (where the sheds are), and, while approaching the automobile, we heard some loud conversation and saw soldiers by the gate, suddenly a shot was heard, - apparently some bastard shot at the car. During the walk we heard several shots. Returned home through the Zoo at 5 o'cl. J[ohnson] met us and announced that Kerensky just escaped from the palace in an automobile, while Svistunov, who also escaped, was detained at the Baltic Station. All Gatchina is surrounded by the Bolshevik troops, and they are searching for Kerensky everywhere. Around 5 1/2 N, A. N. and I went to J[ohnson]'s on foot, where we stayed until 7 3/4, and then went to Elena K's. They range from

our house and notified us that artillerist disarmed our *junker* [cadet] guard and replaced them with themselves. Johnson went to the palace and was supposed to address the new commandant about various issues. We didn't wait for his return and walked home, where we arrived at 12 1/2 and sat down to dinner, or rather supper. Soon J[ohnson] and Ivan Ignatevich arrived with the following information: at the palace the commandant set up a revolutionary committee, under the commandant. The commissar is a sailor of the 2nd Baltic Naval Detachment, the secretary of Gatchina Soviet of soldiers is Borodonosenko, the commandant is the young lieutenant of the Izmailovsky Regiment, Novikov. J[ohnson]'s treatment was polite, and they asked to pass on to me not to worry. But our two motorcars were confiscated. The children arrived at Vyra estate safely, Vedikhov returned at 9 o'cl. We went to bed at 3 o'cl. The weather was overcast, 3°.

2 November. Thursday. Gatchina. Got up late. At 12 1/2 sailors joined the guard. In the afternoon our automobile went to pick up the children to the Vyra estate escorted by a sailor from our guard, - the pass was obtained from the commandant. Natasha, A. N. and I took a walk in the garden, and we spoke with a few sailors. After tea I played the guitar, N. read, while A. N. and J[ohnson] played the billiards. In the evening I played the billiards with A. N. The weather was overcast, it snowed a little during the night, which melted. Commissar Kozar, of the Gatchina Military Aviation Academy was assigned to us, a likable soldier. The head of our small guard is also a very likable sailor. The children had returned from the Vyra estate at 8 o'cl in the evening. They traveled very safely. - At 5 o'cl engineer Rakhinsky arrived and confiscated our last automobile. As it turned out later, he acted on his own accord and wanted to arrest us, for which he later got in trouble with the Soviet.

3 November. Friday. Gatchina. Got up late. A. N. left for Petrograd having stayed with us exactly a week. We did not receive any newspapers either this entire time. The bourgeois press remains silenced. Nadezhda Dmitrievna came over for breakfast and stayed until 3 1/4. Then Natasha and I took a walk in the garden. After tea I lay down on the sofa, then read, and in the evening as well. The weather was dark, 1 1/2°. Today the horses were transported from the palace stables to our place on

Baggovutskaya, while the other part had to be left behind for now. In the morning we learned that some troops are moving from Luga, but which ones is unknown, - presumably they are Kerensky's; there was a battle near Suida. In Gatchina it is peaceful for now. In Tsarskoe [Selo] there were a lot of burglaries and violence. In Petrograd it is relatively quiet. In Moscow an official war is going on, Uspensky Cathedral, St. Basil's and the city duma buildings were destroyed, Tverskoy Boulevard, the Nikitsky Gates and the environs of Arbat Square are on fire, colossal number of victims. There was a search at J[ohnson]'s apartment in the morning, they were looking for machine guns and grenades. Today the guard is from the Military Aviation Academy.

4 November. Saturday. Gatchina. Read in the morning. In the afternoon Natasha, J[ohnson] and I took a walk in the garden, fed the chickens, turkeys and ducks and stopped by the stables. Koton came over for tea. Around 6 o'cl the famous Roshal and Lieutenant Dashkevich arrived completely unexpectedly with the order from the Military-Revolutionary Committee to bring me to Smolny[169] in Petrograd. Koton and J[ohnson] had a long conversation with them and ultimately convinced them not to take me there. Departure was scheduled for after dinner, but in light of our confiscated automobile not arriving and it the late hour, it was decided to transport us tomorrow morning to any private apartment of our choice. The reason was the supposed threat of danger to me from the passing troops, so apparently it won't be for long. In the evening I played the guitar. The weather was dark, 0°. As far as we know, there is a concentration of troops against the Bolsheviks near Luga. It is quiet in Petrograd.

5 November. Sunday. Gatchina and Petrograd. In the morning we were ready to go to Petrograd, as it was agreed, at 11 o'cl, but no one came to pick us up. Before breakfast I took a walk. Nadezhda Dm. came to breakfast and left at 2 o'cl. Then Roshal and War Commissar Dybenko (a sailor from the *Petropavlovsk*). They discussed the question of our trip, -

---

[169] **"Smolny"** – formerly a finishing school for young noblewomen, in 1917 it was requisitioned by the Bolsheviks for use as their Petrograd headquarters. Today it houses St. Petersburg's civil administration.

they still could not find our Packard. They were both polite. In about 45 min[utes] we drove to the palace. After tea Roshal arrived in our Packard, and at 5 1/2 Natasha, J[ohnson] and I finally departed. With us also rode an ensign of the Izmailovsky Regiment, Shidlovsky. Behind us drove a motor with belongings, Chelyshev, Motya and two sailors. At 7 o'cl we arrived on Millionnaya, at the Putyatins,' where we were quartered. In the apartment are staying E. P., M. P., P. P. and Tata, - O. P. is still in Odessa. Soon we sat down to dinner. In the evening I played jacks with M. P. To bed at 1 o'cl. The weather was overcast, it snowed in the afternoon, 0°. Before dinner S. Dolgoruky came over, who left for Ai-Todor at 9 o'cl.

6 November. Monday. Petrograd. Got up very late. In the afternoon Natasha went shopping, she walked on foot. Alexander Nikolaevich came to see me. Natasha returned for tea, also came over Alyosha, Tatiana P and Dvorzhitsky, who arrived from Abas-Tuman about two weeks ago. Around 6 1/4 the guests left, while I took care of business with Alyosha before dinner. The weather was clear occasionally, 1 1/2 [degrees]. We don't have any news.

7 November. Tuesday. Petrograd. Got up late. Had breakfast at around 1 1/4. In the afternoon everyone dispersed to run respective errands, while I took a walk with Alexander N. Walked by the Winter Palace and enjoyed its view, - all the walls are covered with bullet holes, Windows as well; then we reached the end of the embankment, - on the Neva are docked the *Khivinets*, *Dawn of Freedom*, *Aurora*, and *Zarnitsa*. We returned back via Morskaya. With me, about 100 paces away, was a sailor (as a guard who is sitting here in the kitchen). To tea came: Margarita Vasilievna, Alyosha, A. N. Around 6 1/2 M. B. left. After dinner we went to Tata's, and she played the piano. When Birukov came over, we transferred to the study and discussed the question of Derugino. Later the Andreyevs came over. During a political discussion Ekaterina Ivanovna and P. P., were both so wound up and yelled so much that I had to take tough measures, that is to place near me a chairman's bell for restoration of order, and as very last measure - a revolver. The guests left after 12 o'cl. The weather was semi-clear, 1 1/2°.

8 November. Wednesday. Petrograd. Mikhail Pavlovich's birthday. Got up late. Before breakfast Natasha went to a shop and bought flowers for Ekaterina P. At breakfast after practicing - Alyosha, Alexander N, Birukov, besides Margarita V was here. In the afternoon I walked with Putyatin to a photographer on Nevsky, near the Ioffe[170] city Duma, where Natasha and M. V. arrived. Then they went to do errands from there, while we returned home. [Grand Duke] Nicholas Mikhailovich came to tea, he did not stay long, then Andrei I, Praskovia I and commandant of Bologoe Station Lvov came over. Stayed for dinner: Alyosha, Lvov and Alexander N, and also Tatiana P came over. In the evening Abaza and Dulov came over, - the former played the balalaika wonderfully, and the latter accompanied him magnificently. The guests dispersed around 1 o'cl. It was a very pleasant evening. The weather was overcast, it was snowing; sleighs appeared, 4°.

9 November.[171] Thursday. Petrograd. Got up late. Zinoviev stopped by before breakfast (acquaintance of the Abakanoviches) and stayed for breakfast. In the afternoon everyone left to do errands, while I took a walk with Shleifer, - Palace Bridge was open and the *Khivinets* was passing, it dropped anchor at Korpikovo before reaching Troitsky Bridge. At 4 1/2 A. N. left, and Margarita V, the young Prince Putyatin and Dvorzhitsky arrived for tea. From 6 o'cl until 8 o'cl I played the guitar with Domenici. Dvorzhitsky returned for dinner. (Natasha had tea at the Shleifers's and only came back at 8 o'cl). In the evening we sat in the pink room, while

---

[170] **"Ioffe City Duma"** Michael Alexandrovich refers here to Adolf Abramovich Ioffe (b. 1883 - d. 1927), who led the Bolshevik faction in the Duma in the fall of 1917 and was one of the Duma's delegates to the Democratic Conference between 14 and 22 September. Joffe left the "pre-parliament" before the October Revolution, and after the October Days was again the Duma leader. He went on to help negotiate the Treaty of Brest-Litovsk, which ended Russia's involvement in World War I.

[171] **"9 November"** At Ai-Todor, news of Michael's situation had already reached the Dowager Empress who wrote in her diary on the same day: "About Misha's situation, they [Countess Apraksina and Prince Shervashidze] are saying that two Bolsheviks brought him from Gatchina to Petersburg, where, together with his family, he is living at Prince Putyatin's thought he is not under arrest there." (cf. *Dnevniki Imperatritsy Marii Fedorovny*, Bagrius, Moscow: 2006, pp. 221)

J[ohnson] received D. V. Lyarsky. The weather was overcast, 6°. I wrote a letter to Xenia. Today around 12 noon P. P. left for Odessa for Olga P.

10 November. Friday. Petrograd. Around 10 o'cl, Natasha left the house and with J[ohnson] she was supposed to take the Warsaw line to go to Gatchina, but due to a breakdown of the caboose they only reached Alexandrovskaya, where they got a bite to eat and returned to Petrograd via Tsarskoselsky Highway, - got home at 4 1/2. I read before breakfast, and in the afternoon, went to Andrei Ivanovich on Sergeyevskaya with Putyatin. He has a lot of antiques. Before dinner Natasha and I lay down and fell asleep. In the evening we sat in our bedroom. The weather was sunny from 3 1/2 o'cl, 1 1/2°. Alyosha came to tea and had had dinner. In the evening J[ohnson] went to Gatchina to do errands.

11 November. Saturday. Petrograd. Read in the morning. In the afternoon Natasha headed to the shops, while Alexander N came to see me and read to me. At 4 1/2 he left, and Colonel Merchule came to tea. Natasha returned for tea, while Merchule stayed until 6 o'cl. Then I played the guitar with Domenici. In the evening we sat in the pink room. Today J[ohnson] returned from Gatchina around 8 3/4. The weather was damp, it was snowing, 1 1/2.

12 November. Sunday. Petrograd. Read in the morning. Two Englishmen from the embassy came to breakfast - Brooks and Bruce, both very likable. At 3 o'cl they left, and shortly Prince M. P., J[ohnson] and I went to the Shleifers at Izmailovsky, 7. We took a cab for the last chunk, and J[ohnson] went to the train station and to Gatchina. We visited until 7 o'cl. Besides us there were other guests, - Natasha and Ekaterina P came over in a hansom cab. By the way there were: Sergei Petrovich, Filippov and the Mikhailovskys. In the evening we sat around and had lively discussions, - Alyosha and Praskovia I were there. The weather was dark: it was snowing, 1/2°. The situation remains the same - all power remains in the hands of Bolsheviks headed by Lenin and Troitsky; Ensign Krylenko was appointed War [Commissar] and Commander-in-Chief, who judging by newspapers, left for Stavka yesterday to replace Gen[eral] Dukhonin (the latter was replaced for refusing to enter peace talks with the

Germans).[172] All government organizations refuse to recognize the Bolsheviks government and are striking. On all fronts - no changes, but famine is starting. Today the Constituent Assembly[173] elections started.

13 November. Monday. Petrograd. In the morning Margarita V stopped by, and in the afternoon- Andrei I. At 3 o'cl I took a walk with Alexander N. Rybarsky came to tea and stayed until 6 1/2. After that I played the guitar. After dinner Natasha, Putyatins and I took a hansom cab to the Piccadilly cinema, - they showed an Italian drama. Returned at 10 o'cl 20 min. Went to bed early. Waited for J[ohnson], who was supposed to arrive from Gatchina, but apparently his errands delayed him. The weather was sunny from 1 o'cl until 3 o'cl, 3-4°, a nice sleigh path. Representatives of the treaty sovereignties at Stavka gave Gen[eral] Dukhonin a note, in which all the consequences of breaking the ally treaty were laid upon Russia. England is not recognizing the Bolshevik government.

14 November. Tuesday. Petrograd. Read in the morning. Sergei Aleksandrovich, Alyosha and Shleifer arrived for breakfast. J[ohnson] was telling us a very interesting story about his visit to the Smolny last evening - there he saw Trotsky (Bronshtein), Kozlovsky and Menzhitsky [sic. Menzhinsky] - he went there with Roshal and was able to bargain my return to Gatchina.[174] At 3 o'cl everyone left, and I with Alyosha and

---

[172] *"Dukhonin"* – Nikolai Nikolaevich Dukhonin (b. 1876 – d. 1917) was appointed commander-in-chief of the Russian Army after the Kornilov Affair. Removed from command by Lenin for these reasons, he surrendered to Krylenko at Stavka but was then murdered by Krylenko's Red Guard escort, who then used his corpse for target practice.

[173] **"Constituent Assembly"** – The Provisional Government had taken power promising to hold national elections to an assembly to draft a constitution to determine Russia's political future. The election date was set earlier without anticipating that the Bolshevik coup would take place. Lenin's government distrusted the idea but held the elections anyway, hoping either to secure a majority in it or simply tolerate it long enough to seize power. The Bolsheviks received only 24 percent of the votes in the end and in January 1918 dispersed the Assembly after just one day of meetings.

[174] **"return to Gatchina"** On 13 November, 1917 the Petrograd Soviet considered the issue of the transfer of Grand Duke Michael from the capital: "Hearing regarding the 'translation' of Michael Romanov either to Gatchina or Finland. Commissioner Roshal of Gatchina has confirmed that Gatchina and the railway line are entirely in our hands ... It is permitted to transfer Mikhail Romanov to Gatchina under house arrest." (Khrustalëv, n. 389, p.666, citing GARF f. 1236, op. 1, d. 1, l. 83) It is

Shleifer headed out on foot, walked along Nevsky and dispersed to our respective homes. Prince B. A. Vasilchikov and Westfalen came to tea. After dinner, to which Margarita V came, the five is us headed to the Splendid-Palace cinema - the ladies rode in Kreisler's automobile, while the prince and I walked partially, and took a cab partially. Returned home at 10 3/4. The weather was dark, 1°, snow was falling almost all day. There is shooting at the front is some places, in some places there is fraternization, - The 2nd and 3rd Armies have started independent talks with the Germans about separate peace treaty, - the troops, starting from Romania towards the south, did not recognize Krylenko as commander-in-chief.

15 November. Wednesday. Petrograd and Gatchina. Before breakfast Natasha went with J[ohnson] to the State Bank, but it turned out to be closed, as the staff went on strike for three days in a protest against the Bolsheviks.[175] In the afternoon I took a walk along the Embankment to the Palace with Putyatin, then in the Alexandrovsky Gardens, along the Morskaya, Nevsky, and Konyushennaya. Alexander N came over and read to me until tea, and I rested. At hairdresser came over for Natasha. At 4 1/2 Tatiana P, the Mikhailovskys and Pototskaya (Putyatins' sister) came over. They left around 6 o'cl. Domenici came over for a lesson, which

---

interesting to note that Finland was still considered a safe place to keep Romanovs, likely due to its separate constitutional status within the Russian Empire. Six months earlier, in June 1917, Grand Dukes Georgii Mikhailovich and Kirill Vladimirovich and his family had been given permission by the Provisional Government to go to Finland but were refused the right to leave the country.

[175] In her book *Step-Daughter of Imperial Russia*, Nathalie Majolier (Tata) mentions that her mother had tried to go to the bank to retrieve her jewels in case they were to leave the country. "All our valuables and most of my mother's jewels were were at the bank, and the banks had been one of the first things seized by the government." Brasova was later able to retrieve some of her more important things as "she made representation to the authorities that she must be permitted access to her safe on some excuse to do with papers that she had either to examine or procure for them. Someone was detailed to accompany her to Petrograd for this purpose and to take her to the bank. Whether this person was venal or merely careless it would be hard to say, but the result of her expedition was that, after viewing her papers, she returned home with her muff stuffed full of some of her more valuable and portable jewellery." (cf. Nathalie Majolier, *Step-Daughter of Imperial Russia*, Kindle edition, viewed Sept 18, 2018)

didn't take place because my guitar was packed, - and instead he played by himself until 6 1/2. (Forgot to mention that Tata arrived in the afternoon). After a snack Natasha and both Tatas went to a ballet, *Swan Lake*, - the Putyatins went there too separately. J[ohnson] and I drove to the Warsaw Station in the same Kreisler's automobile, and went to Gatchina in the 7 o'cl train, in a private compartment. Got out on Baggovutskaya platform and walked to the house. Baby was still awake and was happy with my return. J[ohnson] and I had dinner, where Miss Neame and Ivan Ig. were present. The weather was overcast, it snowed occasionally, 1° in the afternoon, in the evening 1°. Natasha stayed at Putyatins' until Saturday.

16 November. Thursday. Gatchina. It is strange and unpleasant to be here without Natasha. In the morning copied over the diary. Then took a walk in the garden with Miss Neame. Had breakfast at 12 1/2, J[ohnson] was here and Ivan Ignatevich. In the afternoon, J[ohnson], Miss Neame and I took a walk (past the Warsaw Station to Priorat, made a circle and came out by the *Realnoe* School). J[ohnson] went home. Koton came to tea and stayed until 5 1/2. I tested until 6 o'cl. The last few days I have felt weak. Tata returned from Petrograd at 6 1/2, she liked the ballet. Natasha sent me a letter, and Andrei Iv A - a rosette, a George's cross for civilian dress. Baby dictated his diary to me. After dinner I wrote a letter to Natasha, and then took a ride in a sleigh with J[ohnson] across Priorat, past the palace to Baltic Station and back via Sobornaya. The weather was overcast, although in places the sky was blue, 3-4°, wonderful sleigh path. Gatchina is silent.

17 November. Friday. Gatchina and Petrograd. At 11 o'cl I rode horseback (I have not ridden, I think, since 19 August). Rode in the Zoo and rode along the lake in the palace park. Rode Vityaz. Had breakfast at 12 1/2. In the afternoon Miss Neame dictated to me, and besides that, taught me the new penmanship with the letters slanting to the left. At 4 1/2 J[ohnson] and I went to Petrograd via Warsaw [Station]. From the station we took a hansom cab. Natasha soon returned home and got busy with the hairdresser. At 7 o'cl Alexander N read aloud to me before dinner. To dinner came: Tatiana P, Sergei Petrovich and Bologov commandant Stanislav Lvov. In the evening we had an interesting conversation, while

M. P., A. N. and Lvov played cards. Went to bed late. The weather was semi-clear, strong wind, from 1-3°.

18 November. Saturday. Petrograd and Gatchina. Got up late. Natasha and A.N. Went to the bank and had breakfast at Margarita V's, while A. N. returned to us. In the afternoon A. N. and I took a walk and went to a few shops. To tea came: Tatiana P, Merchanskaya and three wounded officers, Podgursky, Rubenshtein and Belyaev, all three very likable. At 6 1/4 they left, and at 6 3/4 Natasha, J[ohnson] and I went to the Warsaw Station and barely found seats on the train, - sat in the service section and in 3rd class, the train moved slowly. I walked from Baggovutskaya platform. Domenici was awaiting me, and we practiced in the evening until 11 o'cl. The weather was sunny, 4°.

19 November. Sunday. Gatchina. Planned to ride but got so caught up that I did not go, and had the riding horses' shoes removed. From 11 o'cl until breakfast I played with Domenici, who stayed the night here. After breakfast and until 3 1/2 I played the guitar again, then Domenici left. Natasha and I took a walk, walked along Alexandrovskaya and returned via Nikolaevskaya. After tea Elena Konstantinovna came over and stayed until 7 o'cl. Then I wrote Baby's diary. After dinner we went to the cinema (French drama, - there was no program). The weather was dark, 1 1/2°. All these last days the barometer remained at 716.

20 November. Monday. Gatchina. At 9 o'cl 48 min. Natasha went to Petrograd with J[ohnson]. I read. In the afternoon I wrote English dictation. At 2 3/4 I rode on horseback, rode Koko, rode across the closest meadow, then rode past the Grand overpass and came out to the highway, which leads to the Tsarskoslavyanskaya dacha, and rode to the graveyard, then through Zagvostka to Priorat, where I made a circle and returned home at 4 3/4, rode on Olginskaya and Alexandrovskaya. After tea I wrote English dictation. Natasha came back alone at 6 o'cl. After dinner I played the guitar and drew various devils at Miss Neame's request. The weather was dark, damp, it was snowing, 1°.

21 November. Tuesday. Gatchina. From 11 o'cl until 12 o'cl rode horseback, rode at the Zoo along the river and back on Tsagov, a lot of snow, almost to the knees. In the afternoon we hung out the miniatures and

arranged photographs, which were packed the whole time lately. From 3 1/4 and until 4 1/2 I was in the garden, - by the house on Baggovutskaya the children and I sawed off two large branches, and then cleared off snow near our house, and also took a run in the garden. After tea I played the guitar. At 6 1/4 arrived: J[ohnson], his uncle Kreisler and [blank]. They came in an automobile from Petrograd, and it was hard to drive because of snow. They stayed for dinner and left at 10 3/4. The weather was overcast, and from 3 o'cl it roared up, in the morning 4°, and towards the evening 11°. Gen[eral] Dukhonin was killed by a mob of soldiers at his departure from Mogilev, which was relayed by the [new] commander-in-chief, Ensign Krylenko.

22 November.[176] Wednesday. Gatchina. Got up late. In the morning all the staff congratulated me in the billiard room. At 12 o'cl Father Strakhov held a prayer service in the dining room and stayed for breakfast, also Ivan Ig. was there. At 2 o'cl arrived: Ekaterina P, Mikhail P, Dvorzhitsky, the Shleifers, Kulikovsky, Chernyavsky and Mirovich (the last two from the 2nd artillery brigade). A bit later Nadezhda Dm and Birukov arrived, who did not stay long. Reier also did not stay long. Then Elena K came over, while two officers left. We had tea at 4 1/2. Around 6 o'cl Natasha sat down to play *zhelëzka* with the guests, while I played the guitar with Domenici in my study. Around 7 o'cl Dvorzhitsky and I took Elena K home to Baggovutskaya, we walked. After dinner everyone sat down to play cards again. At 9 o'cl rather unexpectedly Alyosha and Olga A arrived from Moscow. I played billiards with Mikhail P. After evening tea everyone continued to play *zhelëzka*. Around 12 1/2 Alyosha went to bed, Kulikovsky and Shleifer went to sleep on Baggovutskaya. I also lay down around 1 1/2. The weather was sunny and mild, 8-10 deg. My table with gifts was in the dining room.

23 November. Thursday. Gatchina. Got up late. In the morning soldiers from the Aviation School arrived and requisitioned, or rather, confiscated, wine in the amount of 80 bottles, and sugar (our personal Derugin sugar). They did all this on the decree of the Soviet. To top it off, they immediately cracked open a few bottles and drank the contents. The Putyatins, who

---

[176] Grand Duke Michael's birthday. He turned 39.

spent the night at J[ohnson's], arrived for breakfast very much delayed. Kirusha arrived in the afternoon, and having fed him, we went into the garden, - Natasha and the princess also came out for a walk together with Olga A. At 4 o'cl the Putyatins went to the train station. After tea, to which Sergei Petrovich came, Kirusha and I played the billiards. After dinner we say in the sitting room. Sergei P left at 12 1/2. Kirusha is staying the night with us. The weather was sunny, 10°.

24 November. Friday. Gatchina and Petrograd. At 9 1/2 Natasha, Olga A, Johnson and I went to Petrograd by train. From the train station went directly to Alyosha's. The children arrived for breakfast. In the afternoon I went to Putyatins with the children and Miss Neame, where the children were settled to stay for now. (Today is Ekaterina P's name day). Found out from Putyatins that since last evening the soldiers have been raiding the Winter Palace cellars, there was a major shootout between the soldiers and the Red Guards, who were guarding the entrance. I left at 4 1/4 from the Putyatins. At Alyosha's I saw Mme Gubareva regarding my hair. After tea Alyosha and I practiced. Alyosha headed to Andreyevs for dinner. Natasha, Olga A and I spent the evening at home. J[ohnson] also went to the Andreyevs, and on the way to them he stopped by to see us and told us of a visit to Smolny, where he went to resolve a few issues. The weather was dark, there was a snowstorm in the afternoon, -1°.

25 November. Saturday. Petrograd. Got up late. Natasha and Olga A went to the bank. Schneider came to breakfast. In the afternoon Sh[leifer] and I walked. He stayed to run errands, while I went to the Putyatins, where I visited with the children, and returned to Alyosha's at 4 3/4 in a cab with Olga Aleksandrovna. Andrei I. was supposed to be there, but couldn't wait and went to the doctor. I wrote a letter to Yulia Vladislavovna, and then practiced with Domenici until 8 o'cl. To dinner came: Praskovia I., Andreyev and Shleifer. (Forgot to mention that Kirusha returned from Gatchina around 7 o'cl). Shleifer left in the evening, - the other guests stayed until 1 o'cl. The weather was overcast, -1°.

26 November. Sunday. (Baby's name day) Petrograd. Got up late. Read in the morning. Around 12 o'cl Nina Dmitrievna stopped by with Yuri (ensign of the Calvary Regiment). Then Alyosha and I walked to

Putyatins, while Natasha and Olga A rode in a cab. Yesterday at 1 in the morning Olga P arrived from Odessa with her husband; they traveled for 5 days. Baby got really friendly with Elisa and is always playing with her; he was happy with his presents. In the afternoon Olga P, P. P., Kirusha and I took a walk (Dvorzhitsky was also with us). Returned for tea, the Shleifers, Ekaterina I. and Praskovia were here. At 6 1/2 Natasha and I returned to Alyosha's, where Mme Gubareva massaged my head and showed this skill to Miss Neame. Had dinner and evening tea at Putyatins. Returned to Alyosha's apartment at 12 1/2. The weather was dark, 1°. The other day they raised the wine cellar at the Winter Palace, and besides that there was another burglary in the palace. Today they still were not allowing pedestrians on the Embankment along the palace.

27 November. Monday. Petrograd and Gatchina. At 12 3/4 Natasha and I went to Putyatins for breakfast. I took the e o'cl train to Gatchina with the children and Miss Neame. I walked to the house from Baggovutskaya platform. After tea I played the guitar. Had dinner with Ivan I., and then played the billiards with him. Natasha and Olga A, who planned on coming tomorrow, changed their minds and came at 12 o'cl., - departed with a 9 o'cl train, which crawled endlessly. The weather was overcast, - 2°. Tomorrow the Constituent Assembly is supposed to open.

28 November. Tuesday. Gatchina. Got up late. Read in the morning. At 1 1/4 I rode in a hunting sleigh with Baranov to Tsarskoslavyansky Forest, - reached the guardhouse and from there walked back with Reit, - I walked around 7-8 versts, that is reached the village Korkozi, there got into a sleigh, and at. 4 3/4 We returned home. The Reiers came to tea. Reier was laid off his position by the new powers. Later I played the guitar and then wrote English dictation. After dinner we went to the cinema for *Through the Fire of Passions* and *France's Duel*. The weather was sunny, mild, it was wonderful in the forest, 10°. The Constituent Assembly was postponed until day after tomorrow.

29 November. Wednesday. Gatchina. At 9 1/2 Natasha, J[ohnson] and Olga A went to Petrograd. I read in the morning. Before breakfast, which was at 12 o'cl, I jogged in the garden. Read in the afternoon, and from 2 o'cl until 4 o'cl I was in the garden, walked and worked by the house on

Baggovutskaya. We with Miss Neame gathered snow into piles. At 4 1/2 Kirusha and Domenici arrived. I played the guitar until 6 3/4. Wrote in English before dinner. Natasha and Olga A arrived at 6 o'cl. In the evening I played billiards with Kirusha and took turns with Ivan Ig. The weather was sunny, from -15° to -11°.

30 November. Thursday. Gatchina. In the morning sledded with Kirusha, reached the Black Gates and returned through Priorat. Then I drove Natasha to Elena K, but she was not home and we returned. Sergei Petrovich came to breakfast. In the afternoon we all took a walk in the garden and went down the hill for a little while, the one by the Baggovutskaya house. Kirusha left at 4 o'cl. Today he is leaving for Moscow, and Natasha, S. P. and I walked in the garden until 4 1/4. I read after tea, then sat with N and S. P. downstairs. After dinner I studied with J[ohnson], then we all sat in the sitting room. S. P. left at 12 o'cl. The weather was dark, from 5 to -2 deg. The Bolsheviks dispersed the Constituents' meeting.[177]

December 1917

1 December. Friday. Gatchina. Read in the morning, then worked in the garden. Nadezhda D. [Lyarskaya] came to breakfast with Sophie. They left around 3 o'cl. Then Natasha and O[lga] A. walked to the palace pharmacy, while I worked in the garden, cleared the pathways, a lot of snow, a triangle passed by, drawn by a little donkey. At 4 1/2 N[atasha] and O A returned, Elena K [Gavriluk] also came over and stayed until 6 o'cl. Then I read, and from 6 3/4 until dinner time, I wrote English dictation. In the evening, we went by sleigh to the cinema in Orlov (Natasha, O A, Miss N[im], Johnson and I), for *The Child of Forest - The Child of Nature*. The weather was dark, it was snowing, -2°.

2 December. Saturday. Gatchina. At 9 1/2, Natasha, OA and J[ohnson] went to Petrograd. I read, then, one hour before breakfast, which was at 12 o'cl., worked in the garden on the large alley. From 2 o'clock to 4 o'cl.

---

[177] As noted above, the Bolsheviks were hostile to the Constituent Assembly, and took numerous actions against the elections to it as well as to its organization and participants even before it met in January 1918.

worked in the garden again. Initially Tata worked with me, then Ivan Ig. came. At 4 1/2, Koton came over. Natasha returned at 6 1/4 with O.A. At the same time, Domenici arrived too, and I studied with him until 7 3/4. Koton had dinner with us and left at 9 1/2. Around 10 o'cl., Alyosha and J[ohnson] arrived, who had dinner with us. In the evening, we looked at magazines. The weather was dark, 1°. In the newspapers we read that Nicky allegedly escaped from Tobolsk,[178] - most likely this is all made up.

3 December. Sunday. Gatchina. Took a walk around the garden with Alyosha before breakfast. In the afternoon, he read to me, and at 3 1/2, Alyosha and I walked Natasha to M. F. Nabokova, and returned via Alexandrovskaya. After tea, Alyosha and I wrote letters (to A.N. Naryshkina, Lavrinsky, Yatzyn and Kravchinsky). Shortly after dinner, we all rode to J[ohnson's] in two sleighs. He played the piano, I the guitar, we had tea. At 12 o'cl, we returned home. The weather was dark, that is simply overcast, -2-5°. The rumour about Nicky's disappearance from Tobolsk was, of course, disproved.

4 December. Monday. Gatchina. Read in the morning, and from 12 until 1 o'cl, walked in the garden. Read from 2 o'cl until 3 o'cl, then walked in the garden, and jogged until 4 1/2, while Natasha and OA were visiting at J[ohnson's], they walked there and back. After tea, I rested for a bit. Then played the guitar, and wrote in English until dinner. In the evening, studied with J[ohnson], then played the billiards with him. The weather in the afternoon was semi-clear, very beautiful sky, -3°.

5 December. Tuesday. Gatchina. At 9 1/2, Natasha, OA and J[ohnson] went to Petrograd. I read, then took a walk in the garden before breakfast. In the afternoon, I read, and at 2 o'cl went to the garden, where I worked in the garden on the large alley with Miss N[im] and Baby. After returning home, I rested. Read after tea. At 6 o'cl, Natasha and Olga A returned.

---

[178] **"Nicky allegedly escaped"** There were such reports at this time, all false. Khrustalëv notes that on 2 December 1917, *Petrograd Voice* reported Nicholas II's escape: "Yesterday at Smolny, the news was received that Nicholas II has managed to escape from Tobolsk. The Military Revolutionary Committee has sent an urgent demand [for] the immediate preparation of a train of 15 carriages to send 500 sailors to Chelyabinsk, suggesting that they take all measures to ensure the train makes haste." (Khrustalëv, n. 392, pp. 667).

Wrote English dictation before dinner. We spent the evening in my study. J[ohnson] returned at 10 1/4. The weather in the afternoon was semi-clear, -6°.

At Brest-Litovsk, peace talks have been conducted over these past few days.[179] Supposedly any day now, German officers will arrive in Petrograd, they say, for demobilisation of the Russian army. This is the kind of shame that Russia lives to see!

6 December. Got up late. Took a walk in the garden. To breakfast arrived: Olga P, Ekaterina P with Mikhail P, then the Andreevs, Alyosha, Alexander N. They all came over to J[ohnson']s, where a grandois table was prepared for tea. (I forgot to mention that Tatiana P arrived at 3 1/2). After tea and until 7 1/2, we listened to music - F. Ramsh played the accordion, Domenici the guitar, and Alexander N took turns on the piano with J[ohnson]. Then we transferred to our house, some in sleighs, others used their own legs, - I, of course, walked. Around 8 1/2, we sat down to dinner, - candles were lit, as electricity refused to turn on. The dinner was very lively, - Ekaterina I. Made two long toasts, Prince M. P. [Putyatin] made one toast, and J[ohnson] as well. At the end of dinner, Domenici and Ramsh played. The guests left at 10 1/4. The weather was overcast, -3-5° deg. The Shleifers and their children stayed the night. (Miss N[im] and Ivan Ig. had breakfast, had tea and dinner with us).

7 December. Thursday. Gatchina. Before breakfast, I took a walk around the garden. Andrei I. arrived for breakfast and stayed until 3 o'cl. Then Nadezhda D came over. Natasha walked her home with Tatiana P. Alexander N and I worked in the garden on the large alley. After tea, I rested, then wrote in English. Before dinner, we all sat in the school room, the children danced, and I did a squat dance, but not very successfully, as I kept hitting the floor. At 9 o'cl, everyone went to the cinema, - while I stayed and played the guitar. The weather was overcast, 4°.

Lately, there are battles on the Don between the Cossacks and Bolshevik units. In Kiev, the Ukrainians have disarmed the Bolsheviks, - the Rada

---

[179] **"peace talks"** Peace talks between the Soviet regime and the Central Powers were in session at Brest-Litovsk from 19 November until 2 December 1917.

[Ukrainian Parliament] will not submit to the Bolshevik government. In Petrograd, the destruction of wine storehouses continues, lots of shooting and drunks.

The Shleifers and their children continue staying here.

8 December. Friday. Gatchina. In the morning, I jogged around the garden several times, then Alexander N read to me before breakfast. At 2 1/2 I went to a hill near the house on Bagovutovskaya, where we slid down with the children, Miss Neame and Alexander N, and I. Ig. came too. We all frolicked like children, and rolled around in snow. Then I took a walk around the garden with Natasha, Tatiana P and Olga A. After tea, I played the billiards with A. N. Then I lay down for 45 minutes. Before dinner, I wrote English dictation. In the evening, I played the guitar, then billiards with Alexander N, moreover I won only one game out of six. The weather was overcast, -4-6°.

9 December. Saturday. Gatchina. Jogged around the garden in the morning, did 6 versts. At 2 1/2, went to the hill, where we slid down with the children and Miss Neame, then we poured water on the hill, Vasily helped us. Returned home at 4 1/2. After tea, I played the guitar with Domenici intil 7 o'cl. Then wrote a letter to Alyosha in the evening, I took turns playing the billiards with A. N., then J[ohnson]. The weather was overcast, windy, -4°,- 6°,- 4°.

10 December. Sunday. Gatchina. Took a walk in the morning, then read. From 2 1/2 until 3 1/2, I slid down the hill with the children and Miss Neame. At 4 o'cl. Tatiana P and I walked to J[ohnson's], while Natasha and O. A. came there in a sleigh. Also Nadezhda D and O. D. Durova came to tea. After 6 o'cl, they left, and soon I too went home, - the ladies later came in a sleigh. In the evening, Nadezhda D and Olga D came over for a game of bridge, while I played billiards with J[ohnson]. I went to bed at 12 1/4, while the guests stayed until 3/4 to one [in the morning]. The weather was overcast, -4-5°.

11 December. Monday. Gatchina. Around 11 o'cl, I went to the hill, where we worked with Miss Neame and Boradulin, we extended the drain in the kitchen garden and poured water. At 2 1/2, the Shleifers left to Petrograd.

At 2 1/2, we worked on the hill again, brought the snow up to the top of the hill, worked until 4 o'cl. O. D. Durova came to tea. Before dinner, I wrote English dictation. In the evening, I played the guitar, we sat in my study.

J[ohnson] came from Petrograd at 10 o'cl with very interesting news. They say that a German peace delegation will soon arrive in Petrograd. The weather was overcast, 10-6 deg.

12 December. Tuesday. Gatchina. In the morning, jogged around the garden, as usual, - now I can easily do 5-6 laps without stopping. Then I read. At 2 1/2, I went to the hill, where worked with Miss N[im] and two horse grooms, while Baby was sliding down this entire time in a basket with Felix. At 4 1/4, I came home. Natasha took a ride in a sleigh with Olga A. After tea, I played the guitar, then wrote English dictation. In the evening, we sat in my study. The weather was sunny at times, 10°.

Received a letter from Xenia in Ai Todor.

13 December. Wednesday. Gatchina and Petrograd. At 9 1/2, Natasha, Olga A, Johnson and I went to Petrograd. In the train compartment we had an interesting conversation with two interlocutors. From the train station, we went to Alyosha's in an automobile, which was sent by good acquaintances. Soon Natasha went to run some errands with O. A. and J[ohnson], while Alyosha and I walked over to Margarita Vasilievna's for breakfast, where others arrived as well. Besides us, there were Zinaida Ivanovna and Lyapunov. After 3 o'cl, I walked to Morskaya, to [see] a mobile exhibit with Margarita V, Lyapunov, Olga A and J[ohnson]; a paucity of paintings and even fewer good ones. From there, J[ohnson] and I headed to the Putyatins' for tea, and at 6 o'cl we went to the Shleifs, where Natasha and Sergei Petrovich were. By 7 o'cl, Natasha, Alyosha, Alexander N, J[ohnson] and I returned to Alyosha's. Olga P, Ekaterina P and Mikhail P [Putyatins] came to dinner. In the evening, we practiced music, - M. P. sang. At 12 o'cl, the guests left. The weather was overcast, it snowed occasionally, 4°.

14 December. Thursday. Petrograd. In the morning I stayed home with Alyosha and read. Natasha with J[ohnson] and Olga A went to the bank,

which turned out to be shut by the soldiers and sailors, just like all other banks as of today. Had breakfast all together at Alyosha's. In the afternoon we all dispersed again, to do our own errands. J[ohnson] and I went to the tailor Grenfeldt, and then to Drozhdin, Kirkhner and Surov shops. Returned to Alyosha's in a cab by 4 1/2. A.N. Frolov came for tea, and a bit later Sergei A[leksandrovich], who arrived from Moscow today. Around 7 o'cl, they both left, and Mme Gubareva came to see me, who showed me how to do electric head massage. At 8 o'cl we went to dinner at the Putyatins, where we stayed until 10 o'cl. By this time Andreyevs, Praskovia I. and Alexander N arrived there to play cards. Natasha, O A and I went to Margarita Vasilievna's (Moika, 99). There besides us were Zinaida Ivanovna and B. Ya. Lyapunov. We sat in front of a fireplace, and looked at albums, M. B.'s pictures. After tea, that is at 12 o'cl, we went to sleep at Alyosha's. The weather was overcast, 2°, there is a lot of snow.

15 December. Friday. Petrograd and Gatchina. Before breakfast Natasha went out with O. A. and J[ohnson]. Sergei A[leksandrovich] came over at 12 o'cl, and we discussed the Brasov business. At 2 o'cl. D Gr Balakhovsky and Rosenberg arrived, - Shleifer also came. We talked about Brasov and Derugin. At 3 3/4 I went to Millionnaya with J[ohnson], - he to the Putyatins, and I to Count P. Benckendorf, where I stayed for 3/4 of an hour, and then returned to Alyosha's with Natasha, where after tea we, i.e. N., O. A., J[ohnson] and I, went to Gatchina on a 5 o'cl 40 min. train. From the station J[ohnson] and I dropped by his apartment, then walked home on foot. Had dinner at 8 o'cl, and in the evening I wrote three days in the diary. The weather was overcast, 2-3°.

16 December. Saturday. Gatchina. In the morning I jogged in the garden. Nadezhda Dmitrievna came to breakfast and stayed until 3 3/4, then Natasha and Olga A walked her home and, besides that, took a walk in Priorat. I only walked in the garden. From 4 3/4 to 7 1/2 I played the guitar with Domenici. J[ohnson] did not have dinner with us, as his sister with husband, daughter and son came to see him. In the evening I wrote English dictation, then helped Natasha and O. A. paste newspaper clippings into an album. The weather was overcast, 4°.

17 December. Sunday. Gatchina. In the morning I jogged in the garden. We were expecting guests from Petrograd for breakfast, but no one arrived. In the afternoon Natasha and O A went to buy flowers from Petrik, while I worked in the garden until 4 1/2. Around 5 1/2 Margarita V and Lyapunov arrived. Koton came to dinner. In the evening Lyapunov played the piano. Margarita V and Lyapunov left at 10 1/2. The weather was overcast, 2-0°.

18 December. Monday. Gatchina. At 9 1/2 Natasha went to Petrograd with J[ohnson] and Olga A (the latter is leaving to Moscow tonight). Before breakfast, which was at 12 o'cl, I jogged in the garden, as usual, only in a sweater and without a hat, and then read the month of May 1908. At 2 o'cl headed across Tatarsky overpass on skis, then to the left via a field to the stone gates, which are at Tsarskoselskoe highway, then turned right at the clearing and walked the entire grove around the edge. Returned home at 4 1/2. I was awfully hot, despite the fact that I was dressed lightly. I walked almost without stopping, - probably walked about 12 versts. After tea I lay down for a bit. Then I wrote English dictation. Had dinner with Ivan Ig, then wrote a short letter to Xenia and a postcard to Mama, and after that I played the billiards with I. Ig. The weather was wonderful, sunny with a full absence of air movement, 9°, 12°. Natasha is spending the night at Margarita V's on Moika.

19 December. Tuesday. Gatchina. Got up late. Read before breakfast and after, until 3 o'cl. In the afternoon Tata rode Fanze, and Baby, in the garden with Ponka, in a tiny sleigh. I walked in the garden from 3 o'cl to 4 o'cl. After tea I played the guitar, then wrote in Baby's diary. Natasha returned at 7 o'cl 10 min. After dinner we read newspapers and looked at English magazines. J[ohnson] arrived from Petrograd at 10 1/2. I wrote two postcards - to Maria V and princess Orbeliani, both to Crimea. The weather was dark, it snowed in the afternoon and evening, 3°. I got a letter from Maria V.

20 December. Wednesday. Gatchina. In the morning I did not stay in the garden for long, then read. At 3 1/4 Natasha and I walked to the Reiers, who have moved to Lutzevskaya, to Burakov house, near *Realnoe* School. There were: Nadezhda D, Father Strakhov, the engineer Ilyin and Shtal

with his wife. We stayed with them until 5 o'cl and had tea. Then I took Natasha to Elena K, and took myself home in a small sleigh. Until 7 1/2 I played the guitar with Domenici. In the evening J[ohnson] arrived from Petrograd, and I played a game of billiards with him, and also we read newspapers. The weather was overcast until 2 o'cl with 1/2°, 4°, 8°.

21 December. Thursday. Gatchina. Spent the morning as usual. Nadezhda D came to breakfast and brought everyone a little gift. Before tea I jogged in the garden. N. D. left at 5 o'cl and Sophie too. Then I played the guitar. Around 6 1/4 Dmitri Mikhailovich Kravchinsky arrived, a charming Lisino hermit. The last time I saw him was in Lisino in 16 June. Before and after dinner we all sat in the sitting room and had an interesting conversation and exchanged photographs. He is spending the night with us, and tomorrow at 8 o'cl in the morning he is going to Petrograd for errands and on Saturday returning back to Lisino. He has lived in Lisino for 33 years, but is now planning on leaving. The local peasants set up a school at the palace, despite the fact that nearby is a large empty house, which would have been much more comfortable. The weather was windy, snowstorm, 6°, barometer 721.

22 December. Friday. Gatchina. At 9 1/2 Natasha and J[ohnson] went to Petrograd, that is, they were supposed to go, but were not able to, as one train, the local, was not released due to the absence of its caboose, and the long distance one was full and its windows were broken. I worked in the garden, cleared the paths, which were under deep snow. Had breakfast at 12 o'cl. Then N[atasha] and J[ohnson] went to the Baltic Station, but they struck out there, specifically: the train cars were not heated so they returned home at 2 o'cl. From 2 to 4 o'cl I worked in the garden, cleared the paths with a shovel, and also walked the triangle with Ponka. After tea Natasha and I took a little walk in the garden, and then played the guitar, and before dinner wrote English dictation. In the evening A. K. Reier came over and stayed until 11 1/2. The weather was sunny, 12°, strong wind.

23 December. Saturday. Gatchina. In the morning I jogged in the garden, and also worked in the garden, cleared the paths. We were expecting two Englishmen - Bruce and Brooks, for breakfast, i.e. at 2 o'cl, but they never came. We sat down to breakfast only at 2 o'cl 20 min. At 4 1/2 I walked

to J[ohnson's] apartment, while Natasha rode there in a sleigh with J[ohnson]. Nadezhda Dm came over, and B. Ya. Lyapunov a little later, and we all had tea. At 6 1/2 I walked N. D. home and returned to J[ohnson's], and at 7 1/4 we were told that Ekaterina P, Mikhail P and Domenici came to our house, and I headed there on foot, while others in a sleigh. Sat down to dinner a little after 8 o'cl. In the evening M. P. played the billiards with J[ohnson], while I played the guitar with Domenici in the sitting room, and also Lyapunov played the piano a little. After tea the guests helped us decorate the fir tree, which turned out looming very festive and fluffy. It was cut down by the gardener Andrei yesterday in the Orlovsky grove. The guests are staying the night with us, while Domenici in another house. Diverged at 1 o'cl 15 min. The weather was wonderful, sunny and mild, 16°, 21°. Horrible things are happening on railroads, from masses of people and drifts full ruin and chaos.

24 December. Sunday. Gatchina. Before breakfast Natasha and I showed the garden to Lyapunov. Then I played the guitar with Domenici for a bit. Just after 4 o'cl the frozen Shleifers came over with the children, they rode on Baltiyskaya for 2 hours 45 min[utes]. The train cars are no longer heated, this is presumably considered a luxury. Around 4 o'cl I took a walk in the garden. At 4 1/2 the following came to see us: Nadezhda D with Sophie and Vera A., as well as Ivan Ig. After tea in school-room we went down and lit up the tree in the dining room, only candles were burning. Before dinner we sat in the sitting room, played the piano, Domenici played the guitar. After dinner, did the same. At 10 1/2 Lyapunov left together with Domenici, while Nadezhda D at 11 1/4. The weather was overcast, windy, snowing hard, 13°, 7°, 13°, barometer 710.

25 December. Monday. Gatchina. Took a walk in the garden before breakfast. Alyosha arrived at 2 o'cl. From 3 o'cl to 4 o'cl I went to the hill with Alexander N, which is now high, and slid down in a new sled, - I slid rather unsuccessfully and buried the radish almost every time. At this time Dvorzhitsky arrived, who was taking a walk with Natasha and Tatiana P. After tea, i.e. at 5 1/4, Father Strakhov arrived to praise Christ, and then along with the deacon they had tea. After their departure Dvorzhitsky, the children, and I built a tower from wooden blocks, and then we all went downstairs, lit up the tree, danced around it and played cat and mouse. The

children put on masks and marched in such a comical manner. Around 9 3/4 we all rode to J[ohnson'] in two sleighs, where we had tea and stayed until 12 1/2. Alyosha and Dvorzhitsky stayed the night at J[ohnson's]. The weather was sunny, 13°, 19°, 16°.

26 December. Tuesday. Gatchina. In the morning I walked on skis for an hour and 1/4, skied down Gernetovskaya and entered the Zoo through a gap in the fence, made a circle on Martyashkin meadow, exited through a gate and walked home past the infirmary. There was so much snow that one may think one is in a forest. To breakfast came: Alyosha, J[ohnson] and Dvorzhitsky, who left for Petrograd at 2 1/4. Alexander N and I went to the Kotons, who recently moved to a government apartment near the palace infirmary. Natasha and the Shleifers came there in a sleigh, and a little later J[ohnson] came as well. We had tea. Koton's brother's wife is living at his house, - besides there was a Cossack (from the Don) and the pilot Alexandrov. The apartment is very cute on the lower floor. At 6 1/4 we left them, - everyone except me rode in sleighs, but I got home at the same time they did. Before dinner I played billiards with A. N. In the evening I played a game of billiards with Alyosha, after which he played most with A. N., while Natasha played the same game with T. P. I went to bed early. The weather was overcast, it was snowing hard, windy in the morning, -16°, -14°, -11°, barometer 720.

27 December. Wednesday. Gatchina. From 11 o'cl until 1 o'cl I skied, entered the Zoo through the Kurakin Gates, reached the Kaskadny Gates, proceeded through the palace park walked to the greenhouses and exited to the street, walked by the palace through Priorat and via Olginskaya walked home. Towards the end of breakfast, Olga P and Praskovia I. arrived from Petrograd. At 4 1/4 Natasha and I went to have tea at M. F. Nabokova's and Nadezhda D's, where O. D. Durova was as well. We stayed with them until 6 1/4, then stopped by J[ohnson's] for Olga P and P. I. and went home with them. J[ohnson] came in a cab. Before dinner we looked at magazines, and after dinner some played most, some the billiards, while Domenici and I played guitars in the billiards room. O. P., P. I. and Alyosha went to J[ohnson's] to spend the night, - departed at 12 o'cl. The weather was overcast, 8°, 14°, 16°. Tonight from midnight was daylight savings, i.e. one hour back.

28 December. Thursday. Gatchina. At 11 o'cl skied down Olginskaya to J[ohnson's]. Around 12 o'cl O. P., P. I., J[ohnson] and I walked back via Alexandrovskaya. Nadezhda D came to breakfast. At 2 o'cl O. P. and P. I. left. The Reiers came to see us. (Forgot to mention that Elena K came to breakfast). Around 4 o'cl Natasha, A. N. and I walked all the guests home. (Forgot to mention that Tatiana P also left after breakfast). After tea Natasha played most with A. N., while I read. After the children's dinner we played with them in the dining room, they danced *à la russe*. In the evening Natasha played kosti with A. N., while I [played] billiards with J[ohnson]. The weather was sunny, mild, -20°, -22°, -16°.

29 December. Friday. Gatchina. At 9 1/2 Natasha went to Petrograd with J[ohnson]. I read with Alexander N upstairs. At 10 1/2 I had breakfast there as well and headed on skis with Vasily across the nearest grove through a ditch and straight across fields to the edge of Tsarskoslavyansky Forest (the bosons and village Bolshoe Zamostie was to the right). At the clearing we went more than a verst into the forest, then turned right at another clearing, crossed Somerskaya road, walked another verst and a half and took the clearing to the right, and walked to the grove via the meadows that spreads from the village Pustoshka to the colonists. We walked through this grove and came out to the road that leads to Zagvozdka. Having reached the Warsaw Station, we carried our skis and walked home on foot. Arrived home at 5 o'cl. In total we walked for 5 hours 45 min[utes] and approximately from 25 to 30 versts. In the forest we saw two capercallies, passing the first current, and besides [saw] that a good amount of elk hoof prints, as well as foxes. Walked without stopping. In the field the wind was very strong. After tea, that is milk, I lay down to rest and fell asleep for an hour. At 8 1/2 I had dinner with A. N., after which he went to Kotons to play cards, while I played the guitar. At 10 1/4 I went to the Baltic Station to pick up Natasha, who it was rumored was supposed to arrive. Two trains came, but Natasha did not arrive, and I returned home at 12 o'cl. A sleigh was also dispatched to the Warsaw Station, but also in vain. I went to bed at 2 o'cl 40. The weather was semi-sunny, a strong and very cold wind, -18°, -16°, -12°, in the evening a snowstorm started.

30 December. Saturday. Gatchina. In the morning I went to the hill and watched the children slide down. After breakfast, which was at 12 o'cl, Aleksei Semyonov stopped by to see me, who returned the other day from the 2nd Cavalry Corps. The Corps practically no longer exists. After that I took a walk, took the streets to Konnetable, then returned via Priorat. Natasha arrived at 3 1/4 and travelled endlessly. Yesterday she had no intention of returning home at all, someone got it all confused. After tea I played the guitar with Domenici until 7 1/2. In the evening N[atasha], Tatiana P and I went to Elena K, where we had tea and stayed until 12 o'cl. At her house were: Kalinin, her niece, Kostya, two Chukhnovskys and two [*Realnoe* students]. The weather was semi-clear, mild, -10°, -16°.

31 December. Sunday. Gatchina. From 10 3/4 to 12 3/4 I walked on skis in the palace park (the Birch Gates, pontoon bridge, long island, past the palace, Admiralty and came out by the Birch Gates again). After breakfast A. N. read to me, and at 3 1/2 N[atasha] and I took a walk down Nikolaevskaya and returned via Alexandrovskaya. I lay down to rest for an hour. At 6 o'cl Father Strakhov led a prayer service, after which he had a snack with us and stayed until 7 1/2. I wrote in the diary until 8 1/2. Then read. At 12 o'cl we sat down to supper and not as much to greet the new year as to see off the cursed year 1917, which brought everyone so much evil and misery. The children were also at the table, of course except Baby. We lit up the tree. Parted around 1 1/2 o'cl. The weather was sunny, mild, in the morning -15°, -20°.

January 1918

1 January. Monday. Gatchina. From 11 o'cl until 1 1/2 Vasily and I skied, - from Gernetovskaya St[reet]. We walked up to the Zoo, walked along Matyashkin meadow, past the Farm to the Black Gates, through parade ground to Priorat, walked quickly through the center of the park. When I got home, everyone was already sitting at the table. Then three officers of 2nd Brigade: Mirovich, Osipov and von Witte, came over with greetings, - they had a snack and stayed until 4 o'cl. After their departure we all walked over to the other house, where they had a Christmas party for the children of the staff, there were 14 children. They each got a book and 5 rubles. After we returned home, Nadezhda D and Reier came over, and we had

tea. The guests left at around 6 o'cl and at this time Boris Ya. L. arrived. Before dinner I played billiards with A. N., and in the evening Boris Ya. played the piano. The weather was wonderful, in terms of beauty, bright sun, all trees covered in snow, -22°, -19°, -22°.

2 January. Tuesday. Gatchina. In the morning I took a bit of a walk on skis through the streets, then sat in the sitting room with Lyapunov. In the afternoon we sat in sitting room, Lyapunov and A. N. took turns playing the piano. Natasha washed her hair until 3 1/2, and by this time I had gone skiing with Vasily. We walked through the entire Tatar crossing and to the right through the field towards the far edge of the grove, then returned home through the ravine across the entire grove we arrived at 5 o'cl. Sat in the sitting room before dinner, looked at albums, and I also wrote English dictation with Miss Neame. In the evening we played billiards. In the morning the weather was sunny, windy, -22°, -16°, -14°, -13°.

3 January. Wednesday. Gatchina. In the morning I took went on skis through town. B. B. Balashev arrived for breakfast and stayed until 4 o'cl. Then I skied (Tatar crossing, to the right through field to crossing, to cathedral and via Nikolaevskaya). Natasha took a walk with A. N. and Boris Ya. After tea we sat in the sitting room and read newspapers. I played a game of billiards with A. N. Before dinner Natasha, Miss Neame and I had a serious talk with Tata. Tata has a very difficult personality. After dinner we went to the cinema for *Slave of Women*. The weather was windy, snowstorm, -4°, -10°. The Council of People's Commissars gave an order to arrest the [Crown Prince] of Romania. In the morning Tatiana P tried to go to Petrograd but unsuccessfully, she got on to the train to Tosno and got out at the Baltic Station, from where she had to walk alone through snow drifts back to Gatchina. She went to Petrograd in the afternoon, and this time, having learned a bitter lesson, she took the right train.

4 January. Thursday. Gatchina. In the morning I walked on skis for an hour and a half with Vasily (Tatar crossing, to the left via meadows until Tsarskoselsky crossing, then along the edge of Orlov grove and home via Krasnoselskaya highway). In the afternoon I played billiards with A. N., and at 3 1/2 Natasha, A. N., Lyapunov and I took a bit of a walk, and at 4 o'cl Lyapunov left, while we went to see our newly purchased cow. After

tea Tatiana P returned. I played the guitar, and then wrote English dictation. In the evening I read, then Miss Neame massaged my head. The weather was overcast, mild, -10°, -13°.

5 January. Friday. Gatchina. In the morning ride horseback, rode around Priorat (Baltiiskaya train station and back through town). Then did gymnastics. After breakfast I received two officers of the [Lifeguard] Jaeger Regiment: Khodnev and Debagory Mokrievich. When they left, Klevezal came over in a very wretched state, - he returned from the front on 2 December, and on the 25th his wife passed away, - lately his life at the front was bad, he lost weight and suffers from dyspnea. From 4 to 5 o'cl I went skiing with Vasily. Walked through the grove, turned right and returned via sleigh road. Reier came to tea and brought buns as a gift, and around 6 o'cl Ekaterina P and Mikhail P and Alyosha came over. After the children's dinner we lit up the tree and played with the children. In the evening everyone played various games, kosti, billiards, I played the guitar. The weather was overcast, mild, -12°, -13°.

6 January. Saturday. Gatchina. At 11 o'cl I went to the *Realnoe* School church with Putyatin and Alyosha. Natasha was feeling a bit unwell, and she got up late. Before breakfast I played billiards with the prince. In the afternoon we played *probka*, and at 3 o'cl I went skiing with Vasily and walked into the grove and returned by 4 1/2. Elena K came over for tea and stayed until 6 o'cl, then I played the guitar with Domenici. The children lit up the tree and danced and played, while we, the musicians, played. Kotons came to dinner. During dinner we lit up the tree for the last time. In the evening we initially played some billiards, *kosti*, and cards, while I practiced music with Domenici, and then almost everyone played lotto in the sitting room, - I did not win even once and was feeling annoyed. The weather was overcast, snowstorm almost the entire day, -7°,- 6°, -1°, -6°. After the lotto game we completely unexpectedly began playing probka and parted only at 2 3/4. Yesterday the Constituent Assembly[180]

---

[180] "**Constituent Assembly**" Elected in November 2017, the Constituent Assembly was intended to draft a constitution for Russia. The Bolsheviks received only 24 percent of the vote, with the Social Revolutionary (SR) Party winning an absolute majority of the seats. It met for little over one day before the Bolshevik forces closed it down by force.

opened under the chairmanship of [Viktor] Chernov, but according to rumors, there was already issued a decree for its dismissal. There were some peaceful demonstrations, which were shot at by the Bolsheviks. The whole fight is between the Bolsheviks and S[ocialist] R[evolutionaries] (but not those on the left).

7 January. Sunday. Gatchina. Got up late. Before breakfast played the guitar with Domenici, and before that with M. P. was learning a song with him. In the afternoon the guests played billiards, and besides that Nadezhda D, Olga D came over, and Sophie came over to see the children, who prior to that recited poetry to me, wonderfully well. After tea I took both ladies home and returned via Baggovutskaya with A. N. and Domenici. (Forgot to mention that at 2 o'cl A. N. Frolov and Dvorzhitsky arrived). Before dinner I played the guitar. In the evening Domenici and I practiced music again, while the others played *kosti* and billiards. At 10 1/2 A. N., Dvorzhitsky and Domenici left. We parted only around 12 o'cl. The weather was sunny and mild, -5°, -10°, -7°. In the morning the children took down the tree.

8 January. Monday. Gatchina. From 10 3/4 to 12 1/4 I went skiing with Vasily (past the cemetery, about three versts toward Tosno, then back home through the grove). I checked the speed with which we moved one verst, - 4 minutes. Natasha did not get up due to a slight cold. After breakfast we sat in her bedroom, and at 3 1/2 I took a ride with Putyatin in Orlov's sleigh, rode through Priorat, past the Baltic Station, the horse stables, the palace and back through town. After tea we went to Natasha and discussed Brasovo issues. At 7 o'cl Alyosha left for Petrograd, while I played billiards with M. P. In the evening E. P. played *kosti* with Natasha. I took a bit of a walk in the street, it was a moonlit night, and then played billiards, after which the prince played *kosti* with N. The weather was foggy, -3°, +1°.

9 January. Tuesday. Gatchina. In the morning jogged around the garden, then read. Natasha did not get up but feels better today. In the afternoon Putyatin and I went to J[ohnson's], who has a very bad cold. We stayed with him for 3/4 of an hour and went back home. Nadezhda D came to see Natasha, who stayed until 5 1/2. Before dinner I wrote English dictation.

J[ohnson] came to dinner after all. In the evening I played billiards with the Prince, and after tea we went to Natasha, who played *kosti* with the prince until 12 1/2. The weather was overcast, mild, +2°.

10 January. Wednesday. Gatchina. From 11 o'cl until 1 o'cl I rode horseback (Krasnoselskaya highway, Gatchina mill, Kipensky highway, past the palace and home). In the afternoon I played the guitar while the prince sang, then we played billiards. Domenici arrived around 5 1/2, and we played with him before dinner. In the evening we went to the cinema for *Unknown Hands*. After returning home, we practiced music for a bit - the prince sang, Domenici and I accompanied him. The weather was overcast, +1°, 1°, 5°. On the night of the 5th-6th [of January] the KDs [Constitutional Democrats][181] Shingarev and Kokoshkin were killed by Red Guards and sailors at the Mariinsky Hospital.

11 January. Thursday. Gatchina. In the morning I rode horseback 3/4 of an hour, then played the guitar with Domenici. After breakfast I played billiards with Mikhail P. At 3 o'cl Natasha went to the palace greenhouses with Ekaterina P. M. P. and Domenici took a bit of walk, while I skied until 4 o'cl. In the field there was wonderful light from the sunset. After tea I played with Domenici, and before dinner wrote English dictation, after which I did gymnastics. In the evening I played billiards with the Prince, then he played *kosti* with Natasha, while I practiced music with Domenici. The weather was wonderful, sunny, mild, 9, 15°.

(From the newspaper *Nashe Vedomosti*)

Destruction of the army.

Chief of Staff of the Supreme Commander-in-Chief Gen[eral] Bonch-Bruevich sent a telegram to Supreme Commander Krylenko:

"Complete anarchy. Many parts of the front are bare. On the Western Front there are only 160 bayonets counted per verst. The reserves are not replacing their comrades in the trenches. Tremendous number of

---

[181] **"KDs"** - The Constitutional Democratic (KDs, or "Kadets") Party was a moderate liberal party that favored a constitutional government for Russia. Outlawed by the Bolsheviks, their members and officials were subject to severe harassment and, in this case, murder.

experienced military commanders left at the elections.[182] The current command staff is not experienced. Staff and organizations will soon automatically end work, as there is no one to work. There is no one from the General Staff. The working conditions of the staff is horrible. The economy is completely devastated. The training and the order of the army is miserable. Orders are not followed. Masses of deserters. Those on leave are not returning. Communication is cut in many areas. Cavalry is almost destroyed. Fortified positions are falling apart. The wire has been removed for easier fraternizing and commerce. The onslaught of the enemy is impossible to endure. The only salvation of the army is to retreat behind natural borders."

12 January. Friday. Gatchina. At 10 1/2 Natasha, the Putyatins and Domenici went to Petrograd via the Baltic railroad (it is now impossible to ride on the Warsaw line, as there is complete disorganization). I had breakfast at 10 1/2 and started to ski, - walked around the entire Malogatchinskaya Grove, - started at the Tatar crossing and walked to the left, then came out on the Tosno branch and on it walked to a road to the cemetery, then turned right and walked straight home. Walked 2 and 1/2 hours. From 2 to 3 o'cl I rested, then read, that is after tea, which I had with the children at 3 1/2. Before the children's dinner I wrote English dictation. Then did gymnastics – "muscle control." At 7 1/2 I had dinner with Ivan Ig., then played the billiards with him and won all three games. After that I read. Went to bed around 11 1/2. Natasha stayed over at Margarita V's. The weather was overcast, 12°, 8°, 1°, +1/2°. Got a letter from Koka in Onnel.

13 January. Saturday. Gatchina. From 10 1/4 to 11 1/4 I rode on horseback, it was very slippery, only rode in town. Before breakfast I did gymnastics, read in the afternoon, then did gymnastics. After tea I wrote English dictation, after which did gymnastics again, muscle control. Had dinner with Ivan Ig., then played the billiards with him, then read. The weather is dark, +1 1/2. Natasha returns tomorrow at 12 o'cl.

---

[182] **"the elections"** – In the early period of Soviet rule, the Russian army was "democratized" and mandated the election of officers by the common soldiers.

14 January. Sunday. Read in the morning, then did gymnastics. At 2 o'cl arrived: Natasha, Margarita V, Alyosha, Johnson, Lyapunov and Dvorzhitsky. They sat down to breakfast. Around 3 o'cl Zinoviev arrived, and a little later Nadezhda D came over with Sophie and the little S. Reier. After tea Dvorzhitsky, Zinoviev and I walked Nadezhda D home and returned. From 7 o'cl until 8 o'cl I did gymnastics. At 10 1/2 Dvorzhitsky and Zinoviev left. Natasha played *kosti* with Alyosha, Boris Ya. played the piano, and J[ohnson] sang into the late hours. The weather was dark, +1 1/2°.

15 January. Monday. Gatchina. In the morning I went out with Vasily, in order to walk on skis, but the snow was falling through due to meltdown, so we returned home and I did gymnastics. Before breakfast Natasha and I came out into the garden with Margarita V and Lyapunov and took photographs. After breakfast I studied with Alyosha for a bit, and at 3 1/2 N[atasha], M. B., B. Ya. and I took a walk. Walked by the Priorat palace and walked past Filkino lake, - got into a sleigh at Kseninsky lane, on the way home B. Ya. fell out of the sleigh due to a jolt and there was a lot of laughter. After tea M. B., B. Ya. and Alyosha left. At this time A. M. Strizhevsky arrived, he was in Petrograd on business and tomorrow is leaving back to Voronezh. He left at 6 o'cl. After the English dictation I did gymnastics. In the evening we sat in my study, and then I played billiards with J[ohnson]. The weather was wonderful, March-like, cloudless, +8° in the sun, +2 1/2° in the shade.

16 January. Tuesday. Gatchina. In the morning I did gymnastics. From 3 1/2 to 4 1/2 o'cl Natasha and I took a walk on Nikolaevskaya, on Baggovutskaya ran into Elena K, who took a walk with us, walked on Lyutsevskaya for a bit, then on Alexandrovskaya and returned home at 4 1/2, and at this time Maria Ferdinandovna with Nadezhda D came over to see us, and also Andrei I. The guests stayed until 6 1/4. After the English dictation I did gymnastics. After dinner J[ohnson] and I played two games of billiards, then Miss Neame massaged my head, as usual. The weather was overcast, 1 1/2°.

17 January. Wednesday. Gatchina. In the morning I did gymnastics. Andrei Ivanovich came to breakfast, he spent the night at his brother's. He

left at 2 3/4, and Natasha and I took a walk, - in priorat by the lake we ran into Ramsh, who walked us almost all the way home. When we were approaching the house, Domenici caught up to us. After tea I played the guitar with him until dinner. In the evening they went to the cinema, while I stayed home with Domenici and played until 10 1/2. The weather was overcast, 3 [degrees]. At the Romanian Front the famous Bolshevik Roshal was executed, the same one who was here in Gatchina in the early days of November.

18 January. Thursday. Gatchina. From 10 1/2 to 12 3/4 I skied with Vasily, - we walked around the entire Zoo in an hour and a half. The poor park now looks dead, not one animal, not one bird can be seen. In the afternoon Natasha and I took a ride in a sleigh across Priorat, past the palace and back through streets. Around 5 o'cl the Reiers came to see us and brought buns as a gift. After children's dinner I wrote English dictation, then did gymnastics. After dinner I played the guitar. The weather was overcast, it rained in the morning, +1.5°.

19 January. Friday. Gatchina. In the morning I did gymnastics. After breakfast Klevezal came to see me, and later N. N. Kalinin. At 3 1/2 Natasha and I went to the Reiers on Lyutsevskaya, where we had tea. Nadezhda D also came to their place. At 6 o'cl we left, walked N. D. home and took Baggovutskaya to our place, it was terribly dark, the lanterns were not lit. Before dinner I wrote English dictation, then did gymnastics. After dinner we read. At 9 1/2 J[ohnson] arrived from Petrograd. The weather was overcast, +1 1/2°. It has been uniformly spring-like for the past few days.

20 January. Saturday. Gatchina. In the morning I did gymnastics. At 12 o'cl Natasha and I went to church of the *Realnoe* School, where there was a memorial service for Olga S. and Vera S. After returning home, we had breakfast with J[ohnson], after which I went skiing with Vasily, - we walked through the railroad crossing, straight in bits across Tosno branch, then to the right on the road, which leads to the bisons, then turned right again and went back, - walked for an hour 3/4. Having changed, Natasha, J[ohnson] and I went to J[ohnson]'s, where Nadezhda D soon arrived, and a little later - Boris Yakovlevich L, Domenici and Ramsh. After tea Ramsh

played the accordion, while Domenici the guitar. Around 8 o'cl we headed home, all in sleighs, while I with Domenici on foot. Sat down to dinner at 8 1/2. In the evening we practiced music, - the musicians enjoyed great popularity while they played *Two Guitars under the Window*. Parted around 11 3/4. Nadezhda D also had dinner with us. The weather was semi-clear, mild, 1 1/2°.

21 January. Sunday. Gatchina. In the morning I walked on skis with Vasily, walked for only 3/4 of an hour in the field. Then I played the guitar before breakfast. Around 2 o'cl arrived: Alyosha, Dvorzhitsky and A. N. Frolov. Sophie and Seryozha P. came to see the children (Reier brought them). In the afternoon Natasha, Boris Ya., Domenici and I took a walk, walked past the Priorat house, where there was a crowd of people (came down the mountains), then we walked on ice of Filkino lake and took photographs, - sat by the big bathhouse. N[atasha] and B. Ya. got into a sleigh by J[ohnson's] apartment and rode through town to the Black Gates and back, while Domenici and I reached home by foot. The other guests, not having any energy, stayed home and walked around the garden. After tea we sat in the sitting room. Before dinner I played for an hour with Domenici. In the evening I took turns playing the billiards with Alyosha, A. N., Dvorzhitsky and Domenici. The weather was wonderful, spring-like, over +6° in the sun, +1.5° in the shade, 1°in the evening. All the guests stayed the night. Petrograd procession of the cross [sic].

22 January. Monday. Gatchina. At 9 1/4 departed: A. N. Frolov, Dvorzhitsky and Domenici. In the morning I read, and also studied with Alyosha for a bit. In the afternoon Natasha, Alyosha, J[ohnson], Boris Ya. and I took a walk, - walked on Baggovutskaya, on Bombardirskaya. Walked to Priorat from the Bolshoy Prospect and walked home from Kseninskaya. After tea, I was showing my snapshots and transparencies, to Boris Ya. After dinner we spent time in the sitting room. The weather was overcast, +1°, -1°.

23 January. Tuesday. Gatchina. Did gymnastics in the morning. After breakfast Boris Ya and I looked at my photography apparatus. Around 3 1/2 Natasha, B. Ya. and I took a ride in a sleigh, rode through the Zoo from Kurakin gates to the black lake, returned home past the palace. After 20

min[utes], i.e. at 4 o'cl 40, Boris Ya went to the train station. N[atasha] saw him off. I wrote English dictation, then did gymnastics. Read in the evening. J[ohnson] and Miss Neame went to the Kotons. The weather was overcast, snowed in the afternoon, 1°.

24 January. Wednesday. Gatchina. In the morning I did gymnastics and read. After breakfast we spoke with the housekeeper who came from Brasovo. A few hamlets were already destroyed there; all Brasovo inventory, horses and cattle were taken by the peasants; they have not touched the house so far. Pereverzev was sent away; he supervises the county land committee, but the peasants are not particularly listening to him and mostly act on their own. Around 4 o'cl Natasha, J[ohnson] and I walked to the corner of Baggovutskaya and Alexandrovskaya, from there J[ohnson] and I got into a sleigh and rode home along Baggovutskaya, - we tried P. I. Arapov's ginger horse, the one he is selling, - Natasha reached home on foot. After tea I played the guitar with Domenici until dinner. In the evening I played billiards with Domenici and then practiced music. The weather was overcast, +1°.

25 January. Thursday. Gatchina. At 10 1/2 Natasha went to Petrograd with Domenici. I had breakfast at 11 o'cl, and at 12 o'cl headed out with Vasily on skis, - went along Krasnoselskaya highway and, having walked 7.5 versts, turned left at the clearing, walked straight through the forest and, having come out at the old Krasnoselskaya road, walked left on it to Repuzi, then past the Gatchina mill, and along the Zoo fence towards home, where we arrived at 4 1/2. At 5 o'cl Reier came over and again brought a gift of buns. Before dinner I wrote English dictation, then did gymnastics for a bit. Had dinner with J[ohnson], then he read to me. The weather was overcast, windy, 4°. Natasha stopped by Margarita Vasilievna's.

26 January. Friday. Gatchina and Petrograd. At 11 1/4 J[ohnson] and I went to Petrograd via the Baltic line - the train departed 25 min[utes] late, traveled for two hours. Went straight to the Moika to Margarita Vas., where Natasha, Balashev and Zinaida Ivanovna were, they were finishing breakfast. In the afternoon Vasily and I went to Grenfeld, then to Lidval. From there I walked to the Putyatins, where we had tea, - a little later the

following came over there: Natasha, Margarita V, Boris Ya and J[ohnson]. Poor Ekaterina P is very ill, strong pain in the stomach. At 7 1/4 we returned to Margarita V's. After dinner Boris Ya and J[ohnson] practiced music, - we were served champagne and cherry cordial. We spent the evening very nicely and charmingly. Went to bed at 2 o'cl. The weather was overcast, I think 0°.

27 January. Saturday. Petrograd. Before breakfast I studied with Alyosha and Birukov, who stayed for breakfast, and besides them there were: darling Naryshkin (who recently returned from the front), Zinoviev, J[ohnson] and Zinaida Iv. From 4 to 5 o'cl, I lay down for a rest in the bedroom. Natasha returned for tea, and besides there were: Naryshkin, Brei, Alyosha and Boris Ya. With the latter I looked at his albums, very good snapshots. At 6 1/2 N[atasha], J[ohnson] and I went to the Baltic Station, where met with Olga P and Praskovia I. Waited for the train for 35 min[utes] and froze in the wind, but it never arrived. Went to the Warsaw Station, wanted to take the 8-o'clock train, but it consisted only of unheated compartments, dark and overcrowded, so we did not get on, and once more went to the Baltic Station, but there too we were unlucky, and the train leaving at 8 1/2 was full. Having said goodbye to our poor invited guests, N[atasha] and I returned to Margarita V's, where we arrived at 9 1/2, having frozen in vain for three hours. They fed us dinner and gave us tea, after which we went to bed, - this was at 12 o'cl. I was sleeping on an ottoman in the dining room. The weather was rather windy, overcast and cold, around 6°.

28 January. Sunday. Petrograd and Gatchina. At 11 1/4 Natasha, Olga P, J[ohnson] and I went to the Baltic Station and met Praskovia I. and Alyosha there. Arrived there 25 minutes prior to train departure, otherwise it's now impossible to find seats, - sat in second class, and everything was full a bit later. Natasha and I talked with a soldier (paramedic) until Krasnoe [Selo], he was a S[ocial]-R[evolutionary]. Dvorzhitsky joined us. Arrived in Gatchina at 2 o'cl and got home in three sleighs. Finished breakfast at around 3 o'cl. From 4 1/2 to 5 1/2 Alyosha, Dvorzhitsky, Domenici and I took a walk, walked around town. Dv. visited until 7 o'cl. While we were passing the Koton's, they joined us. After tea I played with Domenici until dinner, which was at 8 3/4. In the evening we played

billiards, *kosti*, the piano, and then lotto all together in the dining room. Parted late. The weather was overcast, 8°, 3°.

29 January. Monday. Gatchina. At 11 1/2 Olga P, Praskovia I., Alyosha, Domenici and I took a walk, while passing by J[ohnson]'s he joined us, while on Baggovutskaya Nadezhda D joined us. We came home for breakfast. Then I played the guitar with Domenici. Nadezhda D left around 3 1/4. After 4 o'cl we all headed to J[ohnson]'s on foot, - Alyosha and I were late and came around 10 minutes after the others. After 6 o'cl Alyosha and Domenici left to Petrograd via the Baltic rail line. We stayed until 7 1/2, then the ladies went home in sleighs, while J[ohnson] and I went on foot. After dinner I played billiards with J[ohnson]. The weather was overcast, 8°, 10°.

30 January. Tuesday. Gatchina. At 11 o'cl Olga Pavlovna and I took a walk along Baggovutskaya, Bombardirskaya past Konnetable, through Priorat, past J[ohnson]'s and home, - walked for an hour and a half. In the afternoon Natasha, O. P., Praskovia I. and I took a ride, I drove, - drove through the Zoo, i.e. from Kurakin Gates to the black [lake] and home across Priorat. After tea I read, then did gymnastics. After dinner I played the billiards with J[ohnson], the princess and Aunt Paranya sat and watched. Koton stopped by. The weather was overcast, around 6°.

31 January. Wednesday. Gatchina. From 11 o'cl until 12 o'cl 40 min. Olga P and I took a walk, walked along Baggovutskaya, Hospital Lane, Bolshoi Prospect, Priorat, past J[ohnson]'s, who joined us, and home via Alexandrovskaya. At 2 o'cl O.P., Praskovia I. and J[ohnson] went to Petrograd. At this time Pavel P arrived, and Sergei Petrovich a bit later. Around 3 1/2 I took a walk with P. P., - walked along Olginskaya, past the Warsaw Station, and then in Priorat, walked down by the house, and returned home along Baggovutskaya. After tea I played the guitar with Domenici until dinner. In the evening I first played billiards with him, then we practiced music. The weather was overcast, mild, 3°. J[ohnson] returned at 9 1/2. - Sergei Petrovich left at 1 o'cl.

February 1918

1/14 February. Thursday. Gatchina. As of today, the new style [of dates] was introduced. In the morning went skiing with Vasily for two hours. Entered the palace park through the Birch Gates. Went down the hill a few times, the one before reaching Holland, then went down the ledges, the ones near Karpochny pond – from there walked to Priorat and there also went down the hill near the house, there were no people at all. In the afternoon Natasha and I took a walk, walked down Baggovutskaya and returned via Alexandrovskaya. After tea we read, and at 6 ½ went to the *Realnoe* School church for an all-night vigil (tomorrow is the Meeting [of the Lord]). Returned home at 8 o'cl. I received an officer of Cherkessk Cavalry Regiment, Dombrovsky, who is hoping to get into a foreign military service. Read in the evening. The weather was overcast, in the afternoon it got clearer, 10°.

2/15 February. Friday. Gatchina. From 10 ½ until 12 ¾ I went skiing with Vasily, walked through the field directly to Tosno branch, then turned right, returned to the Western edge of the Malogatchinskaya Grove and went home. It was a very nice walk, as the old hard snow was covered with a few *vershki*[183] of fresh [snow]. After breakfast Natasha and I took a short walk, walked along Baggovutskaya and returned via Nikolaevskaya. To tea arrived: Nadezhda Dm. with Olga Dm. and Ilyin, - a bit later Reier came too. The guests stayed until 6 ½. Then we read and talked with Margarita Vasilievna and Boris Yakovlevich Lipupuchikov.[184] After dinner I wrote a letter. The weather was wonderful, sunny, 12°, 10°, 4° in the sun.

3/16 February. Saturday. Gatchina. From 10 ¼ to 11 ¼ skied in the field alone. Then did gymnastics. In the afternoon, Natasha and I rode in a sleigh (past the Priorat house, palace and past the Farm home via Mariinskaya St[reet]). Elena K and Mme Vargina came to tea. Domenici also came over at that time, and from 5 ¾ before dinner we practiced with him. The ladies stayed for dinner and stayed until 11 ¾. The weather was

---

[183] **"Vershki"** – unit of measure equal to 4.445 cm
[184] **"Lipupuchikov"** Michael's affectionate diminutive name for Lyapunov.

overcast, 8°, 4°, 3°. J[ohnson] returned from Petrograd at 9 ½. I played billiards with Domenici, and then the guitar.

4/17 February. Sunday. Gatchina and Petrograd. In the morning I skied with Vasily, - walked through the field, along the edge and back. Then played the guitar with Domenici. At 2 o'cl. 40 min. Natasha, J[ohnson], Domenici and I went to Petrograd by the Baltic line, - we sat in 2nd class, first [class] is no longer heated. In Petrograd we went directly to Margarita Vasilievna's, where we had tea. There were: K. D. Naryshkin, Steiner. Then I wrote a letter. At 6 ¾ we had a snack and then went to the ballet for *Raimonda* - sat in a loge next to the side imperial one, - with us were: Naryshkin, Boris Yak., J[ohnson] and Margarita V. During the break Olga P came with P P and Ta[mara] Karsavina danced. At 11 o'cl. we already returned to Moika. After supper Boris Yak. played the piano. Went to bed late. J[ohnson] went to sleep on Galernaya, while B. Ya. and K. D. stayed the night here. The weather was overcast, 1°.

5/18 February. Monday. Petrograd. Got up late. Alyosha came at 12 o'cl., and we studied. Boris Ya. and Vladimir Vasilevich had breakfast. At 2 ¾ Alyosha and I walked to Millionnaya 11, to see the Dutch ambassador Skavenius. From there went to the Putyatins, where I had tea and stayed until 5 3/4 , then with J[ohnson] and Vasily walked to the Moika. Doctor Westfalen was at Margarita V's. To dinner came: Olga P, Alyosha, Naryshkin and Boris Ya. O. P., Alyosha, V V and J[ohnson] left at 12 ¼. Margarita V danced the tango with Naryshkin. We went to bed only at 4 o'cl. Spent the evening merrily and laughed very much. The weather was wonderful, sunny and mild, 8°.

6/19 February. Tuesday. Petrograd and Gatchina. Got up late. From 12 until 1 ¼ Naryshkin and I took a walk along Morskaya and Nevsky to Anichkov Bridge and back. To breakfast came: Tatiana P, Alyosha and Boris Ya. Then I received, at first Mr. Jurgenson, who arrived from Ai-Todor, - the situation there is serious. After him Mme Etter was with me. Her brother Count Kleinmichel was killed in Evpatoria [Crimea]. After tea, that is at 4 3/4, Natasha, Margarita V, J[ohnson] and I went to the Baltic Station and to Gatchina, where we arrived at 7 1/2. In the evening wrote in the diary. The weather was overcast, 8°. The German High

Command has officially announced the end of the peace treaty with Russia. The German troops resumed maneuvers on the Russian Front.[185] Our troops received a command to resist.

7/20 February. Wednesday. Gatchina. From 10 ½ until 1 o'cl. Vasily and I skied, - we walked through the field, crossed the Tosno branch by the Large Overpass and reached the edge of Tsarskoslavyansky Forest, then back, - walked about 14 versts. In the afternoon I wrote a letter to Uncle Waldemar. Nadezhda D came to tea. Around 5 ½ Boris Yak. arrived. I practiced with Domenici before dinner. In the evening we played as well. The weather was wonderful, sunny, mild, [snow] melted in the sun, 6° in the shade.

8/21 February. Thursday. Gatchina. In the morning did gymnastics. At 3 o'cl. walked on skis alone, walked through the grove and reached the Tosno branch, then walked back on the edge. Reiers came to tea. Before dinner we read newspapers. In the evening J[ohnson] returned from Petrograd. The weather was sunny, 6°, 9°.

9/22 February. Friday. Gatchina. Read in the morning. In the afternoon walked on skis with Vasily, through the field, across the grove and to the right on the edge, back. Before tea I rested for a bit, took a nap. Before dinner I read, then we sat at Margarita V's, who rested on the couch. After dinner we went to J[ohnson]'s, where we had tea, then sat on the sofa, while J[ohnson] and Boris Ya. practiced music. Went home around 1 o'cl. the weather was sunny, 6°, 8°, 11°. The Germans continue offense. The People's Commissars announced holy war [*svennashnaya vojna*].

10/23 February. Saturday. Gatchina. From 11 o'cl. to 1 o'cl I walked on skis with Vasily, - we reached Orlovsky grove via highway, then along the edge walked to the right, crossed the Warsaw railroad and walked to the right also along the edge and then home. After breakfast I walked to J[ohnson]'s where I saw [blank space]. Returned home for tea, and by the house caught up to Natasha and Boris Ya., who were returning from a walk. Reier came to tea. From 6 ½ until dinner I practiced with Domenici.

---

[185] **"resumed maneuvers on the Russian front"** Negotiations of a treaty between Soviet Russia and the Central Powers ended on 10 February, and hostilities resumed.

In the evening we all sat in my study. The weather was sunny, mild, 3° in the sun, 10° in the shade.

11/24 February. Sunday. Gatchina. In the morning I practiced with Domenici for ¾ hour, then walked on skis with Vasily for an hour and a half, walked through the field, around the cemetery, across M. Zagvozdka to Priorat, there we came down the hill between pine trees, walked past J[ohnson]'s and went home. At 2 o'cl. arrived: Alyosha, Dvorzhitsky and Naryshkin. Around 3 ½ Natasha, Margarita V, Dvorzhitsky, Naryshkin, Boris Yak. and I took a walk to Olginskaya, a bit via Priorat and home via Nikolaevskaya. At 5 o'cl. Olga P, Praskovia I. arrived, and also Andrei Ivanovich, and Koton a little later. From 7 until 7 ½ I played the guitar with Domenici. After dinner, having acted out, not particularly well, the Revolutionary Tribunal, Dvorzhitsky and I walked to J[ohnson]'s, while all the rest went in a sleigh. We spent the evening very charmingly, first J[ohnson] sang accompanied by Boris Yak., and after tea I played with Domenici, then Margarita V danced the tango in the dining room with Naryshkin. After a light supper we went home, N[atasha] with Dvorzhitsky, Naryshkin with Domenici, and I with Margarita V and Boris Yak. The night was bright, although the moon was not visible. Went to bed at 4 ½. The weather was sunny only around 1 o'cl., 4°.

12/25 February. Monday. Gatchina. At 11 ½ I walked along Olginskaya to J[ohnson]'s, and from there returned for breakfast with J[ohnson], Alyosha and the ladies. At 2 ¼ Margarita V and Boris Ya. left to Petrograd, while we, i.e. Natasha, O. P., P. I., Naryshkin and I, went to take a walk (Nikolaevskaya, Priorat palace, Baggovutskaya and again Nikolaevskaya). Nadezhda Dm, Alyosha and Aunt Paranya came to tea. – they went to the Baltic Station, but could not go to Petrograd, as they would not allow without identifications, and they returned after an hour. Before dinner I played the billiards with Naryshkin. Around 10 1/4 Olga P, J[ohnson] and I went to J[ohnson]'s for some things. It was a wonderful quiet moonlit night. The weather was sunny from 3 ½ o'cl., 1°, 4°, 11°.

13/26 February. Tuesday. Gatchina. At 11 o'cl Olga P, J[ohnson] and I went to walk on Lutzevskaya. J[ohnson] went home, and we walked past the Priorat palace, Filkin lak and to J[ohnson]'s apartment, and from there with J[ohnson], Alyosha and Aunt Paranya to our house. After breakfast O. P., P. I., Naryshkin and Alyosha went to the Baltic Station, but despite having identification they weren't able to leave, and they all went to J[ohnson]'s, where Natasha and I walked on foot and had tea there. Natasha and I returned home by 6 o'cl. Reier then came over to see us. The guests departed via the Warsaw [Station]. Before dinner I did gymnastics. Read in the evening. The weather was sunny occasionally, 4°, 2°. The Germans occupied Pskov, Polotsk, Bobruisk, Revel.

14/27 February. Wednesday. Gatchina. Read in the morning, then did gymnastics. At 2 o'cl. Margarita V arrived. In the afternoon I took a bit of a walk, at first in the garden, then along Nikolaevskaya and Alexandrovskaya. Nadezhda Dm, Ilyin, and Reier came to tea, and later Elena K. around 5 o'cl. Boris Yak. arrived. Around 6 ¾ the guests left, and I practiced with Domenici before dinner. In the evening Boris Yak. played the piano. The weather was overcast, +2 ½ °.

15/28 February. Thursday. Gatchina. In the morning I went skiing with Vasily for ¾ of an hour. In the afternoon I took a walk, walked half the grove. Having returned home, I found everyone at the house on Baggovutskaya, - Natasha was looking over my old clothes, which were brought from the palace. Then Natasha walked Nadezhda Dm and Reier to the cinema, - Boris Yak. and I followed them and returned together with N. Alerinsky (head of the economics department at the Aviation school). Then I sat at Margarita V's, then did gymnastics. In the evening I dressed in my old sailor uniform which I had since 1895. Margarita V taught me [to dance] the tango in the dining room. Everyone left at 1 o'cl. The weather was sunny from 12 o'cl. until 3 o'cl., 4°, 2°. After the breakdown of the Brest[-Litovsk] talks, which ended with a slogan: "Peace treaty was not signed, the war is over," a week of calm passed, after which the Germans started offense on the entire Northern Front.

March 1918

16 [February]/1 March. Friday. Gatchina. At 11 o'cl. Vasily and I skied to Tsarskoslavyansky Forest and continued walking farther along the edge for about 3-4 versts, then turned right at the clearing and walked to a road

which leads to Chirkinsky guardhouse. We were 2.5 versts from the guardhouse. On the way we went to the house, i.e. to Gatchina. Before reaching the village of Korkozi, we walked to the right through the field and directly home, where we arrived at 3 3/4, - we walked about 25 versts. Having had breakfast, I lay down to rest and got up at 5 1/4 . Maria Ferdinandovna and O. D. Durova came to tea. Before dinner I read. In the evening I read in the study, while Margarita V fell asleep on the sofa, then I played the billiards with Boris Yak. The weather was sunny, but a rather strong wind, 3° in the shade. I walked on skis without a hat and only in a jumper.

17 [February]/2 March. Saturday. Gatchina. In the morning walked on skis with Vasily for an hour, - from Gernetovskaya we entered the Zoo, walked along Berezovyi, then to the left towards the river, along to cascade and back home. In the afternoon we sat and talked with Vladimir Vas., who came to breakfast. To tea came: Znamerovsky,[186] Ilyin and Reier. The guests stayed until 6 1/4, at 6 ½ Natasha went to the cathedral for an all-night vigil with Boris Yak, while I played with Domenici [sic] until dinner. In the evening Natasha, Lyapupunchik, Margarita V (Snowmaiden) and I sat on the sofa cozily squeezed together, and talked. I went to bed early, and at 11 o'cl. I had visitors who stayed for a while. The weather was semi-clear, mild, 2°, 7° in the evening.

18 [February]/1 March. [February]/3 March. Sunday. Gatchina. Lay on the sofa all day due to my stomach pains. Around 12 o'cl Westfalen arrived, - he left after breakfast. In the afternoon A. N. Frolov came ver. Everyone sat with me in the afternoon, after tea and in the evening. We sat upstairs in the little corner room. The weather was sunny, I think around 6°. The Russian delegation decided to sign the Brest peace treaty with Germany's

---

[186] **"Znamerovsky"** Piotr Ludwigovich (b. 1872 – d. 1918) A former gendarme officer from Gatchina, whence he was sent to Perm where he met the Grand Duke Michael again. They stayed in the same hotel. A. A. Volkov notes in his memoirs that "One day, he was called in for questioning. He replied in a sharp tone. He was rudely pushed into the courtyard and shot immediately." (cf. A. A. Volkov, *Okolo Tsarskoi sem'i*, p. 90-91)

new conditions,[187] which were worse in comparison to Hoffmann's[188] ultimatum from 21 February. The worse part consists of Russia losing: Ardahan, Kars and Batum.

19 [February]/4 March. Monday. Gatchina. Again spent the entire day upstairs. Read in the morning. Reier stopped by. In the afternoon Natasha, M.B., B.Yak., J[ohnson] and Koton sat with me. Had tea in the corner room, - Nadezhda Dm was there. Around 6 ½ Olga P and Aunt Paranya arrived. After dinner everyone came upstairs, - part of the evening I accompanied Margarita V, who played the mandolin. The weather was wonderful, sunny, mild, 2.5° in the shade. Everyone left very late. This morning a peace treaty was signed with Germany and its allies. Ioannchik was initiated as a deacon.

20 [February]/5 March. Tuesday. Gatchina. From 11 o'cl. until 4 ½ I stayed on the children's balcony. The weather was wonderful, mild, 21° In the sun. after breakfast Olga P, Aunt Paranya and Margarita V sat with me. We had tea upstairs in the corner room, - Reier was there. Before dinner Koton stopped by. In the evening we sat downstairs in the drawing room. O. P., Aunt Paranya and I went to spend the night at J[ohnson]'s. The weather was sunny all day, 4°. According to rumours, the Germans took Yamburg and Volosovo.

21 [February]/6 March. Wednesday. Gatchina. At 10 ¼ Vasily and I came home from J[ohnson]'s. before breakfast and until 4 o'cl. I sat on the children's balcony, although it was not as warm as yesterday, light wind. In the afternoon Olga P sat with me. After tea Aunt Paranya and Olga P left to Petrograd via the Warsaw [Station]. Around 6 o'cl. Natasha went

---

[187] **"Germany's new conditions"** The signing of the treaty of Brest-Litovsk between Soviet Russia and Germany took place on 3 March. Under the treaty, Russia lost Poland, the Baltic region, parts of what is now Belarus, Ukraine, and the Caucasus, most of which were occupied by German troops. This treaty was ratified by the VI Extraordinary Congress of the Council of Workers, Soldiers, Peasants and Cossack Deputies on 15 March 1918. On 27 August, an additional Russo-German financial agreement was signed in Berlin, in which Russia was obliged to pay Germany 6 billion marks. The Treaty of Brest-Litovsk was annulled by the Soviet Government on 13 November 1918, following Germany's defeat by the Western allies.

[188] **"Hoffmann"** General Max Hoffmann (b. 1869 – d. 1927) was chief of staff of the German armies on the Eastern Front and the principal negotiator at Brest-Litovsk.

with Boris Yak. to the Kotons and to take a walk, while Margarita V and I practiced music, - she played the mandolin, and I accompanied on the guitar, we played until 7 ½ o'cl. in the evening

[There are no diary entries for the rest of February, March and most of April 1918].

May 1918

25 [April]/8 May. Wednesday. Perm.[189] In the morning we read after breakfast, engineer Elzhanovsky and I. At around 3 3/4 o'clock Natasha, J[ohnson] and I went in two cabs to the Tupitsyns, where we had tea and ate a lot of delicious things. At 7 o'cl said goodbye to them, Natasha rode, while J[ohnson] and I walked home. In the evening Pyotr Nilovich Vtorov came to tea. The weather was nasty, windy, from night-time snow was on the ground in some places, 2°, by 5 o'cl the sun appeared for a short while.

26/9 May. Thursday. Perm. Read in the morning, took a walk on Torgovaya, Monastyrskaya in the afternoon, and walked back along the river. After tea Natasha and I lay down to rest. The Znamerovskys came to dinner and stayed until 11 1/2. The weather was partly cloudy, 2°.

27/10 May. Friday. Perm. Around 11 1/2 Borunov and I crossed to the other side of Kama in a boat (the settlement of Srednyaya Kurya), there we walked to the left along the edge of the woods, then, having come out to the river, crossed back. After breakfast the Dutch vice-consul Reed with an Austrian secretary came to see us - we served coffee to them. At 5 1/2 Natasha, J[ohnson] and I went to Petropavlovsk Cathedral, where the

---

[189] **"Perm"** On the evening of the 11 March 1918, on the orders of the Council of People's Commisars, Petrograd's secret police chief Moisei Uritsky despatched Michael Alexandrovich and Nicholas Johnson to Perm, almost 1,000 miles to the east, in Siberia. Michael was initially kept at a local hotel but was quickly jailed by the local soviet. In Petrograd, Natalia fought valiantly to have Michael released, and on 9 April, he was given his freedom, but was not allowed to leave Perm. Natalia arranged for their son, Count George Brasov, to be smuggled out of Russia by Miss Neame and left her daughter with friends. In May, Natalia was granted permission to follow Michael to Perm, where she was allowed to spend Easter Week with her husband. His diary resumes during this period.

Archbishop Andronik[190] served the Easter vespers service, - he served very well. In the evening I played the guitar. The weather was overcast, except in the evening, 2°.

28/11 May. Saturday. Perm. In the morning Borunov and I went headed to the other side of the Kama, where we walked in the forest to the right and reached the polygon. Returned at breakfast. In the afternoon Natasha, J[ohnson] and I went to flower shops unsuccessfully, then to Anna K.'s fish store (The store located at the corner of Bolshaya and Tomilinskaya streets), then we walked to Archimandrite Matvei (rector of the seminary). We liked being at his apartment, as we keep looking for a place to move to. They served us coffee and *paskha* - he was lying in bed, the poor thing, being ill. From there we returned home on foot from Monastyrskaya. At 8 o'cl we went to the theater, where they showed *The Dream of Love*. - Boregar came in to see us in the lower loge. Sergei A[leksandrovich] and Olga Tupitsyn sat with us. The weather was sunny in the morning, and the evening it snowed heavily for a short time, 2°. Ukraine had a coup. The Rada was exiled, General Skoropadsky was appointed Hetman of Ukraine. The Germans took Rostov and Taganrog.

29/12 May. Sunday. Perm. Read in the morning. In the afternoon P. N. Vtorov took photographs of me. Around 4 1/2 Natasha, J[ohnson] and I went to Madame Alina on Sibirskaya, where we had tea, and then they showed us the rooms, the house was very nice. When we returned home J[ohnson] and I took a walk along the river for a bit. J[ohnson] went to the theater at 8 o'cl, today was the final play. I went to bed early. The weather was sunny, 3°. The cabinet in Ukraine consists of Kadets and nonparty [members]. The bread makers' deputation filed a petition to Hetman Skoropadsky for reinstatement of the prerevolutionary country. At the Russo-Ukrainian front a peace treaty was agreed. On 7 May a [peace] treaty between Romania and the Central Powers was signed.

---

[190] **"Andronik"** Archbishop Andronik (Vladimir Nikolsky) shared the fate of the Grand Duke. In his memoirs, N. V. Zuzhgov, (one of the murderers of Grand Duke Michael), he noted that he forced Bishop Andronik to dig his own grave, buried him alive in it, and then shot directly into the ground. (cf. Khrustalëv, *Skorbnyi put' Mikhaila Romanova: ot prestola do Golgofy: Sb. Dokumentov I materialov*, Perm, 1996, p. 215.)

30/13 May. Monday. Perm. Read in the morning. At 3 o'clock Borunov and I headed to the other side of the river, where we walked to the right along the bank, walked about 3-4 versts, reached the dachas - returned partially through the forest. Crossed back on a little ferry-steamer. Returned home at 7 1/4. Before dinner, which was at 9 o'cl, I took a bath. In the evening P. N. Vtorov sat with us. The weather was sunny, pleasant, 8°. The Germans moved from Rostov to the Kuban. The Germans moved Mama to Kiev, probably Xenia, Olga and others are with her.

1/14 May. Tuesday. Perm. In the morning J[ohnson] and I went to see the militia, then sat in the little theater garden. In the afternoon J[ohnson] and I boated over to the other side of Kama, I rowed. We returned on a motor steamer, rather little boat. S. Tupitsyn came to tea. After an early dinner Natasha, J[ohnson] and I head to the theater, Shebuev gave a concert, other performers were in it too. The weather was sunny, mild, 10°.

2/15 May. Wednesday. Perm. Read in the morning. In the afternoon Natasha and I headed to Sredniaya Kurya in a row boat, and took a ferry on way back. Miss Kobyak[191] came to tea. Then I played the guitar. After an early dinner we headed to the theater, for a concert of (trio) musicians from Mariinsky Theater. Znamerovsky and Vtorov sat in the loge with us. After the concert they had tea with us. The weather was nice and sunny, 14°. Apparently besides Mama, everyone who was living in Crimea is also in Kiev now.

3/16 May. Thursday. Perm. Read in the morning. In the afternoon Natasha and I took a walk, went to shops and the small market on Monastyrskaya. After tea I took a walk along the bank for a bit with J[ohnson]. After dinner I played the guitar. The weather was sunny, 14°. In the afternoon we stopped by the Znamerovskys on Kungurskaya.[192] Before breakfast Pyotr Nilovich Vtorov came by to say goodbye, he left for Moscow, via steamer to Nizhny [Novgorod]. In the evening it rained for a bit.

4/17 May. Friday. Perm. In the morning I wrote letters - to Olga Pav[lovna], Alyosha, Tata and Dvorzhitsky. In the afternoon Natasha and

---

[191] **"Miss Kobyak"** The daughter of G. I. and V. K. Kobyak,
[192] **"Kungurskaya"** is back to Kungurskaya now

I took a walk, went to *Gostiny Dvor* [a shopping arcade], then passed by the Church of the Resurrection at the old cemetery, having walked around it via Siberia Street, and returned home. Before dinner I wrote a letter to Snow Maiden.[193] Natasha packed all evening, due to which we went to bed late. The weather was warm and partly cloudy, 14°. Natasha's departure was decided on yesterday, - very sad to be left alone again.

5/18 May. Saturday. Perm. Got up around 8 ½. At 9 ½ Natasha and I rode in a cabby to the 2nd Perm Station, behind us rode J[ohnson] and Ekaterina Danilovna. There we waited for the train on the platform for a long time. Ultimately the Siberian Express was about 36 hours late as it was supposed to arrive in the evening of the third day. Natasha got a seat in a small compartment of the international car, with an unknown lady. The train arrived at 12 o'cl., 10 min[utes]. V. M. Znamerovskaya also went. Natasha is traveling via Moscow. J[ohnson] and I returned in a horse cab. Stopped by the militia, then sat in the little theater garden for a bit. Had breakfast at 1 o'cl. Znamerovsky came over, and at 3 o'clock I took a long walk with him, - we boated to the other side of the Kama and walked along the bank to the train bridge, there we got into a row boat and crossed the river, and then returned home along the other side of the river, where we arrived at 7 o'cl. After dinner J[ohnson] went to see Boregar unsuccessfully, while Znamerovsky stayed another half hour. I played the guitar. The weather was nice, partly cloudy, 14°. I felt very sad after Natasha's departure, so empty, and everything feels different, and the rooms seem different.[194]

6/19 May. Sunday. Perm. In the morning took a walk with Borunov, while J[ohnson] went to run errands, we walked through the park above the river. Znamerovsky came to breakfast. He and I took a walk along the embankment, passed the shaft and returned via Torgovaya. Before dinner, which was at 7 ½ o'cl., I read. At 8 o'cl. The three of us went to the theater for the plays *My Baby* and *Beautiful Woman* – an awful farce. We sat in the lower left side loge as usual, during the break S. Tupitsyn and

---

[193] **"Snow Maiden"** *Snegurochka*, the name of a Russian fairytale character, was Michael Alexandrovich's nickname for M. B. Abakanovich.
[194] **"Natasha's departure"** This was the last time that Natalia and Michael saw each other.

Dobrodin stopped by. In the afternoon a minor thunder storm passed, in the morning 14°, towards the evening 8°. Yesterday after Natasha's departure a letter came in her name from Elena Konstantinovna [Gavriluk], and today [a letter] from Tata, and a postcard from Tatiana Pavlovna.[195]

7/20 May. Monday. Perm. In the morning I walked with Borunov to the shoemaker's shop, which closed right in front of our noses. After breakfast I walked around town with Znamerovsky, we also stopped by at the international panopticon – wax figures. After tea J[ohnson] and I crossed to the other side of Kama, where we took a short walk through the woods, and returned by motor boat. In the evening I played the guitar, while J[ohnson] and Pyotr L[udvigovich] made a report. The weather was occasionally rainy, 12°, In the morning I received a telegram from Natasha in Vologda – she is hoping to be in Moscow tomorrow morning.

8/21 May. J[ohnson], Vasily and I headed to the Perm Regional Extraordinary Commission for Combat Counter-Revolution, Speculation and Sabotage.[196] I received a document where I am requested to show up there daily at 11 o'cl. (Good people, tell me, what is this?) After this occurance I headed home, while J[ohnson] and Vasily went to run errands. After breakfast, Znamerovsky and I went to shop for boots and simple soldiers' staples. After 4 J[ohnson] and I boated to the other side of the river and walked to the right to the polygon and returned partially through the woods. Poor J[ohnson] got a foot stuck in a swamp. At 7 ¼ returned home. After dinner I played the guitar. J[ohnson] went to bed early, while Znamerovsky was counting on abacus. The weather was rainy, 12°. Received a postcard from Olga Pavlovna.

9/22 May. Wednesday. Perm. In the morning J[ohnson] and I walked to the Extraordinary Commission. Before breakfast and after I read. At 4 and ¾ J[ohnson] and I went to Barmin (former Agurov), where they treated us

---

[195] **Tatiana Pavlovna** Princess Tatiana Pavlovna Putyatina, sister of Olga Pavlovna.
[196] **Extraordinary Commission for Combat Counter-Revolution, Speculation and Sabotage** Usually referred to by its Russian acronym, Cheka, this was the Soviet secret police established in December 1917. It was the forerunner of all subsequent secret police organizations, including the KGB.

to some tasty things. Returned at 7 o'cl., I wrote a letter to Natasha in Moscow. Then J[ohnson], Znamerovsky and I went to the theater – a farewell benefit for Boregar, *A Doll's House* (Ibsen's) was playing. Tupitsyn S. sat with us. The weather was frustrating, it was raining, 5°.

10/23 May. Thursday. Perm. In the morning we went to the militia, where they asked why we no longer show up there. We answered that we show up to the Extraordinary Committee lately, where we were told that they would notify the militia, but of course [they] forgot to do this. Returned from the Extraordinary Committee. I read. In the afternoon Znamerovsky and I took a walk-in town. It was not possible to go out of town, there was too much mud. Got a haircut before dinner, an Austrian prisoner of war from Lvov, who seeks to return home, was cutting [hair]. Then I read and played the guitar. In the evening the three of us went to the Triumph cinema. Vasily and Borunov were there too. The weather was repulsive, in the morning there was snow on the rooftops, 4°. Received two telegrams from Natasha in Moscow, they passed it all to me not through telegraph by via Extraordinary Committee. Natasha arrived in Moscow on Monday morning. Poor Kirusha got really banged up on a motorbike. I also got two postcards from him en route.

11/24 May. Friday. Perm. Read in the morning. Read until 3 ½. Then J[ohnson], Znamerovsky and I went to Tupitsyns, where we had tea and stayed until 7 ¼, J[ohnson] played the piano. The Dobrotins and Nikolaevs were visiting them. Walked back along the embankment. After dinner I read. The weather was overcast until 6 o'cl., 1°.

12/25 May. Saturday. Perm. Read in the morning. J[ohnson] and I have been going to sign in every morning at the Extraordinary Commission. In the afternoon Znamerovsky and I headed past the Kama, as they say here, and walked along the bank to the Upper Kuria. Then walked to the polygon along the forest footpath, and returned to the Middle Kuria and to town in a row boat, arrived home at 7 o'cl. After dinner, two Americans came to see me – Mr. O'Brien and Mr. Hess. They are going to Vladivostok, if they can get through. The weather was sunny until 4 ½ in the morning and got cold towards the evening. The water in Kama rose a lot. Only today I found out from Tatiana Pavlovna's letter from Gatchina about the death of dear Prince Shervashidze. He died on 25 March, I think, at Ai-Todor.

13/26 May. Sunday. Perm. Read in the morning. After breakfast received Yablonovsky,[197] of course not for newspaper reports about me but only to have an interesting conversation with him. At 4 ½ the three of us went with the young Dobrotin. There were a lot of relatives – his parents, aunt, brother, sister and brother's wife. Left them only at 7 o'cl. Walked back along Kungurskaya towards the Cathedral. After dinner J[ohnson] went to the cinema with the old guard, while Znamerovsky and I read until 11 o'cl. The weather was sunny from 5 o'cl., 3°.

14/27 May. Monday. Perm. In the morning I read, at 3 o'cl. Znamerovsky and I crossed the river and walked to the polygon into the thicket of the forest towards the country road, on the road left through the forest, then through the clearing came out to Kama across from Sludsky Cathedral, crossed the river in a motor boat. Returned home at 6 ½. I think that we walked around 12 versts. I took a bath before dinner. Read in the evening, also played the guitar. The weather was overcast, except in the morning, 12°.

15/28 May. Tuesday. Perm. Read in the morning, in the afternoon also, until 4 ½, and after tea Znamerovsky and I took a walk on Pokrovskaya., walked to 2nd Perm [Station], made a circle to the right, unfortunately got into some very dirty places, then returned home along Monastyrskaya. Read in the evening, while J[ohnson] went to Boregar with a visit. The weather was sunny in the morning, and then it poured rain a lot, 14°. The leaves on some trees are starting to bud, Spring is awfully late, while in Gatchina the bird-cherry already finished blooming. Perm was declared to be in military situation. During the last few days they sent rather large amounts of Red Army companies to various inner fronts. Got a letter from Olga Pavlovna.

---

[197] **"Yablonovsky"** Sergei Yablonovsky was a journalist who wrote for *Russian Freedom*. He wrote a last account of the last known meeting with Grand Duke Michael by an outsider.

16/29 May. Wednesday. Perm. There were no newspapers from Petrograd for two days already, and for some reason no trains arrived from Moscow today. Read in the morning, and after breakfast played the guitar. At 4 o'clock J[ohnson] and I went to Tupitsyns, another family that lives next to them. They have three daughters, two are married. After tea we stayed a bit longer. Returned home via Naberezhnaya. Before dinner I saw Obydenov, who just returned from Ekaterinburg, apparently the prisoners of war there took power in their own hands and arrested the local soviet government, the same happened in a few other Siberian towns. In general, it is hard to comprehend what is happening, but something major is ripening. In the evening the engineer Andreyev came by. The weather was sunny in the morning for a short while, it rained for a bit, after 5 o'cl. the weather got blustery. 12°.

17/30 May. Thursday. Perm. Read in the morning. In the afternoon, played the guitar. From 5 until 6 ½ Znamerovsky and I took a walk, walked in the garden behind the cathedral above the river. Had dinner at 7 1/4, then the three of us headed to the theater for a showing of *The Abyss*, besides Kazarovsky and Polyakov, all acted badly. Then we watched one act of *The Merry Widow* with piano accompaniment, but, despite the miserable setting, it was pleasant to listen to music especially since the two principals played well. The weather was occasionally rainy. As far as we know, the trains depart from here to Vyatka, but I think they do not reach Ekaterinburg. Got a telegram from Natasha in Moscow.

18/31 May. Friday. Perm. In the morning finished reading *Notes from the Underground*. In the afternoon, Znamerovsky and I took a walk through the old cemetery, beyond it we descended through a wooded canyon, dotted with mines, at the bottom of which was a small winding river, and walked across the village of Gorky and back into town past Petropavlosk Cathedral. After tea I played the guitar. At 9 ¼ we went to the Triumph cinema for *White Doves*. The weather was sunny until 5 o'cl., then it rained for a bit, 13°. Got a telegram from Yulia Vladislavovna, who wrote that although Kirusha's condition is serious, there is hope for recovery.

June 1918

19/1 June. Saturday. Perm. Read in the morning. In the afternoon played the guitar, and after tea Znamerovsky and I took a walk. At first, we went to the pier and wanted to walk around a steamer, but the arriving passengers got in our way, then we made a small circle around town and returned at 5 ½. Read before dinner, and then took a bath. Had dinner at 7 ¼ and went to the theater at 8, but they announced to us there that the play was cancelled as there are not enough people in audience. Very frustrating because the workers were supposed to be acting in it, and it would have been interesting to hear them. Znamerovsky and I took a walk around town and sat in the garden above the river at the end of Sibirskaya, for a rather long time. Returned home at 9 o'cl. and read, I started reading [blank space]. J[ohnson] went to visit the Alins after tea and returned only at 11 o'cl. The weather was sunny, a minor thunderstorm passed around 6 o'cl., and 11° in the evening.

20/2 June. Sunday. Perm. The morning passed as usual. In the afternoon J[ohnson] and I went to see the Dutch vice-consul, saw his secretary Sheifler, a very nice polite Austrian. Returned in a cab. Then I wrote to Olga Pavlovna. At 5 o'cl. Alin (the son) with his wife came to tea. From 7 ½ until 8 ½ Znamerovsky and I took a walk on Naberezhnaya and the garden behind the cathedral, wonderful evening. In the evening I finished the letter to O. P.; then wrote to Snow Maiden. The weather was wonderful, the first really nice summer day, 18°. Got a letter from Snow Maiden, Alyosha, Dvorzhitsky and Klevezal.

21/3 June. Monday. Perm. In the morning I wrote a letter to Alyosha. In the afternoon I continued writing to Natasha. I am sending the letter when I have the opportunity. I think Natasha is still in Moscow. Kobyaks came to tea: mother, daughter and son, - the old man could not come because he fell ill. After their departure, Znamerovsky and I wanted to take a walk, but such a strong wind with dust started that we returned immediately. In the evening we walked to Alinins on Sibirskaya and back. The weather was hot, overcast, and in the evening, it rained for a bit, 18°. There were no Moscow or Petrograd newspapers again, the reason being, I think, that there is a move of the Red Army from West to East, to Ekaterinburg and some other places,[198] but where I do not know.

22/4 June. Tuesday. Perm. Read in the morning. In the afternoon I finished the letter to Natasha, then, that is, for tea J[ohnson] and I went to the Kobyaks, - the old man is an inventor of electrolyte water. They live near Mariinsky School, across from Gostiny Dvor. Having returned, we did not have dinner, but only changed and the three of us went to the theater. *Malva*, based on M[aksim] Gorky's short story was showing. There too was a very weak concert, the breaks were endlessly long due to an auction. The weather was occasionally rainy, sunny in the morning, 18°. Got a telegram from Natasha from Moscow, she figures to leave for Gatchina today. Kirusha's health is better.

23/5 June. Wednesday. Perm. Znamerovsky came over in the morning and brought a letter brought by his wife, who came from Gatchina with the son and brother of Pyotr L. Read in the morning, and after that J[ohnson] and I went to Tupitsyns, walked on Monastyrskaya. There we sat on the terrace the entire time, besides the lady of the house and her children no one was there. J[ohnson] sang in the sitting room for a while. We walked back along the embankment. A doctor came to see Vasily. Vasily will have to stay in bed a few more days, he feels pain in the area of his appendix. After dinner J[ohnson] read the newspaper aloud. The weather was wonderful, 14°, the bird-cherry is starting to bloom. I got letters from: Tata, V. A. Kozerskaya, Vlasov V. N., Andreyevskaya, Koton, Men' and his son. The

---

[198] In the spring of 1918, a combined economic and supply crisis hit Russia. Businesses and industries shut down, and many cities experienced food shortages. Counterrevolutionary actions and peasant uprisings erupted. In the North, South, and the Far East, foreign troops crossed Russian borders. On 25 May, an anti-Bolshevik rebellion of the 50,000 troop strong Czech Legion (comprised of Czech prisoners of war from the Austro-Hungarian army) erupted, urged on by counterrevolutionary speeches. From 25 to 31 May, these forces captured scores of settlements along the Trans-Siberian Railway and approached Perm as well as Ekaterinburg, where Nicholas II and his family were being held, and Alapayevsk, where other Romanovs were detained.

other day we read that a military government emerged on the Don, at the head of which stand Gen[eral] Krasnov. He is also the troops' Hetman.

24/6 June. Thursday. Perm. The morning passed as usual. Read in the afternoon. S. Tupitsyn stopped by for a short time, as well as my godson – the lawyer Nagorsky. After tea J[ohnson] and I went to the town gardens, the one by the Sibirsky outpost, where we sat and listened to music, a string orchestra. Met up with Sheifler. Came home for dinner. Read in the evening. Today I got my infamous stomach pains, therefore went to bed earlier. The weather was tedious, 14°. The other day, by the command of Sovnarkom [the Council of People's Commissars], the clock hand was moved 2 hours forward, that is 2 hours against the sun.

25/7 June. Friday. Perm. At the Extraordinary Committee I had a slight encounter with one "comrade," who was very rude to me. I read in the afternoon, later S. Tupitsyn stopped by, and the three of us went to the Kama via Sibirskaya Street, and were planning to take a ride on a motor boat, but the drivers could not get the motor started, so the ride did not pan out. J[ohnson] and I returned home and had tea at 4 ¼ with the landlady of our rooms at the Korolev [Hotel], where the owners hospitably treated us to wonderful coffee and cake. They have two grown young ladies, an eleven-year-old boy and 8-year-old daughter. At 8 o'cl. J[ohnson] and I headed to the gardens to listen to the string orchestra, which plays there daily. There we walked around the garden an after an hour returned home for dinner. In the evening J[ohnson] went to Kobyaks' and stayed there until 11 o'cl. I read. The weather was wonderful, 20° in the afternoon, one cloud sprayed a little. My belly reminds about itself here and there.

26/8 June. Saturday. Perm. Spent the morning as usual. Read in the afternoon. Around three o'clock engineer Umberto came by. At 7 o'cl. Papa Kobyak came by, with whom we have interesting conversations. After 12 o'cl. I no longer ate, as my pains continue. The weather was rainy, 16°.

27/9 June. Sunday. Perm. Spent the entire day in bed by the window and continued eating nothing since yesterday, that is not even a drop of milk. The pains still appeared occasionally. In the afternoon Znamerovsky stopped by and told a lot of interesting things about the rumors around town.[199] In the evening J[ohnson] read to me. The weather was wonderful, 22°.

28/10 June. Monday. Perm. I was on my feet all day but felt very unwell. Slept in the afternoon. At 6 o'cl. doctor Shipitsin came by. The pains appeared periodically. Drank about one and half glass of milk half with water for the entire day, nothing else. The weather is wonderful, 20°, and during the last few days all the greenery bloomed. I read the same French book all day. Znamerovsky stopped by at dinner hour. Towards the evening an unusually strong but still warm wind started. Got a telegram from Natasha in Gatchina. She arrived there last Wednesday.

29/11 June. Tuesday. Perm. Today the pains were weaker and not as continuous. Read in the morning. In the afternoon took a nap for an hour. Znamerovsky came to tea with my godson Nagorsky (a lawyer), he ate with great appetite, no wonder after the Petrograd famine. Then I wrote to Natasha in Gatchina. Doctor Shipitsin came by around 8 ½. In the evening I read. The weather was partly sunny, in the afternoon it rained for a bit, 13 ½ °, in the evening too. Around 10 my godson the jurist Nagorsky came by to say goodbye, he is leaving for Petrograd today.[200]

[Michael's diary ends here.]

---

[199] **"rumors around town"** The rumors Michael mentions may have concerned the gathering Czech Legion and White Russian forces, which were approaching Ekaterinburg and Perm from two directions. At the end of May, the Revolutionary Headquarters of the Ural Soviet was formed, and on 2 June 1918, the Ekaterinburg Committee announced a general mobilization. In the panic that followed a great many issues were "resolved" locally, and the Perm and Ekaterinburg Soviets took their own initiative to eliminate "counterrevolutionary forces." It was at this time that the orders to execute all the Romanovs began to be formed. (cf. Khrustalëv, p. 678)

[200] Khrustalëv notes that Michael was a daily diarist, and that the absence of the 12 July hints at his fate. Michael was placed under strict arrest on the night of 11 June, and his diary was likely confiscated at this point.

From *Izvestia*, 15 June 1918.
"The Abduction of Mikhail Romanov"

On the night of 12-13 June, at the beginning of the first hour of the new time, three unidentified men in soldiers' uniforms arrived armed in the Royal rooms, where Michael Romanov lived. They entered Romanov's office and presented him with an arrest warrant, which was read by Romanov's secretary, Johnson. After that, Romanov was asked to go with the newcomers. He and Johnson were forcibly removed, put in a closed phaeton, and taken along Torgov [Trade] Street towards Obvinskya.

Members of the Emergency Committee, called by telephone, arrived at the rooms a few minutes after the abduction. An order to detain Romanov was immediately issued. Horse-drawn police units were sent out on all the roads, but no traces could be found. A search of Romanov's, Johnson's, and the two servants' premises did not yield any clues. The abduction was immediately reported to the Council of People's Commissars, the Petrograd Commune, and the Ural Regional Council. Vigorous searches are being carried out.

Grand Duke Michael Alexandrovich and Nicholas Johnson
were executed outside Perm in the early hours of 13 June, 1918.
Their remains have never been recovered.

Bibliography

Books:

Alexander Mikhailovich (Grand Duke). *Once a Grand Duke.* New York: 1931.
Benckendorf, Paul. *Last Days at Tsarskoe Selo.* London: 1927.
Brusilov, A. A. *Moi vospominaniya.* Moscow: 2001
Buchanan, Sir George *My Mission to Russia and Other Diplomatic Memoirs.* Vol I. Boston: 1923.
Buxhoeveden, Sophie. *The Life and Tragedy of Alexandra Feodorovna.* London: 1929.
Fabergé, Tatiana, Valentin Skurlov, and others. *The Fabergé Imperial Easter Eggs.* New York: 2002.
Glinka, Ya. V. *Odinnadsat' let v Gosudarstvennoi dume, 1906 – 1917: Dnevnik i vospominania.* Moscow: 2001.
Gray, Pauline. *The Grand Duke's Woman.* London: 1976.
Hall, Coryne. *To Free the Romanovs: Royal Kinship and Betrayal in Europe 1917-1919.* Stroud: 2018.
Hasegawa, Tsuyoshi. *The February Revolution: Petrograd, 1917.* Chicago: 2017.
Kerensky, A. F. *The Catastrophe: Kerensky's Own Story of the Russian Revolution.* New York: 1927.
Kerensky, A. F. *Rossiya po istoricheskom povorote: Memuary.* Moscow: 1993.
Khrustalëv, V. M. (ed.). *Voennyi dnevnik Velikogo Knyazya Andreia Vladimirovicha Romanova (1914-1917).* Moscow: 2008.
Khrustalëv, V. M. (ed). *Dnevnik i perepiska Velikogo Knyazya Mikhaila Aleksandrovicha 1915-1918.* Moscow: 2012.
Khrustalëv, V.M. *Skorbnyi put' Mikhaila Romanova: ot prestola do Golgofy.* Perm: 1996.
Lieven, Dominic. *Russia's Rulers Under the Old Regime*, New Haven: 1989.
Lieven, Dominic. *Nicholas II: Emperor of all the Russias.* London: 1993.
Lieven, Dominic. *The End of Tsarist Russia.* New York: 2015.
Majolier, Nathalie. *Step-daughter of Imperial Russia.* London: Stanley Paul, 1940.
Maria Feodorovna (Empress). *Dnevniki imperatritsy Marii Fedorovny, 1914 – 1920, 1923 gody.* Moscow: 2006.
Maylunas, Andrei and Sergei Mironenko (eds.). *A Lifelong Passion: Nicholas and Alexandra, Their Own Story.* New York: 1997.
Miliukov, P.N. *The Russian Revolution, Vol. I.* Gulf Breeze: 1978
Nabokov, V.D. *Vremennoe pravitel'stvo: Vospominaniya.* Moscow: 1991.

Nicholson, N. (ed.), Tatiana Fabergé, Valentin Skurlov, and others. *The Imperial Empire Egg of 1902*. New York: 2017.
Nikitin, B.V. *Rokovye gody: Novye pokazaniia uchastnika*. Paris: 1937.
Nolde, Boris. *L'Ancien Régime et la Révolution Russe* Paris: 1927
Paléologue, Maurice. *An Ambassador's Memoirs*. Translated by F.A. Holt. New York: George H. Doran Company, 1925.
Smith, Douglas. *Rasputin: Faith Power, and the Twilight of the Romanovs*. New York: 2016.
Spiridovich, Aleksandr. *Velikaya voina i Fevral'skaya revolutsiya*, New York: 1960-1962.
Steinberg, Mark D. and Vladimir Khrustalëv *The Fall of the Romanovs*. New Haven: 1995.
Steinberg, Mark D. *Petersburg Fin de Siècle*, New Haven: 2011.

Articles:

Glagoleva, O. E. "The Illegitimate Children of the Russian Nobility in Law and Practice, 1700-1860." *Kritika: Explorations in Russian and Eurasian History*. 6: 3 (2005).
Guchkov, A. I. "Alexander Ivanovich Guchkov rasskazyvaet—Vospominaniya predsedatelya Gosudarstvennoj dumy i voennogo ministra Vremennogo pravitel'stva." *Voprosy istorii* (1993).
Hasegawa, Tsuiyoshi. "Rodzyanko and the Grand Dukes' Manifesto of 1 March 1917." *Canadian Slavonic Papers/Revue Canadienne des Slavistes*. 18: 2 (1976).
Koenig, Marlene. "In Favour of Grand Duke Kirill." *Royalty Digest Quarterly*. 1 (2018), p. 6.
Martin, Russell E. "'For the Firm Maintenance of the Dignity and Tranquility of the Imperial Family:' Law and Familial Order in the Romanov Dynasty." *Russian History*. 37: 4 (2010): 389-411.
Matveev, A. S. "Velikii Knyaz' Mikhail Aleksandrovich v dni perevorota" *Vozrozhdenie* (Paris, 1952, No. 24).
E.A. Naryshkina, "Iz dnevnika ober-gofmeisteriny kniagini E.A. Naryshkinoi." *Poslednie Novosti*. (Paris, 10 May 1936).

Index

A

Abakanovich, Margarita Vasilievna "Snegurochka" 80, 127 - 128, 146, 148 - 149, 151, 159, 161, 171 - 172, 176, 179 - 185, 188, 188n., 189, 189n., 193.

Abakanovich, Nikolai Nikolaevich "Koka" 66, 66n., 73 - 74, 76, 78, 80 - 82, 84 - 85, 123, 128, 135 - 136, 171.

Aberino, Praskovia Ivanovna "Aunt Paranya" 15, 15n. - 19, 43 - 44, 59, 73 - 74, 81 – 83, 85 - 86, 94, 129 - 131, 135 - 138, 146 -147, 153 -154, 160, 164, 176 -177, 181 - 182, 184.

Abrikosov, Dmitri Ivanovich 19, 69, 70.

Aleksandr Mikhailovich, Grand Duke "Sandro". 31, 36, 39n., 40, 63.

Aleksei Nikolaevich, Tsesarevich and Grand Duke 53n.

Alexander, Prince of the Hellenes 84, 84n.

Alexandra Feodorovna, Empress of Russia "Alix" 20n., 24, 25, 26n., 28, 36n., 39n., 43, 62n, 112n., 124n.

Andrei Alexandrovich, Prince of Russia "Andrusha" 62.

Andrei Vladimirovich, Grand Duke, 20, 20n., 21, 21n., 26 - 27, 48n., 85n., 126, 126n., 128.

Andronik, Archbishop (Vladimir Nikolsky) 186, 186n.

B

Bagration, Prince Dmitri Petrovich 40, 62.

Bantle, Gustav Adolfovich 1 5, 15n – 16, 18, 68 - 69.

Bennett, Mr. (Groom) 71.

Bennett, Mrs. (Governess) 21, 21n., 44, 59 - 62, 65, 71, 74, 82, 93 - 94, 123, 133.

Boris Vladimirovich, Grand Duke 20, 20n., 21, 24, 28, 34, 37, 37n. - 38, 43, 48n., 62, 62n., 85, 85n., 88, 107 - 108, 126.

Brasov, Count George Mikhailovich "Baby" 17, 23, 25, 28, 39, 41 - 42, 44, 56, 58, 61 - 62, 65, 71, 76, 79, 81 - 84, 87 - 88, 91, 97, 105 - 106, 123, 126, 128 - 129, 150 - 151, 153 - 155, 159, 161, 166.

Brasova, Natalia Sergeevna "Natasha" *in the Crimea* 7, 7n., 8, 10 - 14, *returns to Gatchina via Brasovo* 19 – 23, *attends opera with Michael, Vladimirovichi and Konstantinovichi* 24, *meets Grand Duchess Vladimir* 26, *gambling and* 30, 31 - 33, 37 - 42, *letter with Dmitri Pavlovich* 43n., *during February Revolution* 44, 45, *letter from Michael about the Manifesto of the Grand Dukes* 50, 53n., *letter from Michael during deferral crisis* 54, 56 - 62, *Easter at*

Gatchina 64 - 73, 74 - 76,
arrival of father of 77, 78 - 84,
85, 86, 91, 92, *visits Fabergé
with Michael* 116, *placed under
house arrest with Michael* 117,
117n., *and October revolution*
122-124, *released from house
arrest* 125, 125n., *moves to
Petrograd* 145, *transferred back
to Gatchina* 148 - 148n.,
*attempts to retrieve jewels from
State bank*, 149 – 149n.,
confiscations of staples 152 -
153, *tries to visit bank again*
160, *Michael sent to Perm* 184,
with Michael in Perm,
185, *departs from Perm* 188.
Brusilov, General Alexei
    Alekseevich 8, 35 - 36, 82, 103.
Buchanan, Sir George. 20n., 61, 74.

C

Cantacuzène-Speransky, Prince
    Michael 33, 42.
Carol, Crown Prince of Romania 23
    – 24, 36.
Chelyshev, Vasily Feodorovich 66,
    66n., 145.
Cheremeteff, (Family) 9, 30.
Cheremeteff, Count Sergei
    Dmitrievich, 41.
Constantine I, of the Hellenes
    "Tino" 84, 84n.

D

Dalai (horse) 71, 98 - 99, 103, 108.
Dehn, Sofia Vladimirovna "Sonia
    D." 9, 9n., 12 - 14, 62, 67, 68,
    93, 136, 138.
Derfeldnen, Margarita
    Aleksandrovna 44, 63 - 64, 69.
Dmitry Konstantinovich, Grand
    Duke. 9, 9n., 11, 21.

Dmitry Pavlovich, Grand Duke 21n.,
    28, 43, 43n.
Dobrovolsky, N.A. 15, 22, 34, 111.
Dolgorukov, Prince Vasily
    Alexandrovich "Valya" 31, 108
Dolgorukova, Princess Irina
    Vasilievna. 16, 84.
Domenici, (Guitar instructor) 15,
    15n. - 18, 26, 28, 40, 42, 44 - 45,
    60 - 61, 63 - 64, 67 - 72, 73, 76,
    78 - 79, 82 - 84, 85, 87, 89 - 90,
    92 - 93, 95 - 96, 99, 101 - 104,
    106, 109 - 110, 113, 115, 129 -
    130, 132 - 137, 146 - 147, 149,
    151 - 153, 155 - 158, 160, 162 -
    164, 166, 168 - 171, 173 - 183.
Dvorzhitsky, Georgii
    Konstantinovich, 27, 27n., 42,
    62, 65, 71, 76, 81, 86, 94, 99 -
    100, 102, 107, 116 - 117, 145 -
    146, 152, 154, 164, 169, 172,
    174, 176, 181, 187, 193.

E

Elizaveta Mavrikievna, Grand
    Duchess "Aunt Mavra". 25,
    25n., 51, 52n., 53.
Eristov, Prince Aleksandr
    Konstantinovich 55, 56, 59, 61,
    63, 66, 105, 107, 115.
Erivanskaya, Inna Aleksandrovna
    "Inna A." 21, 39, 57, 66.

F

Fabergé (Firm) 30n., 63, 72, 109n.,
    116.
Feodor Alexandrovich, Prince of
    Russia. 62.
Frolov, Aleksander Nikolaevich 160,
    169, 174, 183.

G

Galitzine, Prince Nikolai Dmitrievich 11, 13n., 46, 52, 62n., 72, 90.
Gavriil Konstantinovich, Prince of Russia 34, 37, 37n.
Gavriluk, Elena Konstantinovna 63, 63n., 76, 81, 83, 87, 103, 129, 130, 155, 189.
Georgii Mikhailovich, Grand Duke 40, 40n., 41, 55, 56 (?), 57, 58, 61 - 64, 68, 69, 70, 70n., 72 - 73, 74 - 75, 79, 84, 86.
Guchkov, Aleksandr Ivanovich 48n., 49n., 52n., 53n. 74, 75n.
Gulesko, Jean 90, 90n.
Guzhon, Yuly Petrovich 30, 88 - 89, 103 – 105, 113.

I

Igor Konstantinovich, Prince of Russia 24, 24n., 25n., 37, 37n,
Imperial Porcelain Factory (Firm) 40, 64
Ioann Konstantinovich, Prince of Russia 24, 24n., 25n.,37, 37n., 184.
Ioffe, Adolf Abramovich, 146, 146n.
Irina Alexandrovna, Princess of Russia, Princess Yusupov 9, 9n., 13, 109, 109n.
Ivanov, Nikolai Nikiforovich (attorney) 47n., 48n., 53n.

J

Johnson, Nicholas. 7, 7n., 9, 10, 16 - 18, 20 - 27, 29, 37, 39, 40, 42 - 45, 54 -55, 58 - 62, 64 - 65, 67 - 68, 70 - 73, 74, 76, 78 - 80, 82 - 83, 84, 87, 91, 92, 94, 95, 96, 97, 98, 99, 100, 101, 103, 104, 105 - 111, 113, 115 – 118, 121, 123, 125 – 130, 132 – 133, 135 – 145, 147 – 165, 169 – 170, 172 – 177, 179 – 182, 184 – 196.

K

Kapnist, Count Aleksei Pavlovich 45, 53.
Kavtarze, Colonel Nikolai Alexeevich 21, 21n., 65, 78.
Kerensky, Alexander Feodorovich. 41n., 53, 54, 54n., 57, 70, 75, 97n., 99, 101, 108, 112n., 114n., 118, 120n., 121, 122, 123, 124, 125, 137, 138, 140, 141, 142, 144.
Khitrovo, Margarita Sergeevna "Rita" 43, 67, 69, 80, 119.
Kirill Vladimirovich, Grand Duke 2, 20, 20n., 36n., 39, 47, 47n., 48n., 49 - 51, 51n., 52n., 59n., 149, 200.
Kleinmichel, Countess Maria Vladimirovna "Mme. Etter" 9n., 12, 179.
Klopov, Anatolii Alekseevich 23, 26, 28 - 29, 38 - 39, 44, 48.
Koko (horse), 111, 112, 151.
Konstantin Konstantinovich, Grand Duke "KR", 25n.
Konstantin Konstantinovich, Prince of Russia 24, 24n., 25n., 87.
Kornilov, General Lavr Georgievich 101, 103, 114, 114n., 120, 120n., 121, 122, 125, 127, 141, 148.
Koton, Konstantin Antonovich 10 - 14, 16 - 17, 23, 66, 72 - 73, 75, 79.
Kulikovsky, Colonel (artillerist) 25, 107.

L

Lvov, Commandant Stanislav 146, 150, 190.
Lvov, N.A. (Architect) 19.

Lvov, Prince Georgiy 46, 54n., 57n., 89, 105.
Lyarskaya, Nadezhda Dmitrievna 44, 68, 70, 99, 101, 105, 114, 129 – 130, 133, 138, 155.

M

Mamontova, Nataliya Sergeevna "Tata" 17, 19, 21n., 23, 26 - 28, 32, 39 - 40, 42, 56, 56n., 58, 63 – 65, 71 - 74, 76, 79 - 81, 83 - 87, 92, 94 – 96, 99 - 100, 103 - 114, 116, 119, 126, 132, 145, 149n., 150, 156, 161, 167, 187, 189, 194.

Mannerheim, General Baron Carl 37, 37n.

Maria Feodorovna, Dowager Empress "Mama". 9, 31, 36, 36n., 63, 78, 78n., 111 – 112, 126, 134, 136, 138, 161, 187.

Maria Pavlovna the Elder, Grand Duchess "Aunt Miechen" 21, 21n. 26, 26n., 27n., 39, 48n., 62, 62n., 78n., 85n., 126n.

Maria Pavlovna the Younger, Grand Duchess, Princess Putyatin 29n., 77.

Matveev, Aleksei Sergeevich "Alyosha" 10 - 30, 34, 37 - 45, 48, 51, 54, 56, 59 – 65, 67 – 68, 70 -74, 76 - 78, 80 – 81, 83 - 84, 86, 88 – 92, 95 – 96, 99 – 102, 104-105, 107 – 112, 114 -117, 121, 126, 127, 129, 131, 133 – 136, 138, 145 – 148, 152, 153 – 154, 156, 157, 158 – 160, 163 – 164, 168 – 169, 172, 174, 176 – 177, 179, 181, 182, 187, 193.

Meltzer, Feodor Feodorovich 13, 13n., 14.

Meltzer, Roman Feodorovich, 40.

Mengden, Countess Zinaïda Georgievna "Zina" 31, 43.

Michael Alexandrovich, Grand Duke *in the Crimea,* 7 – 15, *learns of Rasputin's death,* 15, *arrives at Brasovo,* 15, *guitar playing* (see entry for Domenici), *arrives in Moscow,* 18 – 19, *arrives at Gatchina,* 19, *meets with Vladimirovichi cousins* 20, *meets with Maria Pavlovna the Elder and sons,* 21, *meets with Rodzianko,* 22, 24, *visits opera with the Konstaninovichi cousins,* 24, *meets with Nicholas & Alexandra,* 25, *meets with "Aunt Mavra"* 25, *letter to Nicholas II,* 28, *departs for southwestern front,* 31, *meets with Wrangel,* 31, *letter to Natasha from the front,* 33, *arrives in Kiev,* 36 *returns to Gatchina,* 36-37, *attends ballet with Konstantinovichi and Vladimirovichi,* 37, *meets with Rodzyanko and Grand Duke Alexander Mikhailovich,* 40, *leaves for Petrograd,* 44, *disorders in the capital,* 45 – 47, *and the Manifesto of the Grand Dukes,* 47, *text of the Manifesto,* 49, *letter to natasha regarding the Manifesto,* 50 – 51, *Grand Dukes at the State Duma,* 51, *indicated as successor to the Russian throne after abdication of Nicholas II,* 54, *deferral of the throne,* 55, *text of the Act of the Deferral of the Grand Duke Michael,* 55, *returns to Gatchina,* 55, *GD George Mikhailovich moves in,* 56, *visits Ambassador Buchanan,* 74, *learns of the search of the Dowager Empress at Ai-Todor,* 78, *learns of house arrest of GD Boris*, 84, *notes destruction of property in Petrograd*, 88, *demonstrations in Petrograd*, 91, *notes disintegration of former imperial properties*, 93, *July Crisis of the Provisional Government*, 98, *last meeting with Nicholas II*, 108 – 109, *State Conference in Moscow*, 114, *arrested with Natasha*, 117 – 118, *and development of stomach ulcers and illnesses*, 122-124, *released from arrest*, 125, *learns of Nicholas II and family's removal to Tobolsk*, 129, *and October Revolution*, 138 – 150, *and false report of Nicholas II's escape*, 156, *introduction of new style dates*, 178, *arrested and deported to Perm*, 185, in Perm with Natasha, 185 – 188, Natasha leaves Perm, 188, *meets Znamerovsky in Perm*, 196, *"The Abduction of Mikhail Romanov"*, 197, *murder of*, 197.

Miliukov, Pavel Nikolaevich 41n., 47n., 48n., 54n., 54n., 75.

Mogilev (Army headquarters) 29, 37, 44, 46, 57, 62, 122, 152.

N

Nabokov, Vladimir Dmitrievich 54n., 137n., 142, 147.

Nabokova, Maria Ferdinandovna 156, 142, 156, 164.

Naryshkin, Count Kirill Anatolievich "Kira" 29, 55 - 58, 66, 69, 105.

Naryshkin, Kirill Dmitrievich 60, 61, 106, 176, 181, 182.

Naryshkina, Elizaveta Alekseevna (née Pcss. Kurakina) "Mme. Zizi" 26n., 91n, 92n., 97n., 201.

Neame, Miss Margaret (Governess) 15 - 17, 22 - 23, 39, 40, 45, 60, 64, 70, 72, 74 - 81, 83, 87 – 89, 94, 97, 106, 109, 118, 120, 123, 128 - 137, 142, 150 - 151, 153 - 155, 158, 167 - 168, 172, 175.

Nicholas II Alexandrovich, Emperor, "Nicky" 7n., 10n., 20, 20n., 21n., 25, 25n., 27n., 28, 29, 36, 38, 39, 39n., 43 - 44, 46, 48, 53n., 54n., 57, 58n., 62, 72, 91, 93, 101, 108, 109, 112n., 124n., 129, 131n., 146n., 156, 156n., 194, 197.

Nikita Alexandrovich, Prince of Russia. 62.

Nikolai Mikhailovich, Grand Duke 48, 48n., 51, 52n., 53, 53n.

Nolde, Baron 54n.

O

Olga Alexandrovna, Grand Duchess 9n., 31, 36, 36n., 37, 63.

Olga Konstantinovna, Grand Duchess and Queen of Greece "Aunt Olga", 24, 24n., 25, 68, 72.

Orbeliani, Princess Vera Vladimirovna. 9, 9n., 12 - 14, 67, 106, 108, 109, 112, 134, 161.

P

Paley, Princess Olga Valerianovna 29n., 97n., 125n.

Pavel Aleksandrovich, Grand Duke 47, 47n., 49 - 51, 118- 119.

Pistolkors, (family) 29.

Putyatin, Prince Mikhail
  Pavlovich 43, 57, 159, 168, 169.
Putyatin, Prince Nikolai Sergeevich
  13, 13n., 47.
Putyatin, Prince Pavel
  Pavlovich. 40,, 115, 117, 127,
  145, 147, 149, 150, 152-157,
  159, 160, 171, 175.
Putyatina, Princess Ekaterina
  Pavlovna 57, 146, 147, 168.
Putyatina, Princess Olga
  Pavlovna 15, 15n., 16 - 19, 23 -
  24, 26, 27, 34, 41, 43, 45, 47,
  48n., 53, 54, 61, 63 - 65, 67, 68,
  70 - 72, 85, 115, 117, 145, 147,
  150, 152 -157, 159, 160, 171,
  175, 179, 185.
Putyatina, Princess Tatiana
  Pavlovna 65, 82, 84, 85, 87,
  149, 150, 159, 189.

R

Rasputin, Grigorii Efimovich 13n.,
  15.
Reier, Col. Armii Karlovich. 58,
  58n., 59, 78, 81, 83, 90, 95, 109,
  127, 134, 139, 141, 142, 152,
  154, 161, 162.
Reit (dog) 78, 79, 96, 103, 111, 118,
  120, 154.
Rodzyanko, Mikhail
  Vladimirovich 20, 22, 22n., 24,
  25n., 39n., 40, 41n., 45, 45n., 46,
  47n., 48, 48n., 49n., 50n., 51, 52,
  53, 53n., 54n., 57n., 62n.

S

Shelaputina, Maria Vasilievna
  "Maria V" 7, 7n., 8 - 15, 19, 30,
  37 - 39, 41, 58, 60, 74, 88 - 89,
  103 - 105, 161.
Sheremetevsky, Sergei
  Aleksandrovich 18, 30, 76, 77,
  77n., 80, 86, 148.

Shervashidze, Prince Giorgi
  Dmitrievich 31, 36, 63, 69, 74,
  78, 131, 134, 139, 146, 191.
Shleifer, Aleksandr Nikolaevich (and
  family) 19, 25, 37 - 39, 60, 62,
  69, 72 - 74, 76, 78, 80 – 83, 85 -
  92, 94, 96 - 98, 100 - 107, 110,
  113 - 119, 123, 125 - 126, 134 -
  136, 146 - 149, 152 - 154, 157 -
  158, 160, 163 – 164.
Skoropadsky, Pavel Petrovich 186.
Spiridovich, Alexander Ivanovich 10,
  10n., 13, 20n., 44n.
Stackelberg, Count Gustaf
  Ernestovich 48.
Strakhov, Fr. Viktor
  Maksimovich 42, 64, 119, 126,
  132, 152, 161, 163, 166.

T

Tata (see Mamontova, Natalia
  Sergeevna)
Tatiana Konstantinovna, Princess of
  Russia. 9, 9n.
Taube, Baroness Elena (Helène) 65.
Tolstoy, Countess Elizabeth 12, 68.
Trostyanskoi, Irina 16.
Trostyanskoi, Maria Nikolaevna 15,
  15n., 16.

U

Urusov, Prince Nikolai
  Petrovich 45.

V

Valvin, Mlle. 67, 82, 83, 89, 94, 97,
  109.
Vasilchikov, Prince Boris
  Aleksandrovich 149.
Vasili Aleksandrovich, Prince of
  Russia. "Vasya" 8, 8n., 12, 13.
Victoria Feodorovna, Grand Duchess
  "Ducky" 36, 36n.

Vityaz (horse) 38, 41, 42, 44, 60, 68, 70, 73, 99, 103, 111, 115, 150.
Volchok (dog) 18, 56, 57, 59, 61, 64, 89, death of 109, burial of 110.
Vorontsov, Counts (family), 86.
Vyazamsky, Prince Vladimir Alexeevich 16 - 20n., 22 - 24, 31, 36 - 37, 58.
Vyazemskaya, Princess Alexandra Gastonovna 23.

W

Westfalen, Dr. Herman Georgievich 87, 89, 122, 123, 124, 125, 128, 129, 132, 149, 179, 183.
Wrangel, General Baron Pyotr Nikolayevich 11 - 14, 27, 27n., 28, 29, 31 - 32, 34 - 36, 38, 40, 43 - 44, 48, 61, 75.

X

Xenia Alexandrovna, Grand Duchess 7, 8n., 9, 10, 11, 12, 45, 60 – 63, 68, 74, 95, 112n., 126n., 131, 131n., 134, 138, 147, 159, 161, 187.

Z

Znamerovsky, Piotr Ludvigovich 183, 183n., 185, 187 – 196.

www.ingramcontent.com/pod-product-compliance
Lightning Source LLC
Chambersburg PA
CBHW070942230426
43666CB00011B/2534